Routledge Revivals

Distribution Theory

First published in 1972, *Distribution Theory* follows on from the author's earlier book, *Descriptive Statistics and Probability Theory*, but may easily be followed by any reader who has not studied that particular book but who has gained some knowledge of numerical distributions and basic probability theory. The author has attempted to steer a middle course between those textbooks which concentrate solely on statistical calculations and those which concentrate solely on statistical theory. It is his belief that statistics is best understood through a mixture of practical numerical work and knowledge of the corresponding theory.

In this book, probability distributions are shown to develop out of different physical situations that are commonly met in the physical world. The three most commonly used- the binomial, Poisson, and normal distributions- are dealt in detail, but other less commonly used distributions are also introduced. By showing the different situations to which these distributions apply, their individuality is emphasised. The author then illustrates how these probability distributions are used in sampling theory. The book concludes with a chapter which shows how apparently different parts of statistics can be seen to interrelate through statistical theory. This is an interesting reference work for students of mathematics, statistics and economics.

Distribution Theory

Robert A. Barks

Routledge
Taylor & Francis Group
ROUTLEDGE REVIVALS

First published in 1972
by Hutchinson Educational

This edition first published in 2025 by Routledge
4 Park Square, Milton Park, Abingdon, Oxon, OX14 4RN

and by Routledge
605 Third Avenue, New York, NY 10158

Routledge is an imprint of the Taylor & Francis Group, an informa business

Publisher's Note
The publisher has gone to great lengths to ensure the quality of this reprint but points out that some imperfections in the original copies may be apparent.

Disclaimer
The publisher has made every effort to trace copyright holders and welcomes correspondence from those they have been unable to contact.

A Library of Congress record exists under ISBN: 0091128102

ISBN: 978-1-041-07676-6 (hbk)
ISBN: 978-1-003-64171-1 (ebk)
ISBN: 978-1-041-07681-0 (pbk)

Book DOI 10.4324/9781003641711

Distribution Theory

ROBERT A. BARKS

HUTCHINSON EDUCATIONAL

HUTCHINSON EDUCATIONAL LTD
3 Fitzroy Square, London W1

London Melbourne Sydney Auckland
Wellington Johannesburg Cape Town
and agencies throughout the world

First published 1972

Printed in Great Britain by litho on smooth wove paper
by Anchor Press, and bound by Wm. Brendon,
both of Tiptree, Essex

ISBN 0 09 112810 2 (cased)
0 09 112811 0 (paper)

Contents

Dedicated to George R. Gibson

Introduction

This book is designed to follow on from the first book in the series, *Descriptive Statistics and Probability Theory*, but may be understood by anyone with some knowledge of descriptive statistics and elementary probability theory.

In the introduction to that first book, the various stages of a statistical investigation were outlined and this enabled the expression of the following definition of statistics:

'...the science which deals with the collection, processing and analysing of raw data for the purpose of drawing inferences and making predictions.'

The author also emphasised that the study of statistics could begin at any point in what is now a vast body of knowledge. The point chosen in the first book was the study of raw data – that is descriptive statistics which produced and emphasised the necessity to study probability – and elementary ideas about probability were examined.

These basic ideas about probability enabled us to understand exactly what is meant in statistics by phrases such as 'we can be 95% sure of this result', and so on.

Now that we have these ideas, we can use them to develop further work in probability; this in turn will help us to answer more of the questions which spring from a deeper journey into the field of statistics.

1 Statistical Models

1.1 Statistical Models

Let us consider the following experiment. Two pennies were tossed 100 times and the number of heads appearing on each toss were counted – the results were plotted on the graph:

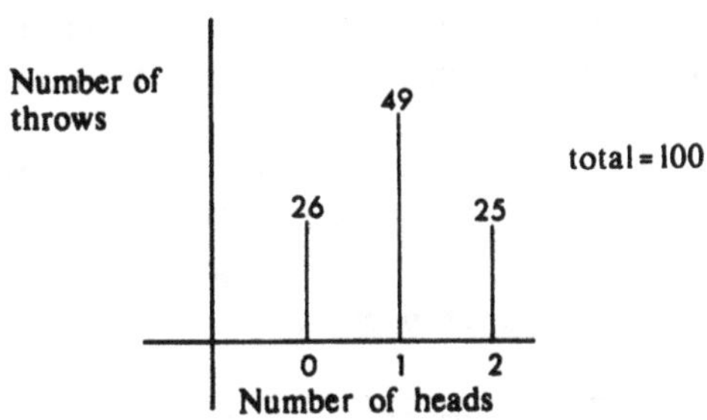

Fig. 1.1 (a)

If we consider the relative frequencies we get

Number of heads	0	1	2
Relative frequency	$\frac{26}{100}$	$\frac{49}{100}$	$\frac{25}{100}$

Fig. 1.1 (b)

The student is now urged to perform a similar experiment for himself and compare his figures with those obtained above.

The first thing that is apparent is that the results are very nearly

Number of heads	0	1	2
Relative frequencies	$\frac{1}{4}$	$\frac{1}{2}$	$\frac{1}{4}$

Fig. 1.1 (c)

and if we use our knowledge of probability (in particular our knowledge of *a priori* probability) we could say that the latter table indicates what we would *expect* to happen in the case of two balanced pennies.

We now have two sets of figures: one set consists of actual figures from an experiment and the other set indicates theoretical figures. The theoretical figures *predict* what should happen in an experiment like this. If we were now to toss the two pennies 400 times we can say that theoretically we should get

Number of heads	0	1	2
Number of throws	100	200	100

Fig. 1.1 (d)

This experiment has been carried out many times and the *actual* results obtained are very close to the *predicted* results. We can now say that the predicted results form a statistical model for the situations of tossing two pennies. Not only that – it also forms a statistical model for any other situation that has the same structure as the tossing of two pennies.

Suppose, for example, a population consists of three types of elements. One element, say e_2, accounts for 50% of the population and the other two, say e_1 and e_3, account for 25% each. If we took a random sample of 100 elements from the population we would expect

type of element	e_1	e_2	e_3
number obtained	25	50	25

and again we used the statistical model to predict what our sample would be like.

Thus it will be seen that a statistical model can be applied to more than one situation. In fact one of the main reasons for finding statistical models is that they may be applied to other situations. If, for example, a fresh situation is discovered and by analysing it further it can be shown to have the same structure as a known model, then the situation does not have to be individually and exhaustively examined – the known results of the statistical model can be used.

It may be apparent now that actual figures derived from experiments suggest various theories. These theories are then formulated and expressed in statistical terminology and so become statistical models. We can now define a statistical model as a theory, expressed formally in mathematical terms, about a physical situation.

Confusion is sometimes caused by the fact that the word 'model' is used in two different senses. The first sense of the word is as explained above, and the second sense is the usual everyday sense of the word 'model', that is, a physical object of some sort. Examples of models of the latter sort are afforded by packs of playing cards, dice, balls in urns, and so on. To be specific an urn containing 19 white balls and one black ball can act as a model for *any* population which can be divided into 95% of one type and 5% of another. An urn containing 10 white, 3 black and 7 yellow balls can act as a model for *any* population which can be divided into 50% of type A, 15% of type B and 35% of type C. An instance of a population to which this model could apply is a voting population where 50% of the voters voted for candidate X, 15% voted for candidate Y, and 35% did not vote. The context should make it clear which use of the word 'model' is intended.

The question now arises as to how we know when two situations have the same structure and so may have the same statistical model applied to them. The answer to this question is to be found in the analysis of the mathematical structure, and a clear statement of that structure. In order to illustrate this point let us take the simplest possible situation.

Consider a car showroom and out of a multitude of possible points of interest let us consider 'the number of cars in the showroom'. Let us analyse the mathematical structure. First we note that the number of cars in the showroom will be a whole number, either $0, 1, 2, \ldots, n$ up to the capacity of the showroom, (say W), and so our point of interest will be expressed in whole numbers including zero. Secondly, fresh cars will be put in the showroom – and this will correspond to addition of numbers. Thirdly, cars will be removed from the showroom – and this will correspond to subtraction of numbers.

If we consider the mathematical sentence $3 + 2 = 5$ we can say this corresponds to the situation where there are three cars in the showroom and two more are put in.

We can now formulate the mathematical structure of our situation in the following assumptions:

(1) we are concerned with the addition and subtraction of discrete objects

(2) the objects themselves undergo no change because of this addition or subtraction

(3) the number of objects subtracted will always be less than or equal to the number of objects from which such subtractions are to be made
(Note that there is no mention of cars or showroom now)

We can condense the above assumption by saying that the appropriate mathematical model is 'the set of natural numbers from 0 to W, together with the operations of addition and subtraction'.

There are, of course, a multitude of situations to which this particular model may be applied – the reader should write out a few – but there are situations to which it may *not* be applied – any situation involving fractions, or negative numbers, for example.

The reader may think it rather pedantic to write out assumption (2) above but consideration of it will help further to clarify the points at issue. Consider a milk churn with a capacity of W pints. Because 2 pints and 3 pints make 5 pints in this situation, then the above model can be applied (provided we are careful to add and subtract exact pints).

But now consider 2 pints of water added to 2 pints of alcohol. At first sight it might appear that the above model could apply, but this is not so. Because of changes that take place when these two substances are combined the resulting mixture is only approximately 3·8 pints. Thus we note the very important point that before applying a mathematical model to a situation we must insure that the situation to which it is applied does fulfill the condition of having the same structure as the model.

There are several reasons why mathematical models are important. The first one is that they are mathematical abstractions and as such may be manipulated within the usual rules of mathematics. This will enable practical experiments to be dispensed with. For example, if we know that a boy holds 537 marbles and wins 232 marbles, then we know he will have a total of 759 marbles. We deduced this result by taking the mathematical model – the same as the one for the car showroom above – and by applying the usual rules of this model, the rules of addition, we arrived at the result.

Secondly, something may be deduced about the situation that was not known or could not be guessed beforehand. This point may not be so easily seen with the examples given above as they are so simple – later chapters will give much more meaning to this point.

Thirdly, the mathematical model may be much simpler to work with than the information which first gave rise to the model. The model cuts away unnecessary detail and allows the mathematician to concentrate upon the important features of the situation without being distracted. This latter point is particularly important in statistics where a welter of numerical detail can obscure the fundamental structure.

We are now in a position to answer a question that may have puzzled the reader. Why is it that any book on statistics always includes sections on throwing dice, drawing cards from a pack, tossing pennies, or drawing balls from an urn? It will now be readily appreciated that these are models, and can be used to study situations which at first sight are apparently different but which in fact have similar mathematical structures. For example, drawing a ball from an urn containing 9 white balls and 1 black ball can be used as a model for examining the daily production of a machine (producing nuts, bolts, light bulbs, television tubes, and so on) which produces on average 10% defective items. An item is selected at random and the question is asked, 'What is the probability that this is defective?', and this corresponds to the random selection of a ball from the urn and the question, 'What is the probability that this ball is black?'.

Selecting without replacement can be used as a model for selecting objects from a small (finite) population, and the selection with replacement can be used as a model for selection from a very large (infinite) population. Selection without replacement can also be used as a model for selecting products which when tested are destroyed, for example light bulbs.

Thus we can see that all these apparently gambling orientated pastimes have a serious use as mathematical models in the theory of probability and its application to statistics. We also see that one of the main points of statistical theory is to formulate models of situations and then investigate the models, with a view to making predictions about the situation, based upon the logical consequences of the model.

We have, in *Descriptive Statistics and Probability Theory*, investigated numerical distributions and in view of what has been said in this chapter it is to be expected that we will seek to find *theoretical* distributions which we can use as models for the distributions that arose as a result of our taking samples. We do this in the following chapters.

1.2 Probability Distributions – Random Variables – Statistical Models

It is worth mentioning explicitely that a prime example of a statistical model is what is known as a probability distribution. The idea of a probability distribution can be approached as follows.

When raw data is grouped and graphed we see how it is distributed. Such a distribution is, as we have seen, a numerical distribution. The theoretical counterpart to a numerical distribution is a distribution which shows probabilities rather than actual data.

Consider the experiment of rolling two dice and summing the numbers shown on the upturned faces. We know that the outcome space for this experiment and the associated probabilities are as shown in the table:

Total	2	3	4	5	6	7	8	9	10	11	12
Probabilities	$\frac{1}{36}$	$\frac{2}{36}$	$\frac{3}{36}$	$\frac{4}{36}$	$\frac{5}{36}$	$\frac{6}{36}$	$\frac{5}{36}$	$\frac{4}{36}$	$\frac{3}{36}$	$\frac{2}{36}$	$\frac{1}{36}$

This is a probability distribution since it shows the expected distribution of the elements of the outcome space. The graph of this appears thus

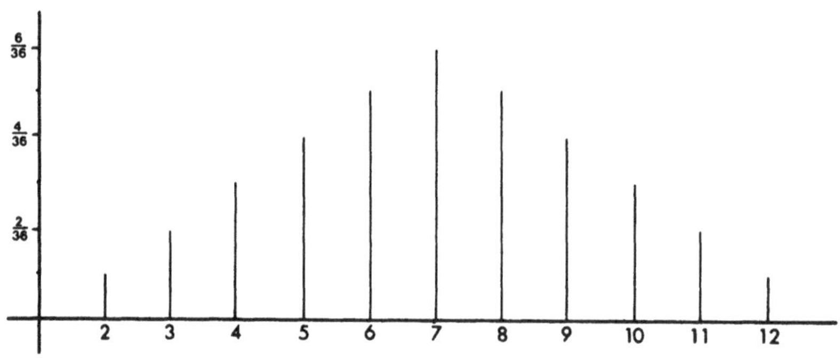

Fig. 1.2 (a)

and we note that merely by looking at the graph we can see how the probabilities are distributed in the same way as when we look at the graph of numerical data to see how it is distributed.

Naturally all the statistics computed for a numerical distribution will have their counterpart in connection with a probability distribution.

Example 1. Find the mean of the above probability distribution.

Answer

The formula $\bar{x} = \Sigma x_i/n$ has to be modified in the following way,

$$\bar{x} = \Sigma x_i P(x_i)$$

Therefore the mean is found by multiplying the value of x_i by the probability of its occurence (rather than the frequency with which it occurs) and then summing in the usual way. Therefore

$$\begin{aligned}\bar{x} &= 2.(\tfrac{1}{36}) + 3.(\tfrac{2}{36}) + 4.(\tfrac{3}{36}) + \ldots + 12.(\tfrac{1}{36}) \\ &= (\tfrac{1}{36})(2 + 6 + 12 + \ldots + 12) \\ &= (\tfrac{1}{36}).252 \\ &= 7\end{aligned}$$

Further statistics for probability distributions will be found in later chapters.

It will be useful now to recall the idea of a random variable as defined in probability work. If a variable $\underset{\sim}{x}$ takes the values $x_1, x_2,, x_2, \ldots, x_n$, with probabilities $P(x_1), P(x_2), \ldots, P(x_n)$ such that $\Sigma P(x_i) = 1$, then $\underset{\sim}{x}$ is a random variable.

In view of this it will be seen that a random variable is in fact a probability distribution; and since a probability distribution is a statistical model it follows that a random variable is also a statistical model.

Exercise 1

1. Repeat the following as often as you find necessary to estimate the theoretical probability distributions they suggest:

(a) divide a circle as shown in the diagram and spin the pointer pivoted at the centre. Record the area where the pointer stops.

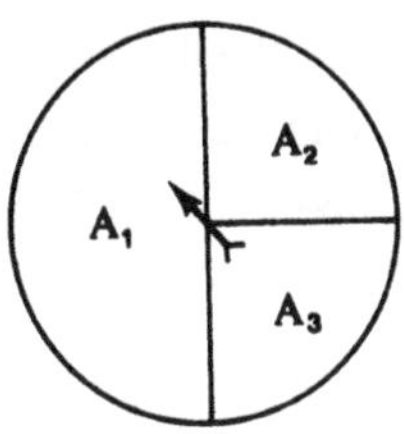

(b) repeat (a) using the diagram

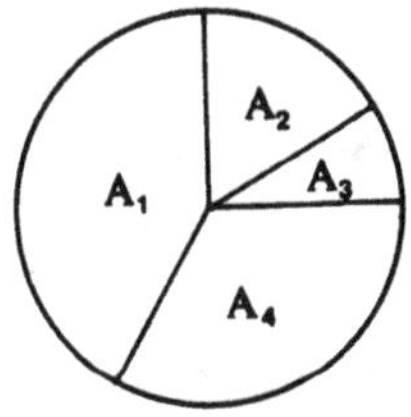

(c) throw two dice and subtract the lower score from the higher

(d) sit by a busy road and record (i) the different types of vehicle using the road (ii) the different makes of cars using the road

(e) draw one dominoe from a set at random and count the total number of dots on it

2. Find situations to which the following probability distributions may be applied:

(a)

0	1
$\frac{1}{2}$	$\frac{1}{2}$

(b)

1	2	3
$\frac{1}{3}$	$\frac{1}{3}$	$\frac{1}{3}$

(c)

0	1	2	3
$\frac{1}{8}$	$\frac{3}{8}$	$\frac{3}{8}$	$\frac{1}{8}$

(d)

1	2	3	4
$\frac{1}{6}$	$\frac{1}{4}$	$\frac{1}{4}$	$\frac{1}{3}$

3. Find models for the following situations:

(a) the number of birthday cards received by someone on their birthday

(b) the position of a diver

(c) the speed of a car

(d) the position of a lift in a large building

(e) a bank account – with and without an overdraft

(f) the number of pages in a book

4. Find situations to which the following models may be applied:

(a) the set of natural numbers and the operation of addition

(b) the set of integers together with addition and subtraction

(c) the set of real numbers together with the operations of addition and subtraction

(d) the set of natural numbers

5. Find situations to which the following mathematical sentences apply:

(a) $8 - 3 = 5$ (b) $3{\cdot}4 + 7{\cdot}35 = 10{\cdot}75$

(c) $13{\cdot}16 - 15{\cdot}47 = -2{\cdot}31$ (d) $3^2 + 4^2 = 5^2$

6. How may relative frequency distributions be used as statistical models?

7. Compare in detail the two formulae $\bar{x} = \frac{\Sigma f_i x_i}{\Sigma f_i}$ and $\bar{x} = \Sigma x_i P(x_i)$

and hence explain the formula for the mean of a probability distribution.

8. Find the variance of the distribution in Section 1.2, using the two formulae

$$s^2 = \Sigma(x_i - \bar{x})^2 P(x_i)$$

and

$$s^2 = \Sigma x_i P(x_i) - \bar{x}^2$$

Discuss any points about these two formulae that you notice.
Answer: 5·83

2 Mathematical Expectation

2.1 Mathematical Expectation

If a man bets on a game of rolling a dice and he wins £1 every time a 6 is rolled, let us investigate his stake money. He will, on average, expect to win every six throws, so if he stakes 50p a throw, in six throws he will pay out £3. In these same six throws he will expect a return of £1 and so he will on average lose £2 every six throws of the dice – we assume that stake money is not returned with a win. If he stakes 25p a throw, by arguing similarly we see that he will lose 50p every six throws. If he bets 12½p a throw he will stand to gain 25p every six throws. A game of this sort is defined to be *fair* if a player stands to gain or lose nothing over a long run, when his expectation is worked out in the way shown above. In this case a stake of $16\frac{2}{3}$p would make the game fair.

Example 1: What price would a man pay for a raffle ticket if 100 tickets are sold and there is a £20 prize?

Answer

With 100 tickets sold the probability of any one ticket winning is $\frac{1}{100}$, a fair price to pay would therefore be $\frac{1}{100}$ of £20, or 20p.

Example 2: What price should a man pay for a raffle ticket if 100 tickets are sold and there are two prizes, one of £20, and one of £5.

Answer

With 100 tickets sold the probability that one ticket will win £20 is $\frac{1}{100}$, and the probability that the same ticket will win £5 is also $\frac{1}{100}$. (We assume that one ticket can win both prizes).

Therefore the expectation of a man holding one ticket is $\frac{1}{100}$ of £20 plus $\frac{1}{100}$ of £5, that is 20p + 5p = 25p.

Note: we could also argue as follows; if we were to divide the whole of the prize money between the ticket holders they would receive 25p each, and so for the draw to be fair as defined above, they must expect to neither win nor lose, so a fair price to pay for a ticket would be 25p.

We now use this idea of what a man might expect to gain, on the average, to lead to the definition of mathematical expectation. If P is the probability that a man will receive an amount S, then his mathematical expectation is defined to be SP.

Example 3: If the probability that a man will win £20 is 0·01, then his mathematical expectation is £20 × 0·01 = 20p. Comparing this with *Example 1* we see that for a draw to be fair the price of a ticket must be equal to the mathematical expectation of the person buying the ticket.

We can now define the *mathematical expectation* of a random variable. The mathematical expectation, $E(\underset{\sim}{x})$, of a random variable $\underset{\sim}{x}$, which takes values $x_1, x_2, \ldots, x_n$, with probabilities $P(x_1), P(x_2), \ldots, P(x_n)$, is defined to be

$$E(\underset{\sim}{x}) = \sum_{i=1}^{n} x_i P(x_i)$$

Example 4: Find the mathematical expectation of the random variable $\underset{\sim}{x}$, defined by the rolling of a die.

Answer

This random variable takes values 1, 2, ..., 6, with probabilities, $P(1) = \frac{1}{6}$, $P(2) = \frac{1}{6}$, ..., $P(6) = \frac{1}{6}$. Therefore, $E(\underset{\sim}{x}) = 1 \times \frac{1}{6} + 2 \times \frac{1}{6} + 3 \times \frac{1}{6} + 4 \times \frac{1}{6} + 5 \times \frac{1}{6} + 6 \times \frac{1}{6} = 3{\cdot}5$.

Note: the expectation gives the same result as the mean, and since expectation was introduced by the idea of 'what to expect on the average' this is not surprising.

We now anticipate a later result by defining the mean of a random variable $\underset{\sim}{x}$ to be the expectation of $\underset{\sim}{x}$, that $\mu = E(\underset{\sim}{x})$.

Example 5: An ice-cream salesman makes £25 a day when the weather is fine, but loses £5 a day when the weather is wet. If the probability of rain for one day is $\frac{2}{5}$ determine his expectation for that day.

Answer

Probability of fine weather is $\frac{3}{5}$, therefore his expectation is £25 × $\frac{3}{5}$ − £5 × $\frac{2}{5}$ (*Note the minus sign for a loss*) which is £13.

Example 6: A bag contains 2 black and 3 white balls. Two people A and B alternately draw a ball (without replacement), A drawing first, and the first to draw a white ball wins £10. Find their expectations and hence determine what price they should pay to enter the game.

Answer

Let A represent a winning draw and A' represent a losing draw by A. Similarly for B and B'.

The probability A wins on the first draw, $P(A) = \frac{3}{5}$

The only time B has a draw is if A draws a black on the first draw leaving 1 black and 3 white balls. Therefore, the probability B wins on the second draw is

$$P(A' \text{ and then } B) = P(A')P(B|A')$$
$$= \frac{2}{5} \times \frac{3}{4} = \frac{3}{10}$$

If B fails to win on his draw it means he has drawn a black ball, leaving only 3 white balls and so A will be certain to win on his draw. His probability of a draw at this stage is

$$P(A' \text{ and then } B' \text{ and then } A) = P(A')P(B'|A')P(A|B' \text{ and } A')$$
$$= \frac{2}{5} \times \frac{1}{4} \times \frac{3}{3} = \frac{1}{10}$$

Therefore the probability A wins $= \frac{3}{5} + \frac{1}{10} = \frac{7}{10}$

and the probability B wins $= \frac{3}{10}$ *(Note sum of probabilities is* 1)

Thus A's expectation $= £10 \times \frac{7}{10} = £7$,

and B's expectation $= £10 \times \frac{3}{10} = £3$

For the game to be fair A should stake £7 and B £3.

Example 7: Prove that $E(k) = k$, where k is any constant.

Answer

Replacing x by k in $E(x) = \Sigma x_i P(x_i)$

gives
$$E(k) = \Sigma k P(x_i)$$
$$= k\Sigma P(x_i)$$
$$= k$$

2.2 Related Random Variables

If we are given a random variable we may form other random variables from it. For example, if we have the random variable x, we may form the random variables $x + 3$, $5x$, or x^2, and so on. These new random variables are called *related random variables*. Let us now take a specific example. If x is the random variable associated with the throwing of a fair die, then we know its outcome space is $\{1, 2, \ldots, 6\}$ and that $P(x) = \frac{1}{6}$, for all x in the outcome space.

In the forming of related variables we must first find the outcome space of the new random variable. For the three examples given above the outcome spaces are tabulated below

Random variable	Outcome Space					
$\underset{\sim}{x}$	1	2	3	4	5	6
$\underset{\sim}{x} + 3$	4	5	6	7	8	9
$5\underset{\sim}{x}$	5	10	15	20	25	30
$\underset{\sim}{x}^2$	1	4	9	16	25	36

Fig. 2.2 (a)

The outcome space for the variable $\underset{\sim}{x} + 3$ was found as follows. When $\underset{\sim}{x}$ takes the value 1, then $\underset{\sim}{x} + 3$ will take the value $1 + 3 = 4$; when $\underset{\sim}{x}$ takes the value 2, then $\underset{\sim}{x} + 3$ will take the value $2 + 3 = 5$; and the remainder of the outcome space was found similarly. The outcome spaces for the variables $5\underset{\sim}{x}$ and $\underset{\sim}{x}^2$ were found by the same method. We now have the outcome spaces of these new variables. To complete the definition of these related variables we need to associate probabilities with the points in their outcome spaces.

We argue as follows. The probability that $\underset{\sim}{x}$ assumes the value 1 is $P(1) = \frac{1}{6}$. Now the probability that $5\underset{\sim}{x}$ assumes the value 5 will, by virtue of the relation between $\underset{\sim}{x}$ and $5\underset{\sim}{x}$, be also $\frac{1}{6}$. Similarly the probability that $5\underset{\sim}{x}$ assumes the value 20 will be the same as the probability that $\underset{\sim}{x}$ assumes the value 4, that is $\frac{1}{6}$. Hence to each point of the new outcome spaces we associate the probability to the corresponding point of the original outcome space.

The notation $\underset{\sim}{y} = \underset{\sim}{x} + 3$, $\underset{\sim}{z} = 5\underset{\sim}{x}$ and $\underset{\sim}{w} = \underset{\sim}{x}^2$ is sometimes used.

Example 1: There are three identical balls in a bag and they have painted on them the numbers -1, 0 and 1. Let the random variable $\underset{\sim}{x}$ be the drawing of one ball from the bag. Define $\underset{\sim}{x}$ and the related variable $\underset{\sim}{y} = \underset{\sim}{x}^2$.

Answer

A random variable is defined when the probabilities have been associated with the points of the outcome space.

For x

Outcome space	x_i	-1	0	1
Probabilities	$P(x_i)$	$\frac{1}{3}$	$\frac{1}{3}$	$\frac{1}{3}$

For $y = x^2$

Outcome space	x_i^2	1	0	1
Probabilities	$P(x_i^2)$	$\frac{1}{3}$	$\frac{1}{3}$	$\frac{1}{3}$

Giving

Outcome space	y_i	0	1
Probabilities	$P(y_i)$	$\frac{1}{3}$	$\frac{2}{3}$

This example serves to bring out two points. First, any related random variable formed must be single valued, that is from any point in the sample space of x it must not be possible to derive more than one point in the sample space of the related random variable, and secondly, if two or more points in the outcome space of the original variable correspond to only one point in the outcome space of the new related variable, then the probabilities of the original points are added and then associated with the new single point.

Example 2: If x is the random variable associated with throwing a fair dice, give an example of a situation to which the associated random variable x^2 may apply.

Answer

The random variable x^2 may apply to situations where players in a game receive an amount equal to the square of the number thrown, for instance if 3 is thrown then the players receive 9 units of whatever the stake units are.

2.3 Expectation of Related Variables

The last example of the previous section ignored the question of what would be a fair amount to stake on a game where players received an amount equal to the square of the number shown on a die. Let us now consider this point. We saw in *Example 4* of section 2.1 that the expectation, $E(x)$, of the random variable x defined by the rolling of a die, is 3·5. The argument of the section also implied that if a player were to receive the amount shown on the die after a roll, then over a long run of throws he would expect to receive £3·5 per throw, and thus a fair price to pay for admission to the game would be £3·5 per throw. We could repeat the arguments of section 2.1 to find a fair price to pay for admission to a game which pays the square of the amount shown on the die, but it would seem reasonable to assume that this amount would be the average, or expectation, of the random variable x^2. This indeed is the case and so we calculate $E(x^2)$. We recall that the expectation of a random variable is the sum of the products of the points in the sample space and the probabilities associated with these points. Thus taking the outcome space for $\underset{\sim}{x}^2$, as shown in section 2.2, and their associated probabilities we get,

$$E(\underset{\sim}{x}^2) = \left(1 \times \tfrac{1}{6}\right) + \left(4 \times \tfrac{1}{6}\right) + \left(9 \times \tfrac{1}{6}\right) + \left(16 \times \tfrac{1}{6}\right) + \left(25 \times \tfrac{1}{6}\right) + \left(36 \times \tfrac{1}{6}\right)$$
$$= \tfrac{91}{6} = 15\tfrac{1}{6}$$

Thus a fair price to pay would be £$15\frac{1}{6}$ per throw.

We now lead to an important theorem in expectation via examples. Let us calculate the expectation of the random variable $\underset{\sim}{x} + 3$ given in Section 2.2. Proceeding in the usual way, we get

$$E(\underset{\sim}{x}) + 3) = \left(4 \times \tfrac{1}{6}\right) + \left(5 \times \tfrac{1}{6}\right) + \left(6 \times \tfrac{1}{6}\right) + \left(7 \times \tfrac{1}{6}\right) + \left(8 \times \tfrac{1}{6}\right) + \left(9 \times \tfrac{1}{6}\right)$$

which can be written

$$E(\underset{\sim}{x} + 3) = \left[(1 + 3) \times \tfrac{1}{6}\right] + \left[(2 + 3) \times \tfrac{1}{6}\right] + \left[(3 + 3) \times \tfrac{1}{6}\right] + \left[(4 + 3) \times \tfrac{1}{6}\right]$$
$$+ \left[(5 + 3) \times \tfrac{1}{6}\right] + \left[(6 + 3) \times \tfrac{1}{6}\right]$$
$$= \left[\left(1 \times \tfrac{1}{6}\right) + \left(2 \times \tfrac{1}{6}\right) + \left(3 \times \tfrac{1}{6}\right) + \left(4 \times \tfrac{1}{6}\right) + \left(5 \times \tfrac{1}{6}\right) + \left(6 \times \tfrac{1}{6}\right)\right] +$$
$$+ \left[\left(3 \times \tfrac{1}{6}\right) + \left(3 \times \tfrac{1}{6}\right) + \left(3 \times \tfrac{1}{6}\right) + \left(3 \times \tfrac{1}{6}\right) + \left(3 \times \tfrac{1}{6}\right) + \left(3 \times \tfrac{1}{6}\right)\right]$$
$$= E(\underset{\sim}{x}) + 3$$

And this result suggests that $E(\underset{\sim}{x} + b) = E(\underset{\sim}{x}) + b$, where b is any constant.

Let us now calculate the expectation of the random variable $5\underset{\sim}{x}$ given in Section 2.2. Proceed as before to get

$$E(5\underset{\sim}{x}) = \left(5 \times \tfrac{1}{6}\right) + \left(10 \times \tfrac{1}{6}\right) + \left(15 \times \tfrac{1}{6}\right) + \left(20 \times \tfrac{1}{6}\right) + \left(25 \times \tfrac{1}{6}\right) + \left(30 \times \tfrac{1}{6}\right)$$

which can be written

$$E(5\underset{\sim}{x}) = 5\left[\left(1 \times \tfrac{1}{6}\right) + \left(2 \times \tfrac{1}{6}\right) + \left(3 \times \tfrac{1}{6}\right) + \left(4 \times \tfrac{1}{6}\right) + \left(5 \times \tfrac{1}{6}\right) + \left(6 \times \tfrac{1}{6}\right)\right]$$
$$= 5E(\underset{\sim}{x})$$

And this result suggests that $E(a\underset{\sim}{x}) = aE(\underset{\sim}{x})$ where a is any constant. Combining the last two results we get the theorem $E(a\underset{\sim}{x} + b) = aE(\underset{\sim}{x}) + b$, the proof of which follows the lines indicated in the examples.

Example 1: If $\underset{\sim}{x}$ is the random variable associated with the rolling of a dice find $E(4\underset{\sim}{x} - 5)$.

Answer

$$E(4\underset{\sim}{x} - 5) = 4E(\underset{\sim}{x}) - 5 = 4 \times 3{\cdot}5 - 5 = 9$$

2.4 Variance in terms of Expectation

If $\underset{\sim}{x}$ is a discrete random variable with mean μ, let us consider the related random variable $(\underset{\sim}{x} - \mu)^2$. In words this says 'subtract the mean from every possible value of $\underset{\sim}{x}$ and then square the result', and we note that this is the first part of the process of finding the variance. The part which would complete the definition of the variance is 'then divide the sum of these squares by n' or 'take the average'. We have seen that the definition of expectation can be considered as the 'taking of the average of the random variable', and so if we take the expectation of the random variable $(\underset{\sim}{x} - \mu)^2$ we will be finding its average. Hence the variance of a random variable $\underset{\sim}{x}$ can be defined as the expectation of the related random variable $(\underset{\sim}{x} - \mu)^2$, that is $\sigma^2 = E[(\underset{\sim}{x} - \mu)^2]$

Note that
$$\left.\begin{aligned} E[(\underset{\sim}{x} - \mu)^2] &= E[(\underset{\sim}{x}^2 - 2\mu x + \mu^2)] \\ &= E(\underset{\sim}{x}^2) - E(2\mu\underset{\sim}{x}) + E(\mu^2) \\ &= E(\underset{\sim}{x}^2) - 2\mu E(\underset{\sim}{x}) + \mu^2 \\ &= E(\underset{\sim}{x}^2) - 2[E(\underset{\sim}{x})]^2 + [E(x)]^2 \\ &= E(\underset{\sim}{x}^2) - [E(x)]^2 \end{aligned}\right] \text{using the results of the previous sections}$$

Note the similarity between

$$s^2 = \frac{\sum\limits_i x_i^2}{n} - \left[\frac{\sum\limits_i x_i}{n}\right]^2$$

and the last result. They are in fact equivalent forms of the same thing namely, a shorter method of finding the variance. Note also the similarity of the algebraic manipulation.

As before the standard deviation is the square root of the variance and so we have a method of finding the standard deviation of a random variable in terms of expectation.

Example 1: A regular tetrahedron has the numbers 1, 2, 3 and 4 on the faces, find the standard deviation of the random variable associated with the 'throwing of the tetrahedron'.

Answer

The random variable $\underset{\sim}{x}$ has outcome space $\{1, 2, 3, 4\}$ with probabilities $P(1) = P(2) = P(3) = P(4) = \frac{1}{4}$. First find the variance.

$$\sigma^2 = E[(\underset{\sim}{x} - \mu)^2] = E(\underset{\sim}{x}^2) - [E(\underset{\sim}{x})]^2$$

$$= \left[\left(1^2 \times \frac{1}{4}\right) + \left(2^2 \times \frac{1}{4}\right) + \left(3^3 \times \frac{1}{4}\right) + \left(4^2 \times \frac{1}{4}\right)\right] - \left(\frac{5}{2}\right)^2$$

$$= \frac{1 + 4 + 9 + 16}{4} - \frac{25}{4}$$

$$= \frac{30 - 25}{4} = \frac{5}{4} = 1{\cdot}25$$

Hence the standard deviation, $\sigma = \sqrt{1{\cdot}25} \simeq 1{\cdot}12$

We shall refer to the variance of a random variable with the notation $\text{Var}(\underset{\sim}{x})$. We now consider the problem of $\text{Var}(a\underset{\sim}{x} + b)$ in the same way as we considered the problem of $E(a\underset{\sim}{x} + b)$. First we consider $\text{Var}(\underset{\sim}{x} + b)$ and to do this we need the mean of the distribution $\underset{\sim}{x} + b$. We find the mean of $\underset{\sim}{x} + b$ by considering its expectation; $E(\underset{\sim}{x} + b) = E(\underset{\sim}{x}) + E(b) = E(\underset{\sim}{x}) + b = \mu + b$. We can now find the variance of the variable $\underset{\sim}{x} + b$.

$$\text{Var}(\underset{\sim}{x} + b) = E\{[\underset{\sim}{x} + b) - (\mu + b)]^2\}$$

$$= E[(\underset{\sim}{x} + b - \mu - b)^2] = E[(\underset{\sim}{x} - \mu)^2]$$

$$= \text{Var}(\underset{\sim}{x})$$

Secondly we consider $\text{Var}(a\underset{\sim}{x})$, and to do this we need the mean of $a\underset{\sim}{x}$.

$$E(a\underset{\sim}{x}) = aE(\underset{\sim}{x}) = a\mu$$

This gives us

$$\text{Var}(a\underset{\sim}{x}) = E[(a\underset{\sim}{x} - a\mu)^2] = E[a^2(\underset{\sim}{x} - \mu)^2] = a^2E[x - \mu)^2]$$

$$= a^2\,\text{Var}(\underset{\sim}{x}).$$

These two results combine to give $\text{Var}(a\underset{\sim}{x} + b) = a^2\,\text{Var}(\underset{\sim}{x})$. The proof follows the lines of the above examples and is left for the reader.

Example 2: Describe in words $\text{Var}(\underset{\sim}{x} + b) = \text{Var}(\underset{\sim}{x})$.

Answer

The random variable $\underset{\sim}{x} + b$ is formed by adding the constant b to all possible values of $\underset{\sim}{x}$. The effect of this addition will be to move the distribution along the axis a distance of b. This addition will not affect the way the distribution is arranged round the mean and hence there will be no change in the variance, Fig. 2.4(a).

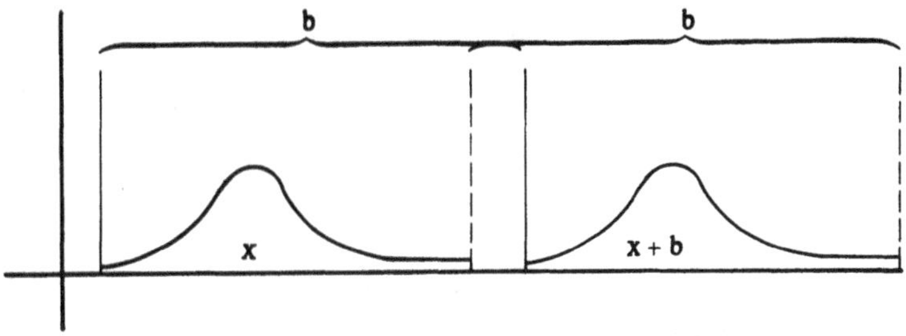

Fig. 2.4 (a)

The student should at all times attempt to put into verbal form the meaning of the symbols with which he is working.

2.5 Moments

Let us now generalise the ideas of the previous sections as follows. If we take $E[(\underset{\sim}{x} - k)^r]$, where k is any constant and r a non-negative integer, then we get what is called the r'th moment of the distribution of **x** about the point k. If $k = 0$ and $r = 1$, we get $E[(\underset{\sim}{x} = \mu$. If $k = \mu$ and $r = 2$ we get, $E(\underset{\sim}{x}) - \mu)^2] = \sigma^2$. Thus it can be seen that by varying k and r all possible variations can be obtained. The term moment is borrowed from physics where it is defined as the product of a force and it's distance from the point about which the moment is taken. If several forces are involved the moment of this system of forces about a point is found by adding all the products of the last sentence. The analogy in statistics is that the probabilities of a function are considered as 'weights' or 'forces' acting vertically downwards on the axis. If one then wishes to take moments about the origin then the sum $\sum_i x_i P(x_i)$ is formed. If moments are taken about the point b on the axis then the sum $\sum_i (x_i - b)P(x_i)$ is formed, and it will be seen how closely these sums resemble ones met earlier in the book, and hence the reasonableness of borrowing the term 'moment'. If the reader has some knowledge of physics this point will be clear, if not, then the term 'moment' should be regarded as a technical term defined as above.

From this it will be noted that first moments can be used to find the mean of a probability distribution, and the second moments can be used to find the variance, and hence the standard deviation. The third moments can be used as a measure of the skewness of a distribution. It may also be seen that the taking of moments about an arbitrary number is equivalent to the device of using an assumed mean to simplify calculations of various statistics. To this end we consider the example

Example 1: $E[(\underset{\sim}{x} - \mu)^2] = E\{[(\underset{\sim}{x} - k) - (\mu - k)]^2\}$

$$= E[(\underset{\sim}{x} - k)^2 - 2(\underset{\sim}{x} - k)(\mu - k) + (\mu - k)^2]$$

$$= E[(\underset{\sim}{x} - k)^2] - 2(\mu - k)E[(\underset{\sim}{x} - k)] + E[(\mu - k)^2]$$

$$= E[(\underset{\sim}{x} - k)^2] - 2(\mu - k)^2 + (\mu - k)^2$$

$$= E[(\underset{\sim}{x} - k)^2] - (\mu - k)^2$$

Note the similarity of this and the expression

$$s^2 = \frac{\Sigma(x_i - K)^2}{n} - (\bar{x} - K)^2$$

which is the method of finding the variance by using an assumed mean K. The similarity of the algebraic manipulation should also be noted.

Example 2: Calculate $E(\underset{\sim}{x})$, $E[(\underset{\sim}{x} - \mu)]$, $E[(\underset{\sim}{x} - \mu)^2]$, $E[(\underset{\sim}{x} - \mu)^3]$ for the random variable defined by the throwing of a tetrahedron.

Answer

The tabulation can be most conveniently arranged in the following table:

x_i	$P(x_i)$	$x_iP(x_i)$	$(x_i - \mu)$	$(x_i - \mu)P(x_i)$	$(x_i - \mu)^2P(x_i)$	$(x_i - \mu)^3P(x_i)$
1	0·25	0·25	−1·5	−0·375	0·5625	−0·84375
2	0·25	0·50	−0·5	−0·125	0·0625	−0·03375
3	0·25	0·75	0·5	0·125	0·0625	0·03375
4	0·25	1·00	1·5	0·375	0·5625	0·84755
	1·00	2·5	0·0	0·000	1·2500	0·00000

$$E(\underset{\sim}{x}) = \Sigma x_iP(x_i) = 2{\cdot}5 \quad E[(\underset{\sim}{x} - \mu)] = \Sigma(x_i - \mu)P(x_i) = 0$$

$$E[(\underset{\sim}{x} - \mu)^2] = \Sigma(x_i - \mu)^2P(x_i) = 1{\cdot}25$$

$$E[(\underset{\sim}{x} - \mu)^3] = \Sigma(x_i - \mu)^3P(x_i) = 0$$

So far we have looked at moments in terms of expectation and probability distributions. In doing so we noted that there was a similarity between them and the formulae used in calculating the mean and variance of a numerical distribution. We therefore take the idea of moments and apply them to numerical distributions. Accordingly we define

$$m_r(k) = \frac{\Sigma(x_i - k)^r}{n}$$

to be the r'th moment about k of the distribution of the set of numbers x_i.

If the x_i's occur with frequencies f_i then

$$m_r(k) = \frac{\Sigma f_i(x_i - k)^r}{\Sigma f_i}$$

Note

$$m_1(0) = \frac{\Sigma f_i x_i}{\Sigma f_i} = \bar{x}$$

$$m_2(\bar{x}) = \frac{\Sigma f_i (x_i - \bar{x})^2}{\Sigma f_i} = s^2$$

just as in the case of expectation.

Example 3: Show that $m_2(\bar{x}) = m_2(0) - m_1^2(0)$

$$\begin{aligned} m_2(\bar{x}) &= \frac{\Sigma(x_i - \bar{x})^2}{n} \\ &= \frac{\Sigma(x_i^2 - 2\bar{x}x_i + \bar{x}^2)}{n} \\ &= \frac{\Sigma x_i^2 - 2\bar{x}\Sigma x_i + \Sigma\bar{x}^2}{n} \\ &= \frac{\Sigma x_i^2}{n} - \frac{2\bar{x}\Sigma x_i}{n} + \bar{x}^2 \\ &= \frac{\Sigma x_i^2}{n} - 2\bar{x}^2 + \bar{x}^2 \\ &= \frac{\Sigma x_i^2}{n} - \bar{x}^2 \\ &= m_2(0) - m_1^2(0) \end{aligned}$$

Example 4: $m_2(\bar{x}) = m_2(a) - m_1^2(a)$ is the moment equivalent of finding the variance by the assumed mean method.

Example 5: Given the distribution shown in the first two columns of the table, find $m_1(0)$, $m_2(\bar{x})$, and $m_3(\bar{x})$.

x_i	f_i	$f_i x_i$	$(x_i - 2)$	$f_i(x_i - 2)$	$f_i(x_i - 2)^2$	$f_i(x_i - 2)^3$
1	1	1	–1	–1	1	–1
2	7	14	0	0	0	0
3	4	12	1	4	4	4
4	2	8	2	4	8	16
5	1	5	3	3	9	27
	15	40	5	10	22	46

Answer

$$m_1(0) = \frac{\Sigma f_i x_i}{\Sigma f_i} = \frac{40}{15} = 2{\cdot}66\dot{6}$$

Because $m_1(0)$, that is the mean, is non-integral, finding higher moments is more conveniently done by using an assumed mean. We elect to take an assumed mean of 2, and this gives us the four right hand columns in the above table.

$$m_2(\bar{x}) = m_2(2) - m_1^2(2) \quad \text{(from \textit{example 4})}$$

$$= \frac{\Sigma f_i(x_i - 2)^2}{\Sigma f_i} - \left\{\frac{\Sigma f_i(x_i - 2)}{\Sigma f_i}\right\}^2$$

$$= \frac{22}{15} - \left(\frac{10}{15}\right)^2 = 1{\cdot}467 - 0{\cdot}444 = 1{\cdot}023$$

By an algebraic process similar to that used in *example 3* it can be shown that

$$m_3(\bar{x}) = m_3(2) - 3m_1(2)m_2(2) + 2m_1^3(2)$$

$$= \frac{46}{15} - 3\left(\frac{10}{15}\right)\left(\frac{22}{15}\right) + 2\left(\frac{10}{15}\right)^3$$

$$= 3{\cdot}067 - 2{\cdot}933 + 0{\cdot}573 = 0{\cdot}697$$

The second and third moments about the mean can be used to measure the skewness of a distribution. To this end we define the

$$\text{moment coefficient of skewness} = \text{M.Sk.} = \frac{m_3(\bar{x})}{\sqrt{m_2^3(\bar{x})}}$$

which, because both $m_3(\bar{x})$ and $m_2(\bar{x})$ are in the units of the variable, will be dimensionless; that is a pure number.

Example 6: Find the moment coefficient of skewness of the distribution in *example* 5.

Answer

$$\text{M.Sk.} = \frac{0{\cdot}697}{\sqrt{(1{\cdot}023)^3}} = 0{\cdot}674$$

The notation $m_r(k)$ will be used for both numerical distributions and random variables (probability distributions). When used for numerical distributions it will be

$$m_r(k) = \frac{\sum_i f_i(x_i - k)^r}{\sum f_i}$$

and when used for a random variable it will be

$$m_r(k) = \sum_i (x_i - k)^r P(x_i)$$

Thus it will be noted in the latter case that $m_r(k) = E[(x_i - k)^r]$.

As a further clarification we note that we talk about 'Expectation' in relation to a random variable only – the term is not used in connection with a numerical distribution.

Exercise 2

1. Find the expectation of the random variable $\underset{\sim}{y}$ defined by the rolling of a tetrahedron.

Answer
2·5

2. An octagonal prism has the numbers 1 to 8 painted one to a face. Find the expectation of the random variable $\underset{\sim}{z}$ defined by the rolling of this prism.

Answer
4·5

3. Plot on a graph the results of number 1 and number 2 together with the expectation of the random variable defined by the rolling of a die. Comment on the results and use your graph to invent and solve similar questions.

4. A raffle has three prizes worth £100, £50 and £20. Determine a fair price for the tickets if (a) 100 (b) 500 (c) 1,000 tickets are sold.

Answer
(a) £1·70 (c) 17p

5. Graph the results of the previous problem and comment.

6. If the ice-cream salesman of *Example 5* of section 8.1 works solidly through the season June to August, how many wet days will make his result for the season a loss?

Answer

77 or more

7. Compare the two formulae $E(\underset{\sim}{x}) = \Sigma x_i P(x_i)$ and $\bar{x} = \dfrac{\Sigma f_i x_i}{\Sigma f_i}$

8. Consider the game of rolling a die. If a win is rolling a six and the bank pays (a) £6 (b) £8 (c) £20 for a win, what should be the stakes for the games to be fair? Assume stake money is not returned. Graph your results.

Answer

(a) $83\frac{1}{3}$p (b) £$1\frac{1}{3}$ (c) £$3\frac{1}{3}$.

9. Two people X and Y roll a die. If a 3 is thrown X gives Y £8, but if a 1, 2, 4, 5, or 6 is thrown then Y gives X £1·60. Is this a fair game? Explain any difference between this result and (b) of the previous question.

Answer

Game fair.

10. A bag contains 2 black and 3 white balls. Three people A, B and C draw in succession (in that order) one ball and do not replace it. The first person to draw a white ball wins £10. Find their expectations hence determine what stakes they should pay.

Answer

£6, £3, £1, for A, B, C respectively.

11. A bag contains 2 black and 3 white balls. Four people draw in succession without replacement and the first person to draw a black ball wins £20. Find their stakes for a fair game.

Answer

£8, £6, £4, and £2 for first, second, third and fourth draws respectively.

12. Given the random variable $\underset{\sim}{y}$ as in number 1, find the probability distributions (that is the outcome space and set of associated probabilities) of the related random variables (a) $\underset{\sim}{y} + 7$ (b) $\underset{\sim}{y}^3$ (c) $\underset{\sim}{y} - 2$ (d) $\underset{\sim}{y} - 2{\cdot}5$ (e) $(\underset{\sim}{y} - 2)^2$

Answer

(a)

8	9	10	11
$\frac{1}{4}$	$\frac{1}{4}$	$\frac{1}{4}$	$\frac{1}{4}$

(b)

-1	0	1	2
$\frac{1}{4}$	$\frac{1}{4}$	$\frac{1}{4}$	$\frac{1}{4}$

(c)

0	1	4
$\frac{1}{4}$	$\frac{1}{2}$	$\frac{1}{4}$

13. Given the random variable $\underset{\sim}{z}$ as in number 2, find the probability distributions for the related random variables (a) $\underset{\sim}{z} - 4$ (b) $(\underset{\sim}{z} - 4)^2$ (c) $(2\underset{\sim}{z} - 8)$ (d) $(\underset{\sim}{z}/2 - 2{\cdot}5)^2$

Answer

(b)

0	1	4	9	16
$\frac{1}{8}$	$\frac{1}{4}$	$\frac{1}{4}$	$\frac{1}{4}$	$\frac{1}{8}$

(d)

0	$\frac{1}{4}$	1	$2\frac{1}{4}$	4
$\frac{1}{8}$	$\frac{1}{4}$	$\frac{1}{4}$	$\frac{1}{4}$	$\frac{1}{8}$

14. Prove $E(a\underset{\sim}{x} + b) = aE(\underset{\sim}{x}) + b$

15. Prove $\mathrm{Var}(a\underset{\sim}{x} + b) = a^2\,\mathrm{Var}(\underset{\sim}{x})$

16. Using the method of expectation, find the mean and variance of the distributions given in numbers 12 and 13.

Answer

	12			13	
	(a)	(c)	(e)	(a)	(c)
mean	9.5	$\frac{1}{2}$	$1\frac{1}{2}$	$\frac{1}{2}$	4
variance	$1\frac{1}{4}$	$1\frac{1}{4}$	$2\frac{1}{4}$	$5\frac{1}{4}$	6

17. Prove (i) $m_2(\bar{x}) = m_2(a) - m_1^2(a)$

(ii) $m_3(\bar{x}) = m_3(a) - 3m_1(a)m_2(a) + 2m_1^3(a)$

18. State and prove a result similar to those in number 17 for $m_4(\bar{x})$.

19. Explain why the moment coefficient of skewness as defined in section 2.5 can be used as a measure of skewness.

20. Find the moment coefficient of skewness for the distribution given in number 2.

Answer

0

3 The Binomial Distribution

3.1 Introduction

The binomial distribution is a theoretical distribution which applies to situations where there are two, and only two, possible outcomes.

Experiment	*Outcome 1*	*Outcome 2*
(a) Tossing of pennies	Head	Tail
(b) Births of babies	Boy	Girl
(c) Driving tests	Pass	Fail

Such experiments consist of a large numbers of trials – the tossing of a penny is one trial, the birth of one baby is one trial, the driving test of an individual is one trial – and these trials can be repeated over and over again – we can toss the penny again, we can observe the birth of other babies, we can observe different individuals taking their driving tests – and because of this it is said that the binomial distribution applies to situations involving *repeated trials*. The repeated trials of course forming the experiment.

Usually in such situations we are more interested in one outcome than the other, and if the subject of our interest occurs we say that the trial was a *success*; if it does not occur, we say that the trial was a *failure*. This usage of 'success' and 'failure' terminology is a hangover from the time when probability theory was considered exclusively in connection with games of chance, and the occurrence of a 'success' was, indeed, a success. Present day use of these terms does not have this connotation. If we are interested in the birth of male babies, then the birth of a female baby will be regarded as a failure. This example makes it quite obvious that a 'success' does not necessarily imply an advantageous or desirable outcome.

3.2 Assumptions underlying the Binomial Distribution

Before the binomial distribution may be applied to experiments consisting of a series of repeated trials, the trials themselves must satisfy two conditions:

(1) The probability of success must be constant from trial to trial

(2) The trials must be independent

Example 1: The tossing of a coin satisfies the two conditions providing that it undergoes no change during the experiment.

Example 2: Rain at a certain point during a period of time. (Here the occurrence of rain on any one day will be counted a success for one trial). It is obvious here that the probability that it will rain on any day will not remain constant from day to day. After a period without rain the probability of rain becomes greater and so condition (1) is not satisfied and the binomial distribution is not applicable.

3.3 Notation

If we let p = the probability of a success in one trial, and q = the probability of a failure for the same trial, then, since we must either get a success or a failure, $p + q = 1$. The two forms, $p = 1 - q$ and $q = 1 - p$, are frequently useful.

Example 1: If the probability of a success in one trial is $\frac{3}{19}$ what is the probability of a failure?

Answer

$$p = \tfrac{3}{19}, \quad q = 1 - p = 1 - \tfrac{3}{19} = \tfrac{16}{19}$$

Consider now a situation where the probability of success in one trial is $\frac{1}{4}$, and hence the probability of failure is $\frac{3}{4}$.

(a) The binomial representing one trial is

$$\left(\frac{3}{4} + \frac{1}{4}\right)^1 = \frac{3}{4} + \frac{1}{4}$$

If we now examine the indivual terms in the expansion, we see that the first term represents the probability of a failure, and the second term represents the probability of a success.

(b) The binomial representing two trials is

$$\left(\frac{3}{4} + \frac{1}{4}\right)^2 = \frac{3}{4}.\frac{3}{4} + 2.\frac{3}{4}.\frac{1}{4} + \frac{1}{4}.\frac{1}{4}$$

If we now examine the individual terms in the expansion we see that the first term represents the probability of two failures in the two trials, and the last term represents the probability of two successes in the two trials. The middle term represents the probability of one success and one failure in the two trials, and since there are two ways in which one success and one failure may occur in two trials – either (s,f) or (f,s) – then the term has the coefficient 2.

(c) The binomial representing three trials is

$$\left(\frac{3}{4} + \frac{1}{4}\right)^3 = \frac{3}{4}\cdot\frac{3}{4}\cdot\frac{3}{4} + 3\cdot\frac{3}{4}\cdot\frac{3}{4}\cdot\frac{1}{4} + 3\cdot\frac{3}{4}\cdot\frac{1}{4}\cdot\frac{1}{4} + \frac{1}{4}\cdot\frac{1}{4}\cdot\frac{1}{4}$$

If we now examine the individual terms in the expansion we see that the first term represents the probability of three failures in three trials; the second term represents the probability of two failures and one success in the three trials and since this can occur in three ways – either (f,f,s) or $(f.s.f)$ or $(s.f.f)$ – then this term has the coefficient 3; the third term represents the probability of one failure and two successes in three trials, and since this can occur in three ways – either (s,s,f) or (s,f,s) or (f,s,s) – then this term has the coefficient 3; the last term represents the probability that there will be three successes in three trials.

(d) The binomial representing n trials is

$$\left(\frac{3}{4} + \frac{1}{4}\right)^n = \left(\frac{3}{4}\right)^n + nC1\left(\frac{3}{4}\right)^{n-1}\left(\frac{1}{4}\right) + nC2\left(\frac{3}{4}\right)^{n-2}\left(\frac{1}{4}\right)^2 + \ldots + nCx\left(\frac{3}{4}\right)^{n-x}\left(\frac{1}{4}\right)^r$$
$$+ \ldots + nCn\left(\frac{3}{4}\right)^0\left(\frac{1}{4}\right)^n.$$

Again examining the individual terms of the expansion we see that the first term represents the probability of n failures in n trials; the second term represents $(n - 1)$ failures and one success in the n trials, and since in the series of n trials this may occur in $nC1$ ways, the term has the coefficient $nC1$; the general term represents the probability of $(n - x)$ failures and x successes in the n trials, and since this may occur in nCx ways, this term has the coefficient nCx; the final term represents the probability of n successes in n trials and since this can happen in $nCn = 1$ way, then this term has the coefficient nCn. The corresponding coefficient for the first term is $nC0 = 1$, which has been omitted.

(e) We now consider the more abstract case where the probability of a success in a single trial is p. The binomial term representing n trials is

$$(q + p)^n = nC0q^np^0 + nC1q^{n-1}p + nC2q^{n-2}p^2 + nC3q^{n-3}p^3 +$$
$$nCxq^{n-x}p^x + \ldots + nCnq^0p^n.$$

The individual items of the expansion representing the probability of

n failures	0 successes
$n - 1$ failures	1 success
$n - 2$ failures	2 successes
$n - 3$ failures	3 successes
$n - x$ failures	x successes
0 failures	n successes

The above form can be abbreviated, using sigma notation, to

$$(q + p)^n = \sum_{x=0}^{n} nCxq^{n-x}p^x$$

Remembering that $q + p = 1$, then $(q + p)^n = 1$,

$$\text{and } 1 = \sum_{x=0}^{n} nCxq^{n-x}p^x$$

The general term of the expansion $nCxq^{n-x}p^x$ represents the probability of $(n - x)$ failures and x successes in n trials with a probability of success p. This will be referred to as

$$B(x;n,p) = nCxq^{n-x}p^x$$

for $x = 0, 1, 2, \ldots, n$. The notation $B(x;n,p)$ is self explanatory

Because this is a mathematical model the distribution that arises is a forecast of what should happen. For this reason it is called a probability distribution – that is what will happen in all probability. Since this distribution takes discrete values only $(x = 0, 1, 2, \ldots, n)$ then it is called a *discrete probability distribution*, or a *discrete probability function.*

Let us now see how the binomial distribution compares with the axioms of probability (as given in Section 7.3, *Descriptive Statistics and Probability Theory*).

(1) $0 \leqslant P(A) \leqslant 1$ for all $A \subset S$
For the binomial, S is the set $\{0, 1, 2, \ldots, n\}$ and A is any subset of S. Taking the general term of the binomial $B(x;n,p) = nCxq^{n-x}p^x$ we see that for all x, $0 \leqslant B(x;n,p) \leqslant 1$, so the binomial satisfies the first axiom.

(2) $P(S) = 1$. Since $q + p = 1$ $(q + p)^n = 1 = \sum_{x=0}^{n} nCxq^{n-x}p^x$ and the second axiom is satisfied.

(3) $P(A_1 \cup A_2 \cup \ldots) = P(A_1) + P(A_2) + \ldots$
If, for example $A_1 = \{0\}$, $A_2 = \{1\}$, $A_3 = \{2\}$, and $A_4 = \{3\}$, then $P(A_1 \cup A_2 \cup A_3 \cup A_4) = P(\{0, 1, 2, 3\}) = \sum_{x=0}^{3} nCxq^{n-x}p^x = P(A_1) + P(A_2) + P(A_3) + P(A_4)$, and again we see that this axiom is satisfied. Any other set of disjoint subsets will give a like result.

We see thus that the binomial probability distribution satisfies the axioms of probability, and we now state that for any distribution to be a probability distribution it must satisfy the axioms of probability.

3.4 Graphs I

If we code success and failure in the following way:

success = 1 failure = 0

then we can make use of cartesian products sets of various dimensions.

(a) $(q + p)^1 = q + p$. The individual terms are of one dimension and so can be represented on a line:

Fig. 3.4(a)

(b) $(q + p)^2 = q^2 + 2qp + p^2$. The individual terms are of two dimensions and so can be represented on a two dimensional diagram of the product set $\{0,1\} \times \{0,1\}$.

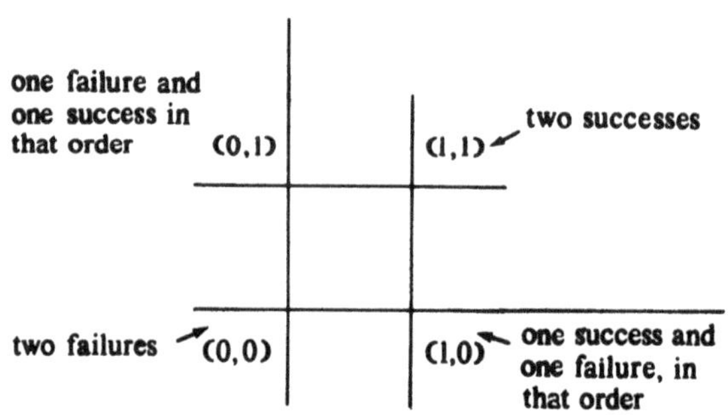

Fig. 3.4(b)

(c) $(q + p)^3 = q^3 + 3q^2p + 3qp^2 + p^3$. The individual terms are of three dimensions and so can be represented on a three dimensional diagram of the product set $\{0,1\} \times \{0,1\} \times \{0,1\}$.

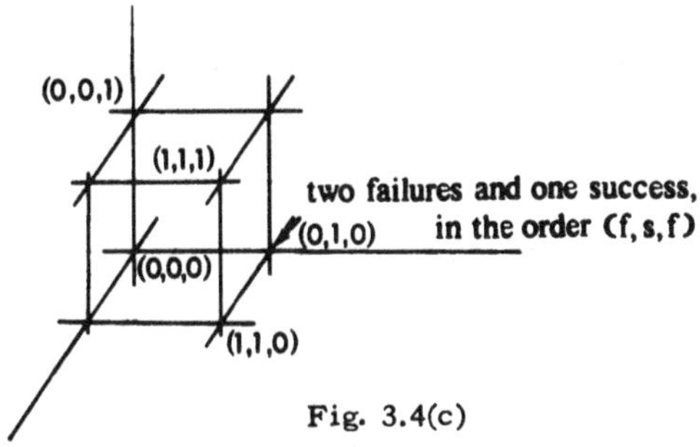

Fig. 3.4(c)

It is obviously not possible to draw diagrams where individual items of a dimension greater than three, but it is still possible to use the product sets. If the experiment consisted of six throws, or trials, then the product set $\{0,1\} \times \{0,1\} \times \{0,1\} \times \{0,1\} \times \{0,1\} \times \{0,1\}$ which consists of the six dimensional elements (0,0,0,0,0,0), (0,0,0,0,0,1) through to (1,1,1,1,1,1) would represent the various combinations of success and failure. For experiments consisting of n trials then the product set consisting of n dimensional elements

$$\overbrace{(0,0,1,0,1,1,1,\ \ldots,\ 1,0,1,1)}^{n \text{ places}}$$

which again represent the various combinations of success and failure in the n trials.

3.5 Graphs II

The graphs of the previous section are of very limited use and so in this section we introduce graphs which are of much wider application. We shall, as examples, graph the distributions given in Section 3.3.

(a) Graph to show the distribution of successes in one trial when $p = \frac{1}{4}$.

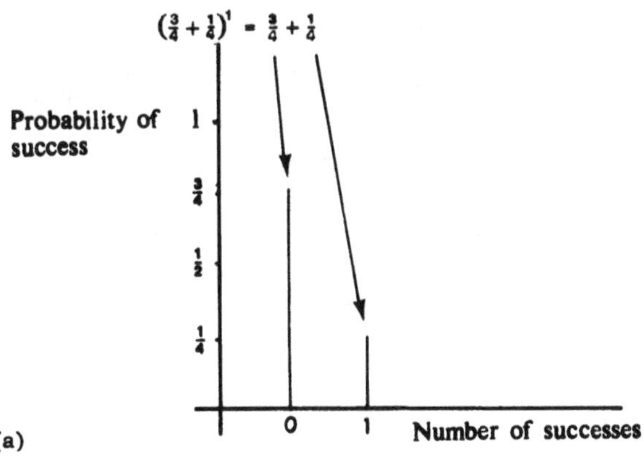

Fig. 3.5(a)

(b) Graph to show the distribution of successes in two trials when $p = \frac{1}{4}$.

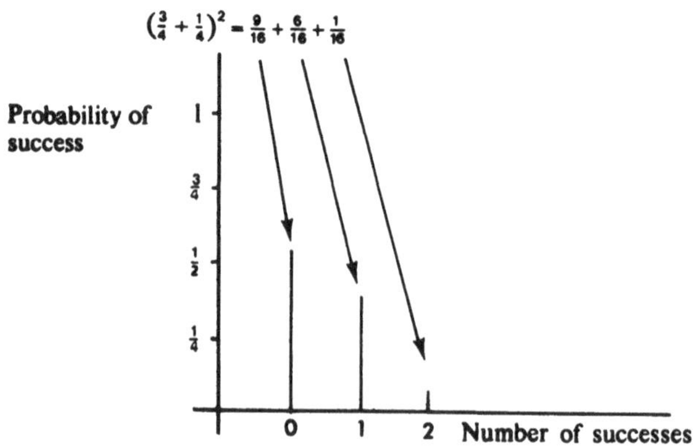

Fig. 3.5 (b)

(c) Graph to show the distribution of successes in three trials when $p = \frac{1}{4}$.

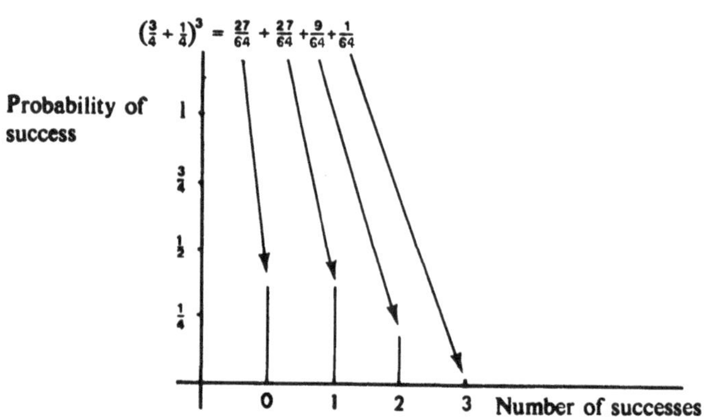

Fig. 3.5 (c)

It will now be seen that since we are graphing the number of successes, and this will be a number between 0 and n, then there is no difficulty in representing binomial distributions of dimension greater than three.

In the graphs just drawn, the general shape is

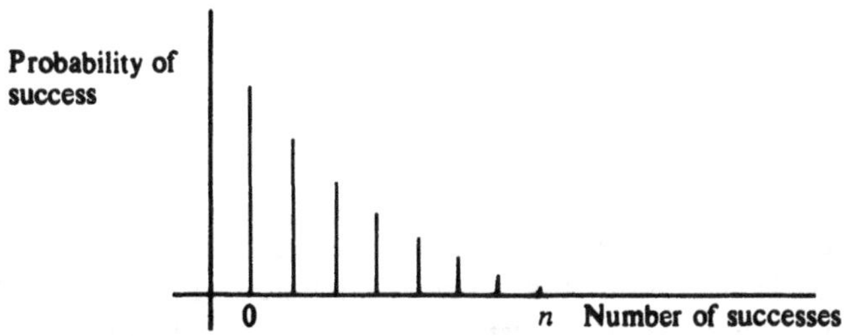

Fig. 3.5 (d)

and we note that $p = \frac{1}{4}$ is fairly small.

If the probability of success were to increase to, say $\frac{1}{2}$, then the general shape of the graph when $(\frac{1}{2} + \frac{1}{2})^n$ is expanded would be:

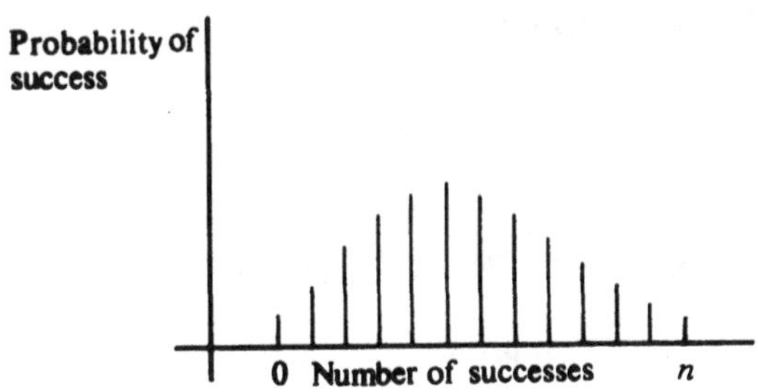

Fig, 3.5 (e)

that is symmetrical. This might have been deduced by arguing that if $p = \frac{1}{2}$, the $q = \frac{1}{2}$, and there is just as much chance of getting a success and a failure, and so the distribution will be evenly balanced.

If the probability of success is high, say $p = \frac{9}{10}$, then the shape of the graph when $(\frac{1}{10} + \frac{9}{10})^n$ is expanded would be:

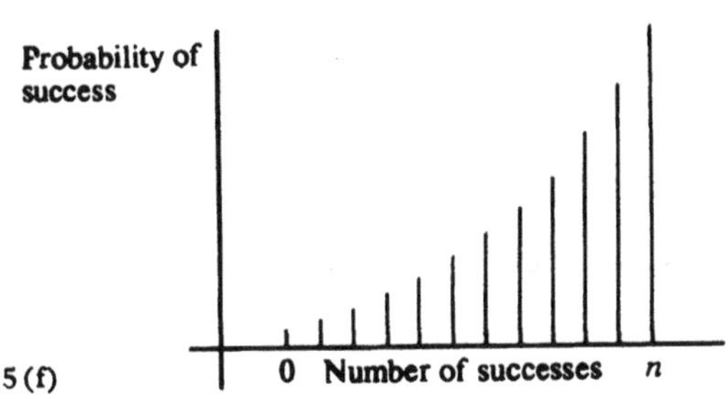

Fig. 3.5 (f)

The student is urged to work through

(a) $(\frac{1}{2} + \frac{1}{2})^1$; $(\frac{1}{2} + \frac{1}{2})^2$; $(\frac{1}{2} + \frac{1}{2})^3$; and so on.

(b) $(\frac{1}{10} + \frac{9}{10})^1$; $(\frac{1}{10} + \frac{9}{10})^2$; $(\frac{1}{10} + \frac{9}{10})^3$; and so on, until he becomes convinced of the truth of these last remarks.

3.6 The Mean

When we have actual numerical data one of the first things about it we wish to find is the mean. Now we have the binomial probability distribution likewise one of the first things we wish to know is the mean.

We might argue as follows: If we have one hundred trials and the probability of a success is $\frac{1}{4}$, then we would expect 25 successes, or $100 \times \frac{1}{4}$. Generalising this we would say that if we have n trials and the probability of a success is p, then we would expect np successes. With this advanced knowledge let us now prove that the mean is in fact np.

Let $\underset{\sim}{x}$ be the binomial distribution $B(x,n,p)$. The mean μ of any distribution is defined as $E(\underset{\sim}{x})$, thus,

$$\mu = E(\underset{\sim}{x}) = \sum_{x=0}^{n} xP(x)$$

but $$P(x) = B(x,n,p) = nCxq^{n-x}p^x,$$

giving $$E(\underset{\sim}{x}) = \sum_{x=0}^{n} xnCxq^{n-x}p^x, \quad x = 0, 1, 2, \ldots, n$$

When $x = 0$, the first term disappears giving,

$$E(\underset{\sim}{x}) = \sum_{x=1}^{n} x \cdot \frac{n!}{(n-x)!x!} q^{n-x}p^x$$

cancelling the x against the first factor of $x!$ gives

$$E(\underset{\sim}{x}) = \sum_{x=1}^{n} \frac{n!}{(n-x)!(x-1)!} q^{n-x}p^x$$

Now factor n from $n!$. and p from p^x (by virtue of our advanced knowledge of the result to be expected)

$$E(\underset{\sim}{x}) = np\sum_{x=1}^{n} \frac{(n-1)!}{(n-x)!(x-1)!} q^{n-x}p^{x-1}$$

$$= np\sum_{x=1}^{n} (n-1)C(x-1)q^{n-x}p^{x-1}$$

now expanding the sigma sign we get

$$E(\underset{\sim}{x}) = np({}_{n-1}C_0 q^{n-1}p^0 + {}_{n-1}C_1 q^{n-2}p^1 + {}_{n-1}C_2 q^{n-3}p^2 + \ldots + {}_{n-1}C_{n-1} q^0 p^{n-1})$$

$$= np(q+p)^{n-1}$$

$$= np \quad \text{since} \quad (q+p) = 1$$

Hence $\mu = E(\underset{\sim}{x}) = np$ as expected.

The reader should not be daunted by the rather difficult algebraic manipulation that is necessary here. At a first reading an understanding of the steps in the proof and *remembering the result* are more important than anything else. As more experience is gained with using the sigma sign in connection with the binomial distribution a clearer understanding of the proof will emerge.

3.7 The Variance and Standard Deviation

The variance is defined as $E[(\underset{\sim}{x} - \mu)^2]$ and using the results of the section on expectation we have

$$E[(\underset{\sim}{x} - \mu)^2] = E(\underset{\sim}{x}^2) - [E(\underset{\sim}{x})]^2$$

We know that $E(\underset{\sim}{x}) = np$ so we only need to find $E(\underset{\sim}{x}^2)$ and we do this now by using methods similar to those of the last section.

$$E(\underset{\sim}{x}^2) = \sum_{x=0}^{n} x^2 nCx q^{n-x} p^x$$

Since we are eventually going to cancel x^2 against a factorial we replace x^2 with $[x(x-1) + x]$ to get

$$E(\underset{\sim}{x}^2) = \sum_{x=0}^{n} [x(x-1) + x] nCx q^{n-x} p^x$$

now taking the sigma sign across the bracket and expanding nCx

$$= \sum_{x=0}^{n} x(x-1)\frac{n!}{(n-x)!x!} q^{n-x} p^x + \sum_{x=0}^{n} xnCx q^{n-x} p^x$$

Now for $x = 0$ and $x = 1$ we find that the first two items of the first summation are zero so we may alter that summation from $x = 0$ to $x = 2$. Doing this and cancelling $x(x-1)$ against $x!$ we get

$$E(\underset{\sim}{x}^2) = \sum_{x=2}^{n} \frac{n!}{(n-x)!(x-2)!} q^{n-x} p^x + E(\underset{\sim}{x})$$

Now factoring $n(n-1)p^2$ (the reason for which will appear in a moment)

$$E(\underset{\sim}{x}^2) = n(n-1)p^2 \sum_{x=2}^{n} \frac{(n-2)!}{(n-x)!(x-2)!} q^{n-x} p^{x-2} + E(\underset{\sim}{x})$$

Now since

$$\frac{(n-2)!}{(n-x)!(x-2)!} = {}_{n-2}C_{x-2}$$

we get

$$E(\underset{\sim}{x}^2) = n(n-1)p^2 \sum_{x=2}^{n} {}_{n-2}C_{x-2}\, q^{n-x} p^{x-2} + E(\underset{\sim}{x})$$

Now expanding the sigma sign

$$E(\underset{\sim}{x}^2) = n(n-1)p^2[{}_{n-2}C_0 q^{n-2}p^0 + {}_{n-2}C_1 q^{n-3}p^1 + {}_{n-2}C_2 q^{n-4}p^2 + \ldots$$

$$+ {}_{n-2}C_{n-2} q^0 p^{n-2}] + E(\underset{\sim}{x})$$

$$= n(n-1)p^2[q+p]^{n-2} + E(\underset{\sim}{x})$$

$$= n(n-1)p^2 + np \quad \text{as} \quad [q+p]^{n-2} = 1 \quad \text{and} \quad E(\underset{\sim}{x}) = np$$

It is now evident that the reason for factoring $n(n-1)p^2$ is to allow the summation to be converted to the expansion of $(q+p)^{n-2}$ which is, of course, 1.

Thus $$E[(\underset{\sim}{x} - \mu)^2] = n(n-1)p^2 + np - n^2p^2$$

$$= np(1-p) = npq$$

(A remark similar to that of the previous section concerning the difficulties of the algebraic manipulation is appropriate here. *Remembering the result* is more important than trying to remember the proof).

Thus the variance of the binomial distribution is npq, and the standard deviation is $\sqrt{npq}$. The mean, variance and standard deviation of the binomial distribution should be memorised.

Example 1: If a machine produces 5% defective items, find the mean and standard deviation for the distribution of defective items in a daily production of 200.

Answer

Here $p = \frac{1}{20}$ where, since we are interested in defective items a defective item will be a success, and 5% expressed in fraction terms is $\frac{1}{20}$ The daily production of 200 is n.

$$\textit{Mean} = np = 200 \times \tfrac{1}{20} = 10$$

$$\textit{Variance} = npq = 200 \times \tfrac{1}{20} \times \tfrac{19}{20} = 9{\cdot}5$$

$$\textit{Standard deviation} = \sqrt{9{\cdot}5} = 3{\cdot}08$$

3.8 Non-binomial Situations

The binomial distribution can be made to apply to situations where there are more than two outcomes by merely dividing all the possible outcomes into two groups. For example throwing a die has six outcomes but if we count a throw of 1 as a success and a throw of 2, 3, 4, 5 or 6 as a failure then the binomial distribution $(\frac{1}{6} + \frac{1}{6})^n$ will apply for n throws under this condition. If we count a throw of 2 or 4 as a success, and a throw of 1, 3, 5 or 6 as a failure then the binomial distribution $(\frac{2}{3} + \frac{1}{3})^n$ will apply for n throws under this condition. These examples go to show that any outcome space may be partitioned into two subsets – one labelled success, and the other failure – and thus the binomial distribution will apply.

3.9 Multiple Repetitions

Example 1: 3 coins are tossed and the occurence of a head counted a success. Find the probability distribution for this experiment.

Answer

3 coins being tossed once is equivalent to 1 coin being tossed 3 times, thus the probable distribution of heads will be given by

$$(\tfrac{1}{2} + \tfrac{1}{2})^3 = \tfrac{1}{8} + \tfrac{3}{8} + \tfrac{3}{8} + \tfrac{1}{8}$$

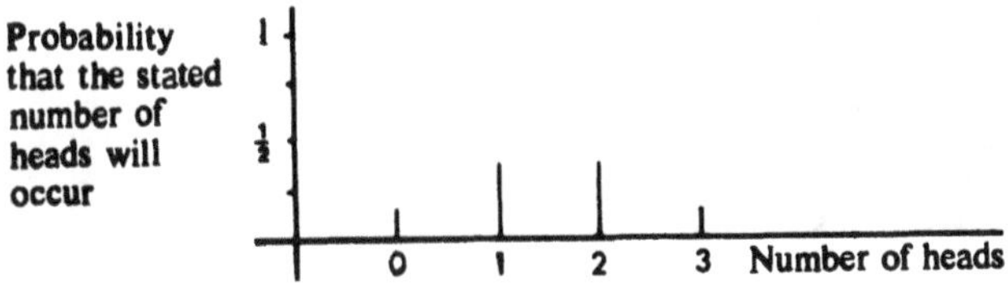

Fig. 3.9(a)

Example 2: If 3 coins are now tossed 8 times, and again the occurence of a head counted a success, find the number of successes to be expected.

Answer

We argue as follows: If we continually toss three coins we can expect from the result of *example 1*, that the number of times no heads will appear will be $\frac{1}{8}$ of the total number of tosses. Similarly we will expect one head to appear in $\frac{3}{8}$ of the total number of tosses. Continuing in this way we can expect

$$8 \times \tfrac{1}{8} = 1 \text{ throw with 0 successes}$$
$$8 \times \tfrac{3}{8} = 3 \text{ throws with 1 success}$$
$$8 \times \tfrac{3}{8} = 3 \text{ throws with 2 successes}$$
$$8 \times \tfrac{1}{8} = 1 \text{ throw with 3 successes}$$

showing this as a graph we get

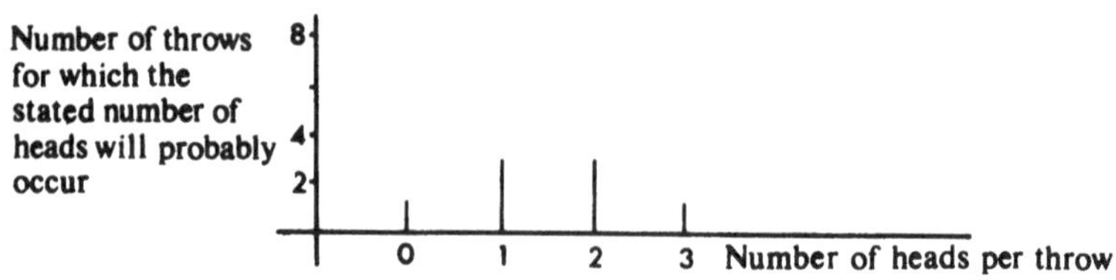

Fig. 3.9(b)

Note that this graph is identical with the probability distribution graph of *Example 1*, except that the probability scale on the vertical axis has been replaced by the number of throws in which the various numbers of successes should occur.

If we were to now toss these 3 coins 16 times we would get the following results

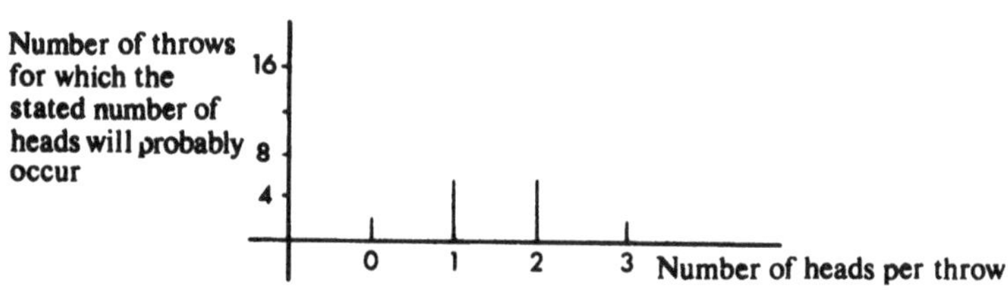

Fig. 3.9(c)

The difference between this graph and the previous one again being in the vertical scale. If the student performs the calculations for this number of throws following the method suggested for 8 throws he will readily understand that in performing experiments of this sort, where multiple repetitions are involved, then if N, the number of repetitions, is chosen so that p^n is a factor of it, the working will produce more convenient whole numbers.

Example 3: If three coins are tossed 16 times draw the graph of the distribution and shade the area representing the expected numbers of times of getting

(a) 3 heads (b) 1 or 2 heads (c) at most 2 heads

Answer

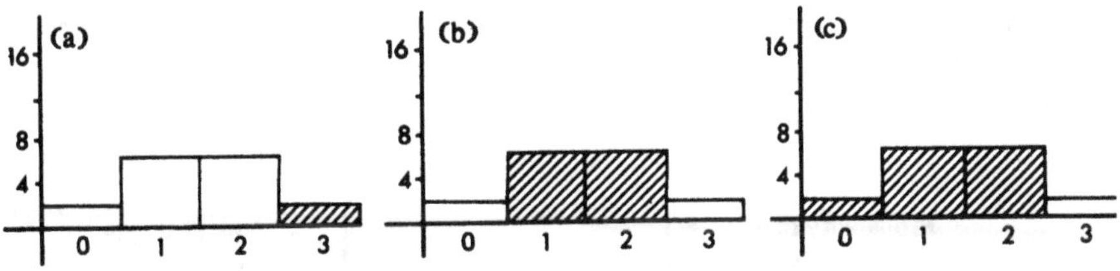

The graphs above are histograms and the shaded parts represent the solutions to the questions. It is quite correct to represent binomial distributions by histograms but there is one point that should be born in mind. The binomial distribution is a discrete distribution and is more naturally represented by line graphs – like those of Fig. 3.9(a), (b) and (c). Representing the binomial distributions with a histogram is open to the error of thinking that there can be some probability associated with points in between the discrete points 0, 1, 2, 3, ... and so on, which the histogram tends to suggest. Use of line graphs in cases like this is recommended.

The work of this section now leads to the result:

If the probability distribution given by the binomial expansion is $nCxq^{n-x}p^x$ for $n = 0, 1, 2, \ldots, n$, and represents the outcome of a trial then the distribution giving the probable outcomes when the trial is repeated N times is $NnCxq^{n-x}p^x$.

Example 4: Two dice are thrown and the occurence of a 6 is counted as a success. Find the distribution of successes if the dice is thrown 720 times.

Answer

The binomial probability distribution for a single trial is given by $(\frac{5}{6} + \frac{1}{6})^2 = \frac{25}{36} + \frac{10}{36} + \frac{1}{36}$ and these three terms give the probability for 0, 1 and 2 successes per throw respectively. Thus $nCxq^{n-x}p^x = 2Cx(\frac{5}{6})^{2-x}(\frac{1}{6})^x$.

If the trial is repeated 720 times then $N = 720$ and

$$NnCxq^{n-x}p^x = 720 \cdot 2Cx(\tfrac{5}{6})^{2-x}(\tfrac{1}{6})^x.$$

For $x = 0$ we get

$$\frac{720 \times 25}{36} = 500.$$

Similarly for $x = 1$ we get 200, and for $x = 2$ we get 20.

A single graph can be used as below where the left hand vertical axis represents the probabilities for a single throw and the right hand vertical axis represents the numbers involved in repetitions of the trial.

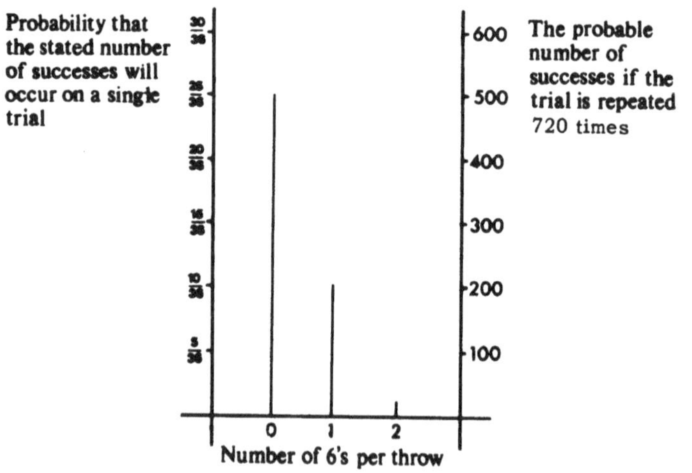

A common difficulty for the beginner is to confuse the two letters n and N. It is essential to remember that n represents the maximum number of successes in a single trial – and N represents the number of times that trial is repeated.

3.10 Quality Control

The tossing of 2, 3, 4, and so on coins N number of times forms a model for an industrial problem. In the nature of things a machine will not produce every component it is set up to make in perfect order. Every so often a component will be produced that is defective. The production of an odd few components that are defective is to be expected and provided that the proportion of defective components is below a certain percentage then the manufacturer is satisfied. If the percentage of defective items is below a certain figure then the machine is said to be 'under control'. When the percentage of defective items produced goes over this figure the machine is no longer under control. It would be possible to examine every item that a machine produced and that way it would be possible to find the exact percentage of defective items, however this 'inspection process', as it is called, would be much too expensive and so more convenient ways of deciding when a machine is under control have been found. The problem of keeping machines under control is the fundamental problem of what has become known as *Quality Control.* Instead of inspecting every item produced by a machine, samples are taken at intervals. The size of the sample varies with the type of component produced but the selection of a sample of 2, 3 or 4, corresponds to the tossing of 2, 3 or 4 coins, and N samples from the product of the machine corresponds to the tossing of the coins N times.

If the tossing of coins were used as a model then the production of the machine would be roughly 50% defective and 50% non-defective. This percentage of defectives is much higher than is normally met with so in order to get a more realistic example let us take a 10% defective margin which is one that is more likely to be met. We now have to construct a 'model' for this and this is done by putting in a jar 9 white balls and 1 black ball. The drawing of a ball is equivalent to taking a sample of one from the machine's production. The probability of drawing the black ball is $\frac{1}{10}$ – and this is counted a success – and the probability of getting a defective item is $\frac{1}{10}$ – and again, because we are interested in defective items, this is counted a success. Hence the binomial distribution $(\frac{9}{10}+\frac{1}{10})^n$ will apply, where n is the size of the sample.

Example 1: A machine produces 10% defective items. Show how taking samples of 3 can be used to determine whether or not the machine is 'under control'.

Answer

A sample of 3 is represented by the binomial distribution $(\frac{9}{10}+\frac{1}{10})^3$.

$$\left(\frac{9}{10}+\frac{1}{10}\right)^3 = \frac{729}{1000} + \frac{243}{1000} + \frac{27}{1000} + \frac{1}{1000}$$

This tells us that out of 1000 samples we can expect 729 to contain 0 defective items; out of 1000 samples we can expect 243 to contain 1 defective item. The results are tabulated below.

Number of defective in sample of three	0	1	2	3
Number of samples	729	243	27	1

Any marked deviation from these figures would suggest that the machine is no longer producing only 10% defective items.

Let us assume that the next 1,000 samples of 3 produce the following figures:

Number of defective in sample of three	0	1	2	3
Number of samples	512	384	96	8

Then we could see straight away that the machine is producing a much higher percentage of defectives than 10%. However in practice it is not possible to wait for a thousand samples before taking action. By the four hundredth sample the machine may have been out of control and so methods have been devised to get a much 'earlier warning' than this. These basic ideas are further developed and refined in methods of quality control and the interested reader is referred to the literature of the subject.

3.11 Fitting Theoretical Distributions to Given Figures

From figures found by experimenting we need to construct a theoretical distribution which will act as a model for the situation from where the figures were obtained. In constructing these theoretical distributions from actual figures we will also be answering the question implied in the last section, that is 'If the machine is not producing defective items at the rate of 10%, then at what rate is it producing defective items?' We show the solution to this problem by example.

Example 1: The following figures for defective items produced by a machine were obtained in the taking of samples of 2. Calculate the proportion of defective items, and assuming that the binomial distribution is applicable, construct a theoretical binomial distribution and compare it with the given figures.

Number of defective in sample of two	0	1	2
Number of samples	178	124	18

Answer

Total number of defectives will be

$$(0 \times 178) + (1 \times 124) + (2 \times 18) = 160$$

$$\text{Proportion of defective items} = \frac{160}{320 \times 2}$$

$$\text{i.e. } \frac{\text{total defectives}}{\text{total produced}}$$

$$= \tfrac{1}{4}$$

This suggests that the machine is producing 25% defective items and the binomial distribution which would fit the given figures would be $(\frac{3}{4} + \frac{1}{4})^2$, the index two being takem because the samples are of size 2. $(\frac{3}{4} + \frac{1}{4})^2 = \frac{9}{16} + \frac{6}{16} + \frac{1}{16}$, therefore 320 samples of size 2 should yield the following figures:

Number of defective in sample of two	0	1	2
Number of samples	180	120	20

The figure 180 was obtained by taking $\frac{9}{16}$ths of 320. The other figures were similarly obtained.

We see immediately that the difference between the actual figures and the theoretical figures is very small and this suggests that we have obtained a good theoretical distribution. Two points in the question are worth mentioning. First the question asked for the proportion of defective items, so giving the clue to the answer; and secondly, the question states 'assuming the binomial distribution is applicable', a point which must always be born in mind when attempting to fit a binomial distribution to a given set of figures.

3.12 Distribution Function

We saw in *Descriptive Statistics and Probability Theory*, Section 1.12 that there are cases when it is of value to know how many varieties fall below a particular score and various cumulative frequency graphs and tables are developed for this purpose. The same idea has a counterpart in probability terms where it is of interest to know that the probability that a random variable $\underset{\sim}{x}$ assumes a value $\underset{\sim}{x}$ – in its outcome space – is less than or equal to a real number s. This is written $P(x \leqslant s)$ and is read, 'the probability that x is less than or equal to s'.

Example 1: If $\underset{\sim}{x}$ is the random variable associated with the rolling of a die, then

$$\begin{array}{llll} P(x \leqslant 0) = 0 & & P(x \leqslant 4) = \frac{4}{6} \\ P(x \leqslant 1) = \frac{1}{6} & & P(x \leqslant 5) = \frac{5}{6} \\ P(x \leqslant 2) = \frac{2}{6} & & P(x \leqslant 6) = \frac{6}{6} \\ P(x \leqslant 3) = \frac{1}{6} & & \end{array}$$

Graphing this we get

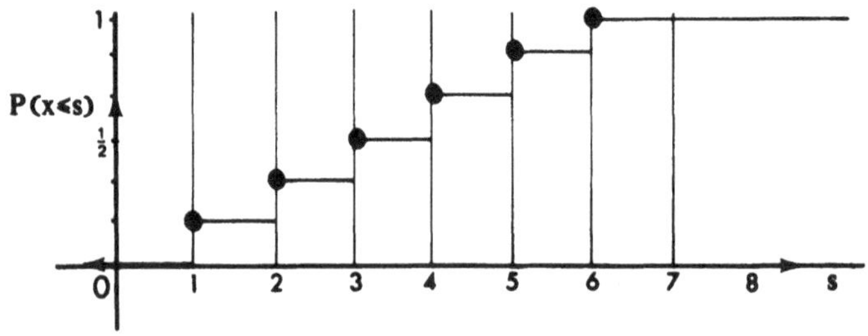

Fig. 3.12(a)

From the graph we see that although the domain of $\underset{\sim}{x}$ is discrete, s can take all real – that is continuous – values, and it makes perfectly good sense to write $P(x \leqslant 2{\cdot}5)$ even though $\underset{\sim}{x}$ cannot take the value 2·5. We may look at this in a slightly different way, for example

$$\begin{aligned} P(x \leqslant 2) &= P(x < 2) + P(x = 2) \\ &= \tfrac{1}{6} + \tfrac{1}{6} = \tfrac{2}{6} \end{aligned}$$

and

$$\begin{aligned} P(x \leqslant 2{\cdot}5) &= P(x < 2) + P(x = 2) + P(2 < x \leqslant 2{\cdot}5) \\ &= \tfrac{1}{6} + \tfrac{1}{6} + 0 \\ &= \tfrac{2}{6} \end{aligned}$$

By virtue of the fact that we are considering values of $\underset{\sim}{x}$ *less than or equal to* s the points $(1,\frac{1}{6})$, $(2,\frac{2}{6})$, $(3,\frac{3}{6})$ and so on, are on the graph, but the points $(1,0)$, $(2,\frac{1}{6})$, $(3,\frac{2}{6})$, $\ldots,(n,\frac{n}{6})$ are not. At the points of discontinuity, that is 1, 2, . . ., 6, the graph is continuous from the right but not from the left. This is indicated by the dots.

Definition: For a discrete random variable $\underset{\sim}{x}$, the function $F(s) = P(x \leqslant s)$ is called the *cumulative distribution function* or more usually, the *distribution function*.

The domain of $F(s)$ is usually taken over the real line, $-\infty < x < \infty$, but its range will be the set zero to one, $0 \leqslant F(s) \leqslant 1$.

The following is an alternative way of writing the definition

$$F(s) = P(x \leqslant s) = \sum_{x_i \leqslant s} P(x_i)$$

and is useful in working out values of $F(s)$.

It will be readily seen that $F(s)$ is, in the discrete case, always a step function, and also

(1) $F(-\infty) = 0$
(2) $F(\infty) = 1$
(3) $F(s)$ remains constant or increases as s increases.

Example 2: Graph the distribution function, $F(s)$, of $\underset{\sim}{x}$, where $\underset{\sim}{x}$ is the Binomial distribution $B(x; 3, \frac{1}{4})$. (See 3.5).

$$F(s) = \begin{cases} 0 \text{ for } s < 0 \\ \frac{27}{64} \text{ for } 0 \leqslant s < 1 \\ \frac{54}{64} \text{ for } 1 \leqslant s < 2 \\ \frac{63}{64} \text{ for } 2 \leqslant s < 3 \\ 1 \text{ for } 3 \leqslant s \end{cases}$$

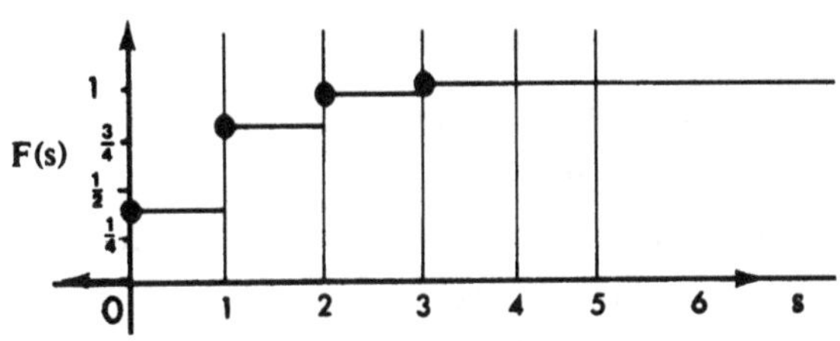

Fig. 3.12 (b)

The above values are simply found as follows:

$$F(0) = P(x \leqslant 0) = 0$$
$$F(1) = P(x \leqslant 1) = P(0) = \frac{27}{64}$$
$$F(2) = P(x \leqslant 2) = P(0) + P(1) = \frac{54}{64}$$
$$F(3) = P(x \leqslant 3) = P(0) + P(1) + P(2) = \frac{63}{64}$$
$$F(4) = P(x \leqslant 4) = 1$$

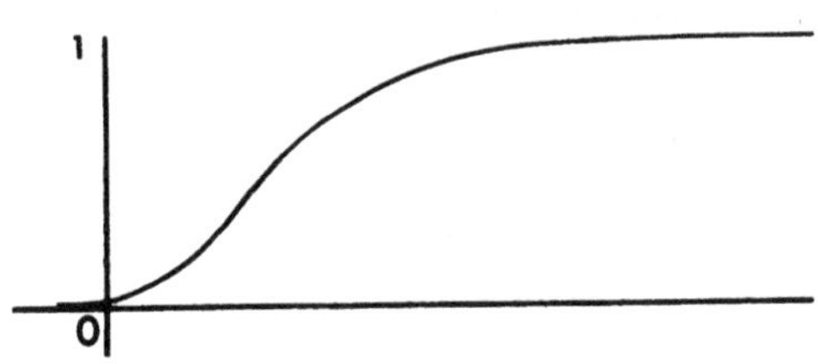

Fig. 3.12 (c)

If $\mathbf{x}$ were a *continuous* random variable then the shape of the graph of its distribution function would be similar in general shape to the above examples but it would be continuous, as in Fig. 3.12(c).

This will be further examined in a later chapter.

Exercise 3

1. State which of the following are binomial situations.
   Show clearly what a trial and a success are in each case.

   (a) Tossing a coin
   (b) Throwing a die
   (c) Accidents on a stretch of road
   (d) Defective bolts from a machine
   (e) An operation in a hospital
   (f) A driving test
   (g) Rain at X-town
   (h) An electricity failure
   (i) An exam score of a pupil
   (j) Height of London policemen
   (k) A defective car being passed as non-defective
   (l) Life of a television tube
   (m) A one-armed bandit
   (n) The weight of a loaf
   (o) Spectators arriving for a game
   (p) People in a queue for a meal at a self service cafe
   (r) Weight of apples on trees in a large orchard
   (s) I.Q.'s of a school population
   (t) I.Q.'s of a school staff
   (u) Particles emitted from a radio active source
   (v) Purchase of certain articles in a large store
   (w) Rifleman shooting at a target
   (x) Cars calling at a garage for petrol
   (y) Scoring of a goal from a penalty kick
   (z) Distress calls to a motoring organisation

2. Expand (a) $(q + p)^5$ (b) $(q + p)^{12}$

3. Expand (a) $(\frac{1}{2} + \frac{1}{2})^5$ (b) $(\frac{2}{3} + \frac{1}{3})^5$ (c) $(\frac{1}{3} + \frac{2}{3})^5$

4. In tossing a fair coin 5 times find the probability of 0, 1, 2, 3, 4, 5 heads. Draw a graph of the results.

5. A fair coin is tossed 6 times, find the probability of getting

(a) 1 head

(b) 1 or 2 heads

(c) 1, 3 or 5 heads

(d) At least 2 heads

(e) At most 2 heads

(f) Exactly 2 heads

Answer

(a) $\frac{6}{64}$ (b) $\frac{21}{64}$ (c) $\frac{32}{64}$ (d) $\frac{57}{64}$ (e) $\frac{22}{64}$ (f) $\frac{15}{64}$

6. A set of 6 fair coins is tossed once. Repeat the previous question.

7. Four fair coins are tossed 64 times. How many times would you expect 0, 1, 2, 3, 4 heads per throw to appear? Draw the graph. Perform the experiment of tossing four coins 64 times and see how your results compare with the expected ones.

Answer

4, 16, 24, 16, 4.

8. Out of 64 families with four children how many would you expect to have 0, 1, 2, 3, 4 boys, assuming that the probability of the birth of a boy is $\frac{1}{2}$? Would you expect the answer to be different if the question read 'girls' instead of 'boys'?

Answer

4, 16, 24, 16, 4. No.

9. A die is thrown and a success counted if a 1 or 2 appears. What iss the probability of one success on (a) 1 throw (b) 2 throws (c) 3 throws (d) 4 throws (e) 5 throws?

Answer

(a) $\frac{1}{3}$ (b) $\frac{4}{9}$ (c) $\frac{4}{9}$ (d) $\frac{32}{81}$ (e) $\frac{80}{243}$

10. A die is thrown and a success counted if a 3 or a 4 appears. What is the probability of 0, 1, 2, 3, 4, 5 successes in 5 throws?

11. A cube has the letters a, b, c painted twice each on its faces. A success is counted if, in rolling, an *a* appears. If 5 such cubes are thrown 125 times, how many times would you expect 0, 1, 2, 3, 4, 5 successes to appear? Draw the graph. Perform the experiment and compare your results.

12. The probability that a 30 year old man in good health will live to at least 65 is $\frac{2}{3}$. If a company sells policies to 5 such men under a 35 year contract what is the probability that before the end of the term

(a) they will have payed out on all policies

(b) they will have payed out on only 2 policies

(c) they will have payed out on at least 2 policies

(d) they will have payed out on at most 2 policies

Answer

(a) $(\frac{2}{3})^5$ (d) $\frac{64}{81}$

13. The probability that a student entering college will graduate at the end of his course is $\frac{9}{10}$. Find the probability that out of 10 students admitted at the same time

(a) all 10 will graduate

(b) none will graduate

(c) between 2 and 9 inclusive, will graduate

(d) between 5 and 6 inclusive, will graduate

How many out of an intake of 350 would you expect to graduate?

14. A population has a frequency distribution $f(x) = \frac{1}{3}$ for $3 \leqslant x \leqslant 6$. What is the probability that a sample of 1 will be (a) bigger than 5 (b) less than $3\frac{1}{2}$ (c) less than 2. If a sample of 2 is taken what is the probability that both of them will be (d) bigger than 5 (e) less than $3\frac{1}{2}$? Repeat for samples of 3, 4 and 5, and at the same time vary the popul ation values.

Answer

(a) $\frac{1}{3}$ (b) $\frac{1}{6}$ (c) 0 (d) $\frac{1}{9}$ (e) $\frac{1}{36}$

15. A recursive formula for use with the binomial probabilities for calculating $P(x+1)$ from $P(x)$ is given by

$$P(x+1) = \frac{n-x}{x+1}\frac{p}{q}P(x)$$

Show that this formula is correct and use it for the binomial distribution $(\frac{7}{8}+\frac{1}{8})^{12}$. Is this method any easier than previous ones?

16. A machine normally produces 5% defectives out of a daily production of 250. To check that the machine is under control a sample of 20 is taken and if there are 2 or more defectives the whole of the days production is examined. What is the probability that the days production will be examined and the machine was working correctly?

17. Find the mean and variance of the following binomial distributions:

(a) $(\frac{1}{4} + \frac{3}{4})^x$ $x = 1, 2, 3, 4, 5.$

(b) $(\frac{2}{3} + \frac{1}{3})^y$ $y = 3, 4, 5, 6, 7$

(c) $(\frac{1}{2} + \frac{1}{2})^z$ $z = 6, 7, 8, 9, 10, 20, 30$

Note any patterns.

Answer

	means	variances
(a)	$\frac{3}{4}, 1\frac{1}{2}, 2\frac{1}{4}, 3, 3\frac{3}{4}$	$\frac{3}{16}, \frac{6}{16}, \frac{9}{16}, \frac{12}{16}, \frac{15}{16}$
(b)	$1, 1\frac{1}{3}, 1\frac{2}{3}, 2, 2\frac{1}{3}$	$\frac{6}{9}, \frac{8}{9}, \frac{10}{9}, \frac{12}{9}, \frac{14}{9}$
(c)	$3, 3\frac{1}{2}, 4, 4\frac{1}{2}, 5, 10, 15$	$\frac{6}{4}, \frac{7}{4}, \frac{8}{4}, \frac{9}{4}, \frac{10}{4}, \frac{20}{4}, \frac{30}{4},$

18. A binomial distribution has a mean of 30 and a variance of 5. Find p, q and n. Repeat for values of your own.

Answer

$n = 36, p = \frac{5}{6}$

19. An examination paper consists of 10 questions. Each of these questions has 5 possible answers and the candidate indicates his choice of correct answer by a tick. If a candidate ignores the questions and ticks his answers at random, what is the probability that he will get (a) 5 questions correct (b) 6 or more questions correct?

Answer

(a) 0·00551 (b) 0·00637

20. What is the probability of getting at least 6 heads in 10 tosses of a fair coin?

Answer

0·377

21. Look up Pascal's Triangle and explain how it is linked to the binomial distribution.

22. Take a two dimensional cartesian grid. Start at the point (0,0) and count the number of different routes that may be taken to get to the points (1,0), (0,1), (1,1) and so on. Work out enough points for you to answer the question, 'How is this connected to the binomial distribution?'

23. A politician has the support of only two fifths of his electorate. If he were to stop six people at random in his constituency, calculate his probability of stopping 0, 1, 2, ..., 6 supporters. If 10 of his supporters each similarly stopped 25 groups of 6 people, how many of these

groups would you expect to contain (a) all non-supporters (b) all supporters (c) 4 or more supporters?

Answer

(a) 10 (b) 1 (c) 45.

24. Can you invent a game which involves a single, or multiple repetitions of a binomial situation?

25. The following distributions were obtained experimentally. Fit a binomial distribution to each one and comment on the differences between the actual figures and those indicated by the binomial distribution.

(a)

x_i	0	1	2	3	4
f_i	13	35	34	15	3

(b)

x_i	0	1	2	3	4	5
f_i	458	370	148	15	6	3

(c)

x_i	0	1	2	3	4	5	6
f_i	90	178	148	64	17	2	1

26. Given $F(s)$ is a distribution function, prove that $F(a) \leqslant F(b)$ for $a < b$.

27. Find the distribution function for the experiment of tossing 3 coins and counting the number of heads.

Answer

$$F(s) = \begin{cases} 0 \text{ for } s < 0 \\ \frac{1}{8} \text{ for } 0 \leqslant s < 1 \\ \frac{4}{8} \text{ for } 1 \leqslant s < 2 \\ \frac{7}{8} \text{ for } 2 \leqslant s < 3 \\ 1 \text{ for } 3 \leqslant s \end{cases}$$

28. Find the distribution function, and draw the graphs, for the following binomial distributions: (a) $B(x; 3, 0{\cdot}4)$ (b) $B(x; 4, 0{\cdot}2)$ (c) $B(x; 6, 0{\cdot}35)$

4 The Poisson Distribution

4.1 Underlying Assumptions of the Poisson Distribution

Although the binomial distribution is the most commonly used one in statistics, it is by no means the only one, and other distributions have been developed to act as models for situations to which the binomial distribution is not applicable. One such distribution is the Poisson distribution and it is applicable to situations where events of a certain kind occur in an interval of time.

Example 1: People using a lift.
The event of interest here is 'a person using the lift' and the interval of time is one of our own choosing; it may be the time when the lift is used most frequently such as 8.30 – 9.30 in the morning or it may be the time when the lift is used infrequently. In all cases the choice of the unit of time – 1 hour, $\frac{1}{2}$ hour or $\frac{1}{4}$ hour – is the one that is most convenient for the problem in hand.

Example 2: Goals in a football match.
The event of interest is the scoring of a goal, and the time interval – not controlled by the statistician – is the 90 minutes playing time.

The same terminology is used as was used for the binomial distribution. Each interval of time is counted as one trial, and the occurence of an event in which we are interested is counted a success. Thus the number of successes that can occur in one trial are $0, 1, 2, 3, \ldots, n$ that is whole numbers, therefore the Poisson distribution is another discrete probability distribution.

Just as with the binomial situation any situation to which the Poisson distribution may apply must satisfy certain conditions. They are:

(1) the expected number of successes that will occur during the trial must be constant from trial to trial

(2) trials must be independent.

(3) there is no upper limit to the number of successes which may occur in a trial

(4) the successes must be 'scattered at random' over the time interval of the trial.

There may, or may not, be time intervals between the trials. If, for instance, we were investigating the calls through a switchboard during the period 2 p.m. to 3 p.m. each day, then there would be a 23 hour interval between each trial; if, however, we were investigating the number of cars using a certain road, then we might make the trial a period of 24 hours, and successive days would be successive trials without a time interval between.

Although the term 'success' is used to denote the occurence of an event which is the subject of interest, and this term is also used in the binomial distribution, there is no equivalent to the term 'failure' in connection with the Poisson distribution. Indeed the whole point of the exercise is to find out how many times certain events will occur and we are not interested in how many times they will not occur.

4.2 The constant e

Before we can describe the Poisson distribution we need some slight knowledge of a mathematical constant which is universally designated by the letter e. It is defined as follows:

$$
\begin{aligned}
e &= \frac{1}{0!} + \frac{1}{1!} + \frac{1}{2!} + \frac{1}{3!} + \frac{1}{4!} + \ldots, + \frac{1}{n!} \quad + \ldots \\
&= \sum_{r=0}^{\infty} \frac{1}{r!}
\end{aligned}
$$

Since $0! = 1$ the above five terms are respectively, 1, 1, 0·5, 0·16667, 0·04167, and continuing in this fashion the value of e may be worked out to any desired degree of accuracy. Correct to 5 decimal places e = 2·71828.

If we wish to raise e to a power, for example e^2, e^3, $e^{3 \cdot 4}$, e^{-1} and so on, then we use the following definition:

$$
e^x = \frac{x^0}{0!} + \frac{x^1}{1!} + \frac{x^2}{2!} + \frac{x^3}{3!} + \frac{x^4}{4!} + \ldots, + \frac{x^n}{n!} \quad + \ldots
$$

and since $x^0 = 1$, we can calculate the value of e^2 as follows:

$$
\begin{aligned}
e^2 &= 1 + \frac{2}{1!} + \frac{2^2}{2!} + \frac{2^3}{3!} + \frac{2^4}{4!} + \ldots + \frac{2^n}{n!} + \ldots \\
&= \sum_{r=0}^{\infty} \frac{2^r}{r!} \\
&= 7 \cdot 389 \text{ to three decimal places.}
\end{aligned}
$$

Note the $e^2 = (2{\cdot}71828\ldots)^2$. Any value of e^x may be calculated by the use of the exponential tables at the back of the book.

The following four important results are quoted:

(a) The limit of $\left(1+\frac{1}{n}\right)^n$ as $n \to \infty$ is e.

(b) The limit of $\left(1-\frac{1}{n}\right)^n$ as $n \to \infty$ is e^{-1}.

(c) The limit of $\left(1+\frac{x}{n}\right)^n$ as $n \to \infty$ is e^x.

(d) The limit of $\left(1-\frac{x}{n}\right)^n$ as $n \to \infty$ is e^{-x}.

For proofs of these the reader is referred to an algebra text book where he will see the binomial theorem used.

4.3 Definition of the Poisson Distribution

We are now in a position to define the Poisson distribution. If a is the average number of events under consideration to be expected in a time interval (trial) of length T, then the probability of $0, 1, 2, 3, \ldots, x, \ldots$ events occuring in any T is given by

$$P(x) = e^{-a}\frac{a^x}{x!} \quad \text{and will be referred to as } P(x;a)$$

Example 1: If $a = 2$, compute the probabilities of 0, 1, 2, or 3 events occuring in T.

Answer

If $a = 2$, then

$$P(0) = e^{-2}\frac{2^0}{0!} = 0{\cdot}1353$$

$$P(1) = e^{-2}\frac{2^1}{1!} = 0{\cdot}2706$$

$$P(2) = e^{-2}\frac{2^2}{2!} = 0{\cdot}2706$$

$$P(3) = e^{-2}\frac{2^3}{3!} = 0{\cdot}1805$$

Example 2: Find the probability of there being more than 3 events in T for *Example 1*.

Answer

The probability of either 0, 1, 2 or 3 events is given by the addition of the results in *Example 1*, that is 0·857. The probability of there being more than three is given by 1 − 0·857, 0·143.

Since the outcome space of a Poisson distribution is the set {0, 1, 2, 3, ...} then the number of points in the outcome space is infinite. We can now look at the ascription of probabilities in this sort of case. For every point in the outcome space of the Poisson distribution the probability is defined by the formula given above, but what happens to these probabilities when x becomes very large? Let us take the case of *Example 1* and see what happens when x is large. Let us take $x = 1000$.

$$P(1000) = e^{-2}\frac{2^{1000}}{1000!}$$

$$= e^{-2}\frac{2}{1000} \times \frac{2}{999} \times \frac{2}{998} \times \frac{2}{997} \times \ldots, \times \frac{2}{3} \times \frac{2}{2} \times \frac{2}{1}$$

Rather than try and work this out in full let us get an idea of what is happening. We know $e^{-2} = 0{\cdot}1353$ and so we look at the other terms. There are 1000 terms here and only one of them is bigger than 1, the remainder are less than 1. When two numbers less than one are multiplied together, the product is another number less than one and smaller than either of the two numbers, for example $\frac{1}{4} \times \frac{1}{3} = \frac{1}{12}$. Let us now multiply $\frac{1}{12}$ by $\frac{1}{2}$ and get $\frac{1}{24}$. Now we have multiplied only three numbers less than one and yet have got a product $\frac{1}{24} = 0{\cdot}0416$ which is quite small. Turning back now to the above we may say that the product of these 1000 numbers will be very small indeed. The result of this is that once x becomes very large for all practical purposes the probability ascribed to point x of the outcome space is zero. Here then we have a case where a probability of zero is ascribed to a point in an outcome space although it is possible for the event associated with the point to occur. This is the situation where we say that 'it could happen, but only once in a million years'. This concept of ascribing a probability of zero to a single point or points in an outcome space will be taken up again when we consider continuous random variables.

We know that the total of the probabilities assigned to the sample space of a random variable must be unity so let us examine the total of the probabilities in the definition above.

$$\sum_{x=0}^{\infty} P(x) = \sum_{x=0}^{\infty} e^{-a}\frac{a^x}{x!} = e^{-a}\sum_{x=0}^{\infty}\frac{a^x}{x!}$$

$$= e^{-a}\left\{\frac{a^0}{0!} + \frac{a^1}{1!} + \frac{a^2}{2!} + \frac{a^3}{3!} + \ldots \right\}$$

$$= e^{-a}e^{a} = e^{0} \text{ (by the usual exponent laws)}$$

$$= 1$$

and so the sum of the probabilities is unity.
Attention is drawn to the following which may be useful as a memory aid.

$$e^{-a}\left\{\frac{a^0}{0!} + \frac{a^1}{1!} + \frac{a^2}{2!} + \frac{a^3}{3!} + \ldots \right\}$$

Probabilities of $\;\uparrow 0 \quad \uparrow 1 \quad \uparrow 2 \quad \uparrow 3\;$ occurences of the event.

It is obvious that Axiom 1 of the Axioms of probability, as given in Book 1, is satisfied by the poisson distribution, and Axiom 2 is shown as satisfied by the above work. It is left as an exercise for the reader to see how Axiom 3 is satisfied.

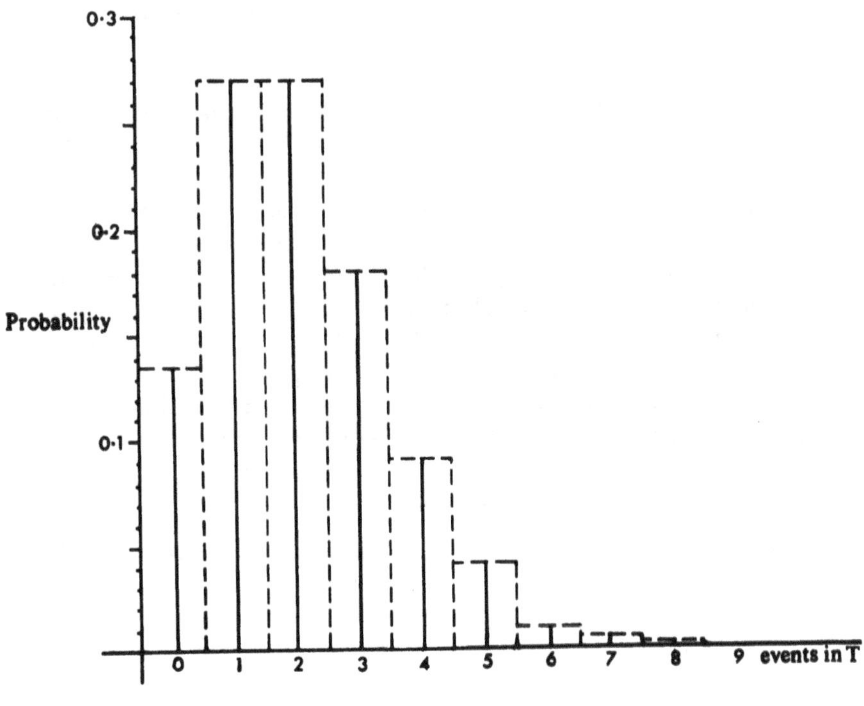

Fig. 4.4(a)

4.4 Graphs of the Poisson distribution

It is left as an exercise for the reader to draw the graphs of the Poisson distribution for $a = 1, 3, 5, 10$. By doing this the reader is able to 'see for himself' what happens to the graph as a varies. The graph when $a = 2$ is given above.

Again it is pointed out that the best type of graph to use for a discrete probability distribution is a line graph, but it is possible to use a histogram – shown dotted in Fig. 4.4(a) – providing the warning given in connection with the binomial distribution is born in mind.

4.5 The Mean of the Poisson Distribution

If x is a poisson random variable and a is the expected number of events to occur in the time interval T, then the mean $= E(x)$

$$= \sum_{x=0}^{\infty} xP(x) = \sum_{x=0}^{\infty} xe^{-a}\frac{a^x}{x!} = e^{-a}\sum_{x=1}^{\infty} x\frac{a^x}{x!}$$

$$= ae^{-a}\sum_{x=1}^{\infty}\frac{a^{x-1}}{(x-1)!}$$ that is factoring a and cancelling x (c.f. binomial distribution)

$$= ae^{-a}e^{a} = a$$

hence the mean of the poisson distribution is a. In the above working the summation $x = 0$ can be changed to $x = 1$, since for $x = 0$ the first term is zero.

There is an important difference between finding the mean for a binomial distribution and finding a mean for a poisson distribution. In the case of the former it is possible to find the mean by theoretical considerations only – it merely involves multiplying p (found by *a priori* methods) by n, the number of possible successes. However in the case of the poisson distribution it is not possible to find the mean other than by empirical methods. Data has to be examined and an average value found to serve as the main parameter of the distribution.

4.6 The Variance of the Poisson Distribution

As with the binomial distribution the finding of the variance $m_2(\mu) = m_2(a)$ is simplified by first finding the moment $m_2(0)$.

$$m_2(0) = \sum_{x=0}^{\infty} x^2P(x) = \sum_{x=0}^{\infty} x^2e^{-a}\frac{a^x}{x!} = e^{-a}\sum_{x=0}^{\infty} x^2\frac{a^x}{x!}$$

$$= e^{-a} \sum_{x=0}^{\infty} [x(x-1) + x] \frac{a^x}{x!}$$

$$= e^{-a} \left\{ \sum_{x=0}^{\infty} x(x-1) \frac{a^x}{x!} + \sum_{x=0}^{\infty} x \frac{a^x}{x!} \right\}$$

$$= e^{-a} \left\{ a^2 \sum_{x=2}^{\infty} \frac{a^{x-2}}{(x-2)!} + a \sum_{x=1}^{\infty} \frac{a^{x-1}}{(x-1)!} \right\}$$

(in the first term in the bracket a^2 has been factored and $x(x-1)$ cancelled against $x!$, and in the second term the same device as was used in the previous section has been applied)

$$= e^{-a} \{ a^2 e^a + a e^a \}$$

$$= a^2 + a$$

We now use the fact that

$$m_2(a) = m_2(0) - [m_1(0)]^2$$

giving

$$m_2(a) = a^2 + a - a^2$$

$$= a$$

hence the variance $= a$, the same as the mean.
The standard deviation is $\sqrt{a}$. The results of the last two sections are usually easily remembered.

4.7 Poisson Probability Chart

There are many cases when it is required to know the probability of getting *at least* x successes in a trial rather than the individual $P(0)$, $P(1)$, and so on. As we have seen *at least* x means x *or more*, and to calculate this from the individual probabilities it would be necessary to either:

(a) find $P(x)$, $P(x + 1)$, $P(x + 2)$, and so on, and add them, or

(b) find $P(0)$, $P(1)$, ..., $P(x - 1)$, add them, and subtract the result from 1. Both these ways are tedious and time consuming. To overcome these difficulties what is called a 'Poisson Probability Chart' has been developed. It is shown in Appendix 2, and a description and explanation now follow.

The chart has three features:

(a) the scale along the horizontal axis which shows values of a from 0·1 up to 100

(b) the scale along the vertical axis which shows probabilities from 0·000001 up to 0·999999

(c) curves running across the chart labelled $c = 1$, $c = 5$, $c = 10$, and so on, up to $c = 150$

Its use is explained by example, and we take $a = 2$ and see how the results compare with Example 1 of Section 4.3.

Look along the horizontal axis for $a = 2$. Having found this 'travel' up the vertical line which represents $a = 2$ until the curve $c = 1$ is met. Then look horizontally across the paper to the probability scale and get the reading 0·865. This now tells us that the probability of getting *1 or more* successes in a trial when $a = 2$ is 0·865. We now move up the line $a = 2$ to where it cuts the curve $c = 2$. Again looking horizontally to the probability scalle we get 0·58. This tells us that the probability of getting *2 or more* successes in a trial when $a = 2$ is 0·58. Continuing in this fashion we get *for* $a = 2$

the probability of *1 or more* successes	= 0·865	0·8647
the probability of *2 or more* successes	= 0·59	0·5941
the probability of *3 or more* successes	= 0·32	0·3235
the probability of *4 or more* successes	= 0·14	0·1430
the probability of *5 or more* successes	= 0·0145	

The second column in the above table shows the results obtained using the figures from Example 1, Section 4.3 and it will be seen that there is close agreement.

Generally then to use the Poisson Probability Chart it is necessary to first find the value of a and then read off the probabilities on the vertical scale where the curves $c = 1, 2, 3$, and so on cut the vertical line representing this particular value of a. The probabilities will be the probabilities of *c or more* successes in a trial.

Note: It is always possible to find the probabilities of *x or more* successes from the individual $P(0)$, $P(1)$, and so on; and likewise it is always possible to get the individual probabilities from the chart by using the facts that $P(0) = 1 - [P(1)$ or more], $P(1) = 1 - [P(0) + P(2)$ or more] and so on. In practice it is rare to use either of these operations as the situation under discussion will dictate which is required, for example either the values of *x or more* or the individual probabilities.

4.8 Fitting Theoretical Distributions to Given Data

As in the previous chapter with the binomial distribution it is necessary to fit a theoretical distribution to given data and we now consider this for the poisson distribution.

Example 1: An 8 hour working day was divided into 5 minute intervals and the number of telephone calls passing through a switchboard counted for each interval. Assuming the situation satisfies the conditions for a poisson distribution, calculate the frequencies to be expected from a theoretical distribution and compare them with the given figures.

Number of calls, x	0	1	2	3	4	5	6
Number of trials in which there were x calls	7	21	25	20	11	7	5

Answer

As with the binomial example we first need to calculate the average number of calls to be expected per trial, that is the mean. Now

$$a = \frac{\text{the total number of calls}}{\text{the total number of trials}}$$

$$= \frac{(0 \times 7) + (1 \times 21) + (2 \times 25) + (3 \times 20) + (4 \times 11) + (5 \times 7) + (6 \times 5}{7 + 21 + 25 + 20 + 11 + 7 + 5}$$

$$= \frac{240}{96} = 2{\cdot}5$$

Proceeding to calculate the values of $P(0)$, $P(1)$, . . . , $P(6)$, in the manner already shown we get, $P(0) = 0{\cdot}082$, $P(1) = 0{\cdot}205$, $P(2) = 0{\cdot}256$, $P(3) = 0{\cdot}215$, we leave the remainder for the reader to calculate. We now come to calculating the frequencies to be expected with this theoretic distribution for the 96 trials. We can expect that 0·082 of the 96 trials will contain no successes, that is 0·082 of the 96 five minute intervals to be free from telephone calls. $0{\cdot}082 \times 96 = 7{\cdot}872 \simeq 8$ calls. Similarly we can expect 0·205 of the 96 trials to contain only one success, that is, one telephone call. $0{\cdot}205 \times 96 = 19{\cdot}68 \simeq 20$. Carrying on in this way the following figures were obtained:

Number of calls, x	0	1	2	3	4	5	6
Number of trials in which there were x calls (theoretically)	8	20	25	21	13	6	3

Comparing these with the original figures we note there is close agreement. In these circumstances we infer that the Poisson distribution with $a = 2{\cdot}5$ is a good distribution to take as a model for this particular case.

Note the similarity of this method and the method for the binomial distribution. In both cases the mean was found first, and then the theoretical frequencies were found by multiplying the theoretical probabilities by the number of trials.

It is now pointed out that in terms of actual practice the procedure as outlined in the above example would not be followed as such. Because the variance of the Poisson distribution is the same as the mean it is possible to discover in advance if a Poisson distribution will be anything like a reasonable fit. This is done by calculating not only the mean of the given distribution, but also the variance. If these two statistics turn out to be similar in value then that indicates that a Poisson distribution may well be a good fit to the given figures. If the reader now calculates the variance for the above figures he will find it to be 2·42 which is quite close to the 2·5 of the mean. This indicates that it would be worth while carrying on with the calculations to find a theoretical distribution. Had there been a marked difference between these two numbers then it would not have been worth while continuing and a distribution other than the Poisson would have had to be used.

4.9 The Poisson Distribution in 1, 2 and 3 Dimensions

We can think of the length of the time interval T as being represented by a line. Each instant of time is represented by a point of the line, and if we think of time as flowing from left to right then the left hand point represents the start of T and the right hand point represents the end of T.

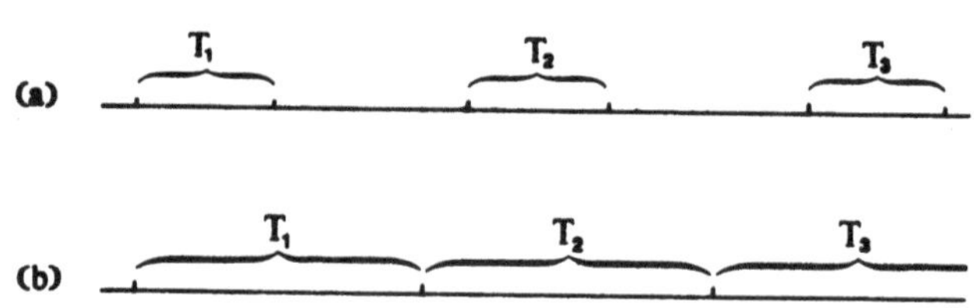

Diagram (a) shows the case when there are gaps between trials and diagram (b) shows the case when there is no gap between trials.

Clearly we have now put the Poisson distribution into spacial terms and the line representing the time interval can easily represent any one dimensional space, for example a road or railway line. Thus the Poisson distribution can be used to determine the probability that x objects of a specified kind are in a unit of space given that a is the average number of objects in each unit of space. The reader will no doubt see that there is no reason why, having made this move, the Poisson distribution should be restricted to one dimension. It can easily be extended to two and three dimensions. In each case the unit of space has to be defined together with the average number of objects for each such unit. The reader should adapt the assumptions underlying the poisson distribution given in 4.1 to these new cases.

Example 1: Examples of spaces of different dimension.
One dimensional Flowers by a railway line.
Two dimensional Rabbit holes in a field. Trees of a certain girth in a forest.
Three dimensional Molecules of a gas in a certain volume. Impurities suspended in a given liquid.

Example 2: At a fair ground the surface is divided by black lines into 100 squares. Pennies are rolled onto this surface and a success occurs when, at the end of its roll, the penny clears the black lines. During one day the following figures were recorded:

Number of successes	0	1	2	3	4	5
Number of squares	23	35	24	12	4	2

Total = 100

(a) Say why the Poisson distribution might apply

(b) Assuming the Poisson distribution does apply, calculate a, and hence calculate the theoretical frequencies.

(c) What consequences might flow from this situation?

Answer

(a) The Poisson distribution will apply because this situation satisfies the assumptions of the Poisson situation as given in Section 4.1.

(b) The average number of successes is 1·45 – the remainder of the calculations are left to the reader.

(c) The owner of the stall would have to decide what values he would attach to the squares. In the light of this evidence he might well attach a high value to the 23 squares where there were no successes so that the customer would be attracted by the prospect of high return.

There are also numerous other points here that the reader may wish to consider.

4.10 The Binomial and the Poisson Distribution I

The reader will have noticed certain similarities between the binomial and the Poisson distributions – both are discrete probability distributions and their fundamental assumptions are alike. There are obvious points of difference – for example an infinite outcome space for the Poisson whilst a finite outcome space for the binomial – but in this section we wish to consider their similarities.

The reader may have noticed already – in the drawing of their graphs – that for certain values of n and p in the binomial, and for certain values of a in the Poisson, their graphs are remarkably alike. When a is small – say less than 5 – then the Poisson distribution graph is skewed to the right and the binomial has this same characteristic if p is small and n fairly large. It would seem reasonable to suppose that when two probability distributions have very similar graphs then one may be used in preference to the other – the simpler one being chosen. This is the case here. The Poisson distribution is 'used in preference to the binomial' because it makes for simpler calculations. In statistical terminology we say that 'the Poisson distribution is used to approximate to the binomial distribution'.

Since there is an infinite number of both Poisson and binomial distributions we are now faced with the problem of deciding which Poisson distribution will be used to approximate which binomial distribution. In practice the binomial distribution arises first and we have to select a Poisson distribution. Again it would seem reasonable that if one distribution is used to approximate to another then their 'centres' should coincide. This is in fact what is done. The mean of the binomial is found, say w, and then the Poisson distribution with a mean of w is used.

In the binomial distribution if p is small, say $\frac{1}{100}$, and n large, say $= 50$, then to calculate the probability of getting 4 or more successes we would have to evaluate

$$\sum_{x=4}^{50} {}_{50}C_x \left(\frac{99}{100}\right)^{50-x} \left(\frac{1}{100}\right)^x$$

truly a formidable task. Thus we note that the binomial distribution becomes difficult to manage in this case. But note that the mean is easy to calculate, $\mu = np = 50 \times \frac{1}{100} = \frac{1}{2}$, and also, when the mean of a Poisson distribution is $\frac{1}{2}$ then the probability of 4 or more successes can be read off the Poisson probability chart in seconds. It is 0·002. Thus it would seem that when p is small, n large, and np finite we might use the Poisson distribution to approximate to the binomial. This is in fact what is done and in the next section we shall put these intuitive ideas into mathematical form and make the required deduction.

4.11 The Binomial and the Poisson Distribution II

The Poisson distribution may be used to approximate to the binomial distribution when the following conditions hold:

(1) p is small – usually less than $\frac{1}{10}$

(2) n is large – usually bigger than 40 or 50

(3) np is finite.

We show that this approximation is possible by considering the general term of the binomial distribution, applying the above conditions, and deriving the general term of the Poisson distribution. Starting then with

$$B(x;n,p) = nCxq^{n-x}p^x = \frac{n!}{(n-x)!x!}(1-p)^{n-x}p^x \text{, since } q = (1-p)$$

$$= \frac{n(n-1)(n-2)\ldots(n-[x-1])(n-x)(n-[x+1])\ldots3\times2\times1}{(n-x)(n-[x+1])\ldots3\times2\times1.x!}(1-p)^{n-x}p^x$$

now cancelling $(n-x)(n-[x+1])\ldots3\times2\times1$ and using the fact that

$$(1-p)^{n-x} = (1-p)^n(1-p)^{-x} = \frac{(1-p)^n}{(1-p)^x}\text{, we get}$$

$$B(x;n,p) = \frac{n(n-1)(n-2)\ldots(n-[x-1])}{x!} - \frac{(1-p)^n}{(1-p)^x}p^x$$

Now $n(n-1)(n-2)\ldots(n-[x-1])$ has x factors and so has p^x so we may write

$$= \frac{np(np-p)(np-2p)\ldots(np-[x-1]p)}{x!}\ \frac{(1-p)^n}{(1-p)^x}$$

We now equate means of the two distributions, $a = np$ and get $p = \frac{a}{n}$. Substituting these in the above gives

$$\frac{a(a-p)(a-2p)\ldots(a-[x-1]p)}{x!(1-p)^x}\left(1-\frac{a}{n}\right)^n$$

We now use the following approximations

(a) If p is small then $(1-p)^x \simeq 1$

(b) If p is small then $a(a-p)(a-2p)\ldots(a-[x-1]p) \simeq a^x$

(c) If n is large $\left(1-\frac{a}{n}\right)^n \simeq e^{-a}$ (see para 4.2).

and get $\dfrac{a^x e^{-a}}{x!}$ which equals $P(x;a)$

Thus the Poisson distribution $P(x;a)$ may be used to approximate to the binomial distribution $B(x\,;n,p)$, where $a = np$.

Another point in favour of the Poisson distribution is that it involves only one constant a, whereas the binomial distribution involves two, n and p.

Example 1: Compare the probability distributions of $B(x, 19, \frac{1}{10})$ and $P(x;\ 1{\cdot}9)$

Answer

Note $a = 1{\cdot}9 = 19 \times \frac{1}{10} = np$

x	$B(x;19,\frac{1}{10})$	$P(x;1{\cdot}9)$
0	0·1351	0·1496
1	0·2852	0·2842
2	0·2852	0·2700
3	0·1796	0·1710
4	0·0798	0·0812
5	0·0266	0·0309
6	0·0069	0·0098
7	0·0014	0·0027
8	0·0002	0·0006
9	0·0000	0·0001
10	0·0000	0·0000

Although here p is not particularly small and n is not particularly large the results are quite close. The reader is urged to work out $B(x;38,0{\cdot}05)$ and see how much more closely the figures obtained agree with those of $P(x;1{\cdot}9)$. This brings out the point that the smaller p is then the more satisfactorily a poisson distribution can approximate a binomial distribution *even for small values* of n. If p is small enough then a satisfactory approximation can be obtained for n as small as 12 or even 10. Of course the larger n is the more accurate the approximation, but it is useful to note that for fixed p the better approximation comes with increasing n, and for fixed n the better approximation comes with decreasing p.

Example 2: The probability that a person will die undergoing an operation is 0·000 001. If 200 000 such operations are performed what is the probability of 2 or more deaths?

Answer

In binomial terms the probability is given by

$$\sum_{x=2}^{200\,000} 200\,000Cx(0\cdot999\,999)^{200\,000-x}(0\cdot000\,001)^{x}$$

Truly a formidable task!

$$a = np = (200\,000)(0\cdot000\,001) = 0\cdot2.$$

Therefore the probability of 2 or more deaths is given by

$$\begin{aligned} 1 - [P(0) + P(1)] &= 1 - (0\cdot8187 + 0\cdot1637) \\ &= 0\cdot0176 \end{aligned}$$

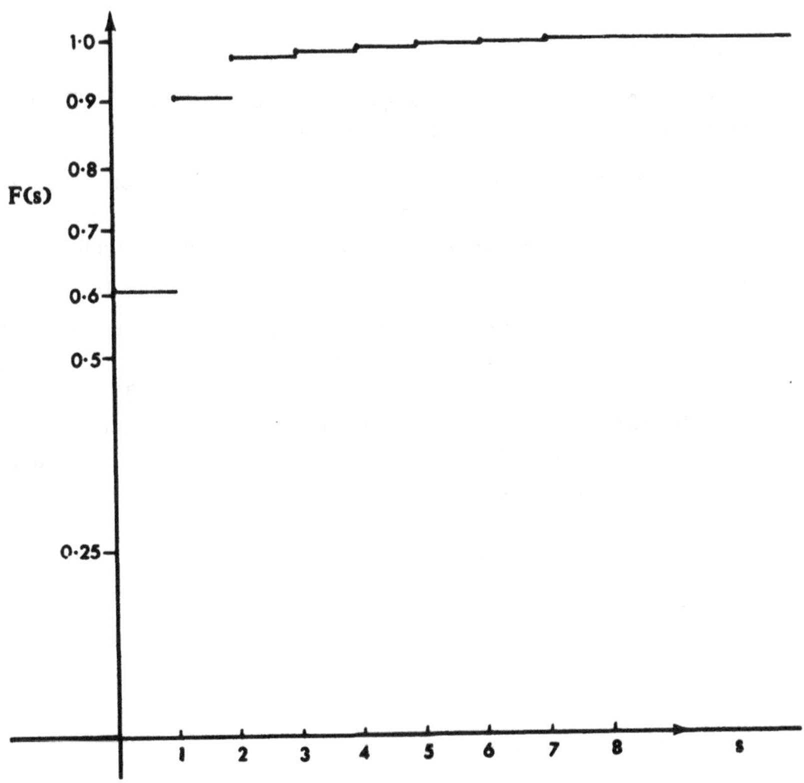

Fig. 4.12(a)

4.12 The Distribution Function of the Poisson Distribution

The distribution function of the Poisson distribution follows the same principles as laid down in Section 3.12. As an example we find, and graph, the distribution function of the Poisson distribution with $a = 0{\cdot}5$

Recalling that $F(s) = P(x \leqslant s) = \sum_{x_i \leqslant s} P(x_i)$ we get

$$
\begin{aligned}
F(0) &= P(x \leqslant 0) & &= 0{\cdot}000 \\
F(1) &= P(x \leqslant 1) = P(0) & &= 0{\cdot}607 \\
F(2) &= P(x \leqslant 2) = P(0) + P(1) & &= 0{\cdot}910 \\
F(3) &= P(x \leqslant 3) = P(0) + P(1) + P(2) & &= 0{\cdot}986 \\
& \qquad\qquad \text{up to} \\
F(7) &= P(x \leqslant 7) = \sum_{x_i \leqslant 7} P(x\ ) & &= 1{\cdot}000
\end{aligned}
$$

and the graph is as above.

Exercise 4

1. Study again the examples of Question 1 of Exercise 3. Which are Poisson situations? Again describe carefully a trial and a success.

2. Assume you are a garage owner and wish to give your customers a good service. Describe what evidence you would collect so that you could arrange the employment of your mechanics and attendants most effectively.

3. A telephone switchboard averages 3 calls a minute during the working day. Find the probability that for any particular minute there will be (a) 0 (b) 1 (c) 2 (d) 3 (e) more than 3, (f) less than 2 calls. Find also the probability that in two consecutive minutes there will be (g) 0 (h) 1 (i) 2 (j) 3 calls. Repeat for 5 consecutive minutes. Repeat for 5 non-consecutive minutes.

Answer

(a) 0·05 (b) 0·15 (c) 0·22 (d) 0·22 (e) 0·35 (g) 0·0025 (h) 0·015 (i) 0·046

4. A teams away record averages 1·2 goals per match. What is the probability that in their next away game they will score (a) 0 (b) 2 (c) more than 3 goals?

Answer

(a) 0·3 (b) 0·22 (c) 0·032

5. Find the value of e^x for (a) $x = -1{\cdot}98$ (b) $x = -3{\cdot}35$ (c) $x = -6{\cdot}8$

Answer

(a) 0·1367 (b) 0·0351 (c) 0·0011

6. On a certain stretch of road the police are called to an average of 913 accidents per year. What is the probability that on any particular day they will be called to (a) 0 (b) 2 (c) 4 or fewer accidents? Comment on the practical aspect of this question.

Answer

(a) 0·08208 (b) 0·2565 (c) 0·8911

7. A forest covers 800 square miles. A timber company will break even on an investment if it cuts 30,000 trees with girths greater than 40″. If it can cut 36,000 trees it will make a 10% profit and if it can cut 40,000 trees it will make a 20% profit. Sample counts of 10 quarter mile squares yielded 3, 2, 0, 1, 2, 3, 3, 4, 2, 3 trees bigger than the required size. What is the probability that the company will (a) make a loss (b) make a profit?

Answer

(a) 0·596 (b) 0·404

8. A Poisson distribution is given by

$$P(x) = \frac{(0 \cdot 7)^x e^{-0 \cdot 7}}{x!}$$

Find (a) $P(0)$ (b) $P(2)$ (c) $P(4)$

Answer

(a) 0·497 (b) 0·122 (c) 0·005

9. The probability that a paratrooper will injure himself on landing or be hit by the enemy in the air is 0·001. If 2,000 paratroopers are dropped what is the probability that (a) 0 (b) 1 (c) 2 (d) more than two will be incapacitated?

Answer

(a) $\frac{1}{e^2}$ (b) $\frac{2}{e^3}$ (c) $\frac{2}{e^2}$ (d) $1 - \frac{5}{e^2}$

10. Ten per cent of T.V. tubes produced by a company are defective. A sample of 10 is chosen at random. Use the binomial distribution and a Poisson approximation to find the probability that exactly 2 will be defective.

Answer

Binomial 0·194, Poisson 0·184.

11. A manufacturing company produces an average 6% defective steel valves. Find the probability that a lot of 50 valves will contain (a) 0 (b) 2 (c) 3 (d) 5 (e) more than 5 (f) less than 3 defective items.

Answer

(a) 0·05 (b) 0·224 (c) 0·224 (d) 0·1 (e) 0·084 (f) 0·423

12, Between the hours of 1 p.m. and 6 p.m. on a Saturday the average number of motorists calling for petrol at a garage is 8 per 5 minute interval. Find the probability that during any particular 5 minute interval there will be (a) 0 (b) 1 (c) 2 (d) 3 (e) 4 (f) 5 or more (g) more than 8 motorists calling. Comment on some practical points in the application of probabilities in this case.

Answer

(a) 0·0003 (c) 0·0107 (e) 0·0573 (g) 0·4075

13. A commercial traveller averages 30 calls during a 5 day week. What is the probability that he will make (a) more than 3 calls on any one day (b) less than 5 calls on one day (c) a total of more than 3 calls on two consecutive days?

Answer

(a) 0·85 (c) 0·99822

14. A certain piece of radio active material emits 150 radio active particles per hour. What is the probability that in any one minute it will emit (a) 1 (b) 3 (c) more than 6 particles?

Answer

(a) 0·2052 (b) 0·2138 (c) 0·0142

15. Twelve and a half per cent of a certain make of central heating boilers need adjustment within 1 month of installation. Eight houses have these boilers fitted. Find the probability that 5 houses will not need to be visited by the adjustment engineer in the first month. Use a Poisson approximation.

Answer

0·061

16. The following table shows the number of articles handed in as lost each day during a 100 day period. Fit a Poisson distribution to the data.

Number of articles lost	Number of days
0	3
1	16
2	23
3	21
4	18
5	11
6 or more	8

Answer

Expected figures 5, 14, 22, 23, 17, 10, 9.

17. Find and graph the distribution functions for the Poisson distributions with (a) $a = 0{\cdot}4$ (b) $a = 0{\cdot}6$ (c) $a = 1$ (d) $a = 2$.

5 The Normal Distribution

5.1 Introduction

Having now looked at discrete probability distribution as statistical models for physical situations we must extend the ideas to continuous data. We recall that discrete data only takes certain values such as 0, 1, 2, ... and so on, but that continuous data can (theoretically) take any value. In practice, of course, the values it takes depend upon the accuracy of the measuring instruments available. We also recall that when we have discrete data we can graph it in different ways, for instance a line graph or a bar graph will serve equally well, but when we come to continuous data we must use a histogram. Now the fundamental point about the histogram is that the area represents the frequency of the readings. It will help if this idea is kept in mind. We now proceed to find statistical models for continuous data. We recall that after the collection of continuous data we have a choice of which class interval to use in the drawing of the graph of the data. We could use wide class intervals and the data might look like

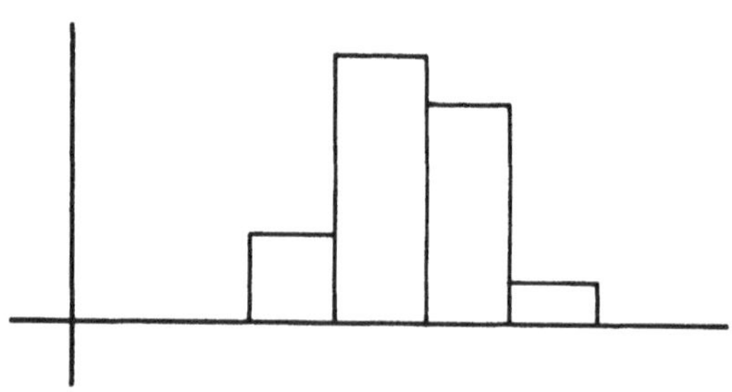

Fig. 5.1 (a)

or we could use narrower class intervals and the data might look something like

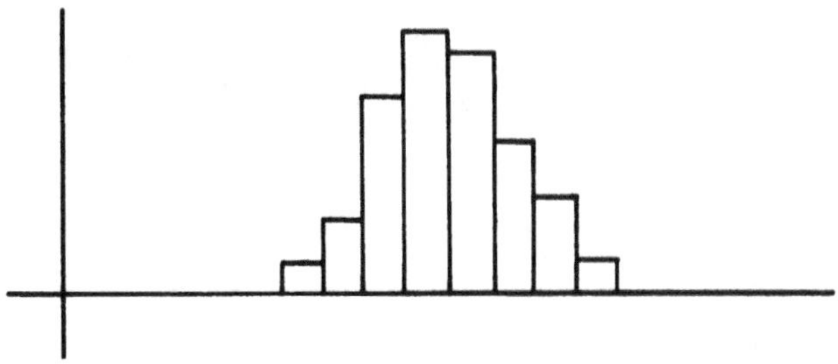

Fig. 5.1 (b)

If we now take even smaller class intervals we get the following graph (provided we either altar the vertical scale or increase the number of items in the data).

Fig. 5.1 (c)

Let us now look at the frequency polygons of these three figures.

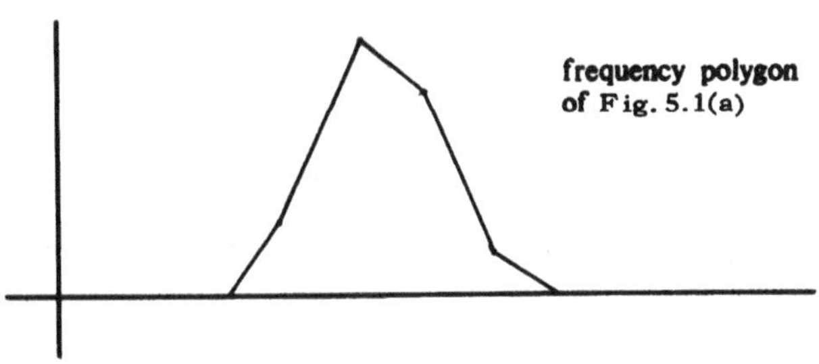

Fig. 5.1 (d)

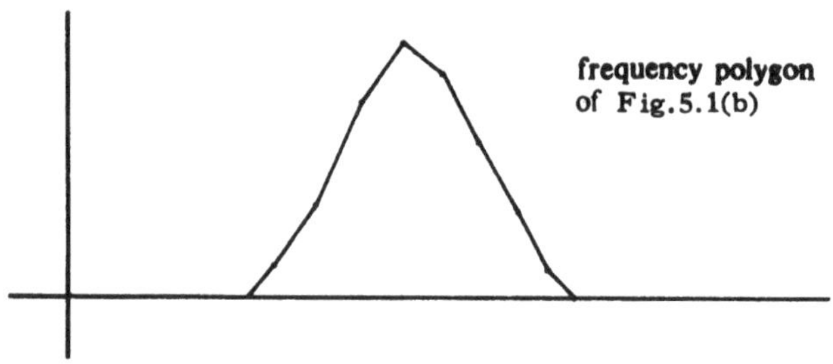

Fig. 5.1 (e)

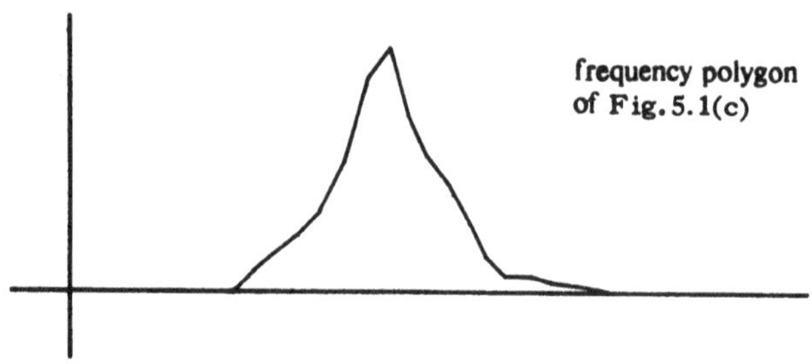

Fig. 5.1 (f)

From these figures we can see that as we use narrower class intervals the frequency polygon approaches more closely to a curve. If we were to carry on in this way then eventually it would become a continuous smooth curve.

Fig. 5.1 (g)

We therefore consider the correct model for a continuous variable to be a continuous curve. Now any smooth curve like the one above is the graph of a mathematical function and so we see that finding a model for continuous data means finding a mathematical function. In general the problem of finding exactly which function forms a model for a specific set of data is difficult so we content ourselves with only giving the outline as above.

If we now consider the frequency polygons as graphs of samples from a population we can consider the curve which results from the limiting process as described above to be a description of the population from which the samples were taken. Just as with a discrete variable continuous populations will vary in the way they are distributed and so different models will have to be used to act as models for different populations.

One of the most important of the continuous probability distributions is the so called *normal distribution.* This name comes from the time when eighteenth century scientists noticed that their errors could be approximated by a continuous curve which they called 'the normal curve of errors'. We investigate the normal distribution in the following sections.

5.2 The Normal Curve

The reader who has worked through examples and exercises connected with continuous data will have noticed that many of the distributions have the general shape

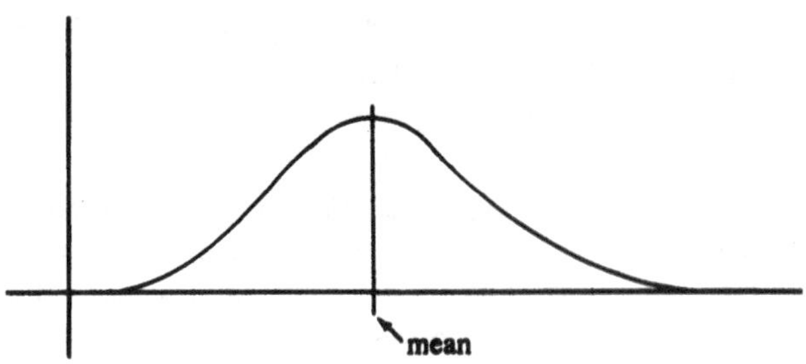

Fig. 5.2(a)

and this bell shaped curve, symmetrical about the mean, is the normal curve.

Its equation is given by

$$y = f(x) = \frac{1}{\sigma\sqrt{2\pi}} e^{-\frac{(x-\mu)^2}{2\sigma^2}} \qquad -\infty < x < \infty$$

where μ and σ^2 are the mean and variance respectively. e is as defined previously and π (frequently known as the ratio of the circumference to the diameter of a circle) is 3·1416 to four decimal places.

The area under the curve represents the probabilities associated with the corresponding points of the outcome space and in the case of the normal curve the outcome space is the real line, that is x may take any value whatsoever. In practice the values of x lie within a certain range but the model for these practical cases allows for every possible range.

In the diagram below the shaded area represents the probabilities associated with the points between a and b in the outcome space.

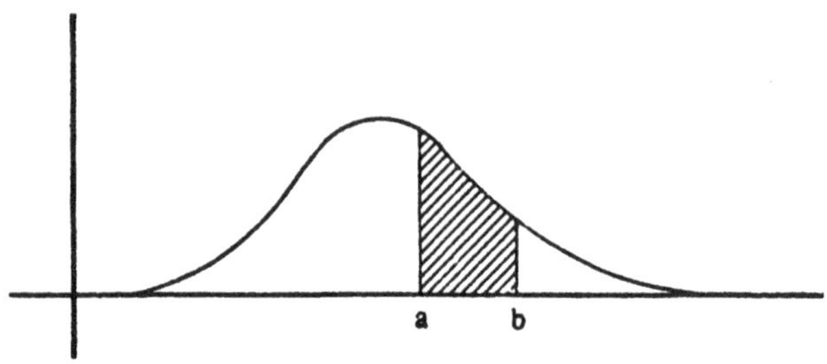

Fig. 5.2 (b)

This is just the same idea of an area representing probabilities as was seen in the previous chapters on the discrete random variables. We recall that the total of all the probabilities associated with the points of the outcome space must be unity and so the area under the normal curve is counted as one.

When x is very small or very large, then $f(x)$ – the probabilities associated with these values of x – is very close to zero; in fact $f(x)$ is asymptotic to the x axis and for all practical purposes they may be counted as zero. This is again the idea that these values may be obtained but the events associated with them are extremely rare.

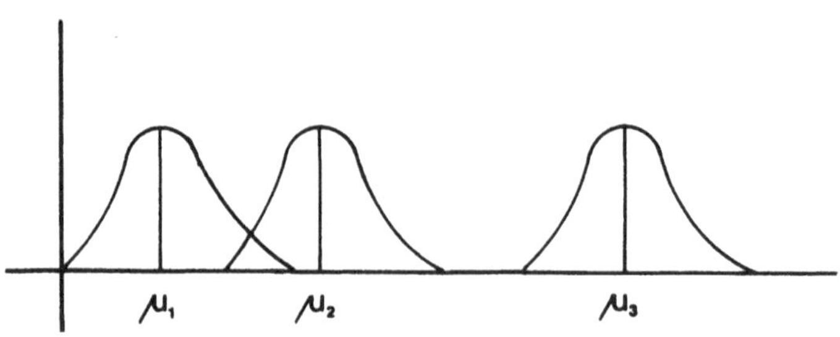

Fig. 5.2 (c)

The Figure 5.2 (c) represents three normal probability distributions with the same variance but with different means $\mu_1 < \mu_2 < \mu_3$. They are the same shape because their variances are equal.

The following diagram shows three normal probability distributions with the same mean but with different variances

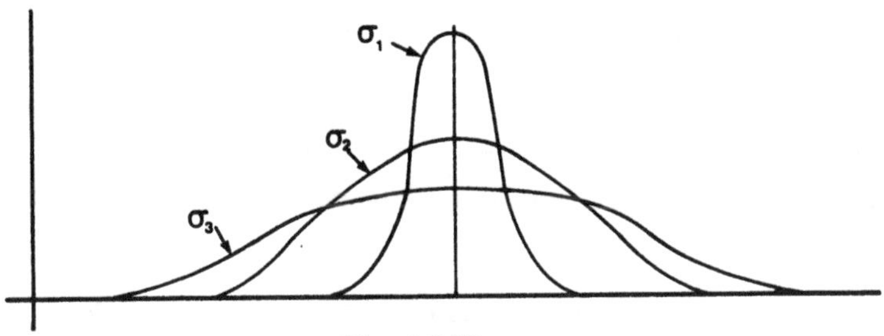

Fig. 5.2 (d)

They are different in shape because they have different variances. The total area under each curve is unity and so the curves have different maximum heights.

Example 1: Calculate the value of

$$f(x) = \frac{1}{2\sqrt{2\pi}} e^{-\frac{(x-2)^2}{8}}$$

for $x = 0, 1, 2, 3, 4$. Plot the points and draw the normal curve through these points.

Answer

The work may be conveniently arranged as in the following table:

x	$e^{-\frac{(x-2)^2}{8}}$	$\frac{1}{2\sqrt{2\pi}} e^{-\frac{(x-2)^2}{8}}$
0	$e^{-\frac{1}{2}} = 0{\cdot}6065$	0·121
1	$e^{-\frac{1}{8}} = 0{\cdot}8875$	0·177
2	$e^{-0} = 1$	0·199
3	$e^{-\frac{1}{8}} = 0{\cdot}8875$	0·177
4	$e^{-\frac{1}{2}} = 0{\cdot}6065$	0·121

and the graph drawn as below.

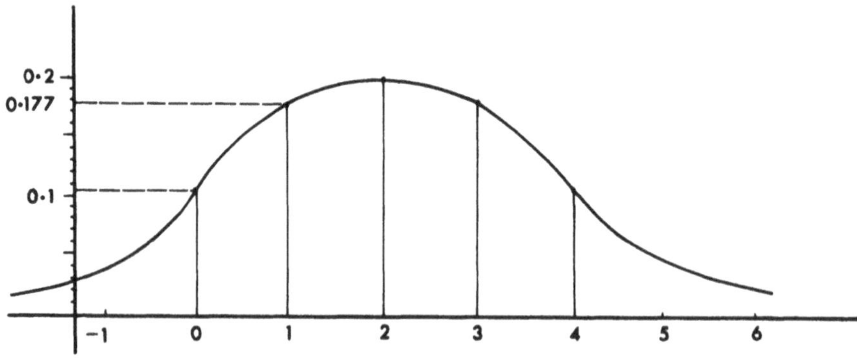

Fig. 5.2 (e)

Using notation similar to the discrete case we now take $\underset{\sim}{x}$ as the random variable whose probabilities are given by $f(x)$, $\underset{\sim}{z}$ as the random variable whose probabilities are given by $g(z)$, and $N(\mu,\sigma^2)$ will stand for a random variable which is normally distributed with mean μ and variance σ^2.

Note: It will have been noticed that in the binomial and Poisson distributions the move from the situation in the world to the derivation of a model for that situation could be fairly easily understood. However, now we have to come to the normal distribution the equation is given without comment as to its derivation. The reason for this is that the derivation of a theoretical curve to fit a set of data normally distributed is mathematically very difficult, and beyond the scope of this book. However it is recognised that a curious reader might wish to know how this is done in outline without necessarily going into detail. This note is added for that reader.

We recall that for a function to be a random variable then every point in the outcome space (domain) must have a probability bigger than or equal to zero associated with it, and also the sum of the probabilities must be unity. Mathematically this means that $0 \leqslant f(x)$ and $\int_a^b f(x) = 1$ where a and b are the least and highest values in the outcome space. Note that the integral sign is used with a continuous variable in just the same way as the sigma sign was used with a discrete variable. We now look at one outline of deriving the normal curve.

We know that the curve will be completely above the x axis, $0 \leqslant f(x)$, and that it must be bell shaped. It is well known among mathematicians that the curve e^{-x^2} has these two properties.

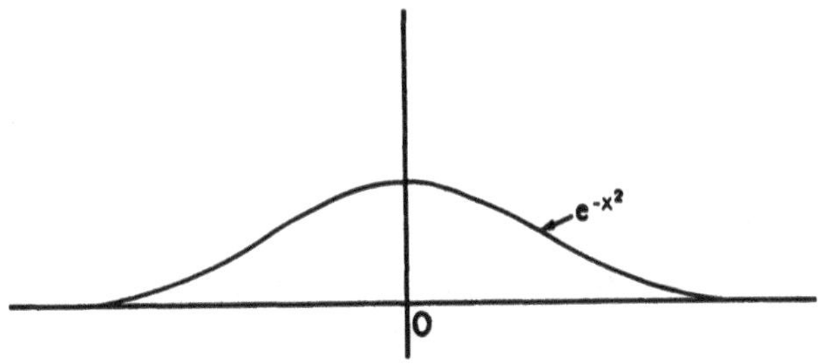

Fig. 5.2 (f)

However since not all distributions have their centre at 0, e^{-x^2} must be adapted so that its centre will be any point desired. This is done by changing the exponent to $(x - \mu)^2$, and so we get

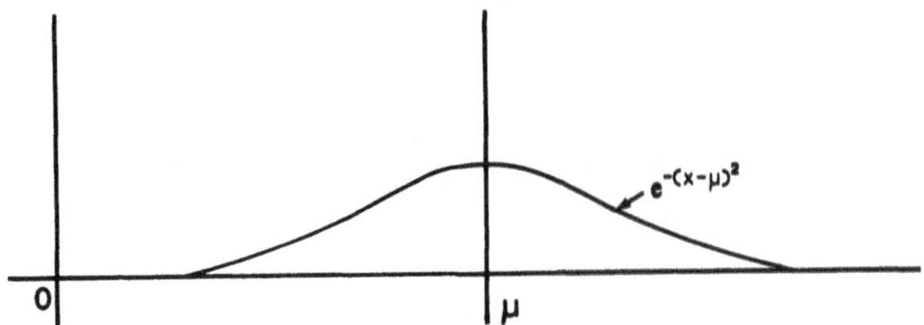

Fig. 5.2 (g)

and as μ changes so does the position of the curve.

Now we must look at the spread of the curve to allow it to be used for distributions with large or small variances. This is again done by changing the exponent. This time to

$$-\frac{(x - \mu)^2}{2\sigma^2}.$$

The final step now is to ensure that the area under the curve is unity and so we must find a constant C such that

$$\int_{-\infty}^{\infty} Ce^{-\frac{(x-\mu)^2}{2\sigma^2}} = 1$$

When this integral is performed – by changing the variable and then using double integrals – the constant C turns out to be $\frac{1}{\sigma\sqrt{2\pi}}$.

Thus we finally get

$$f(x) = \frac{1}{\sigma\sqrt{2\pi}} e^{-\frac{(x-\mu)^2}{2\sigma^2}}$$

5.3 Area Under the Normal Curve

One of the most important features of the normal curve is the relationship between the area under the curve and the standard deviation of the curve. If, for example, a normal curve has mean 30, and standard deviation 5, then we get Fig. 5.3 (a).

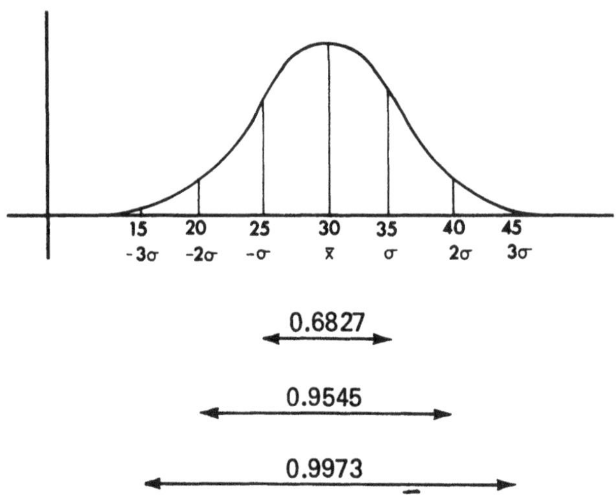

Fig. 5.3 (a)

The diagram shows that 0·6827 of the area under the normal curve lies between $-\sigma$ and $+\sigma$, that is 68·27% of the area lies within one standard deviation of the mean. Similarly 0·9545 of the area lies between -2σ and $+2\sigma$, and 0·9973 of the area lies within three standard deviations of the mean.

The importance of this is that if, by virtue of sampling, we can infer that a certain population is distributed normally, then we will be able to say that 95·45% of the population lies within two standard deviations of the mean. The reader is now in a position to appreciate why the mean and the standard deviation have become the two most important measures of a distribution. The normal curve is one of the most commonly occuring distributions and it may be quite accurately indicated by its mean and standard deviation.

Example 1: A population is normally distributed and has mean 30 and standard deviation 5. What percentage of the population lies between 20 and 35.

Answer

Since the standard deviation is 5 then 20 is two standard deviations below the mean, and 35 is one standard deviation above the mean. The proportion between 20 and 35, shown shaded in the figure,

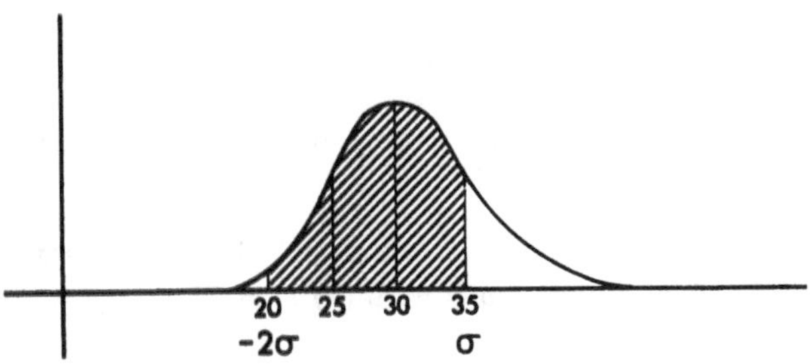

Fig. 5.3 (b)

will be given by the area from -2σ to $+\sigma$. Between $-2\sigma = 20$ and the mean is 0·4772 of the area or half of 0·9545. Between the mean and $+\sigma = 35$ is 0·3413 of the area or half of 0·6827. The total area therefore will be 0·4772 + 0·3413 = 0·8185. Thus 81·85% of the population lies between 20 and 35.

Example 2: In Example 1, what percentage of the population lies between 30 and 32·5?

Answer

Since the standard deviation is 5 then 32·5 is half a standard deviation away from the mean, obviously the area between 30 and 32·5 is bigger than the area between 32·5 and 35 so it is not possible to take half of 0·3413 as the answer. At the moment we do not have sufficient information to answer this question and so we proceed to fill this gap.

5.4 Area Under the Normal Curve 2

The area under the normal curve has been extensively tabulated and the table is shown in Appendix 3. The letter z is used to indicate the distance *in terms of standard deviations* between the point x and the mean.

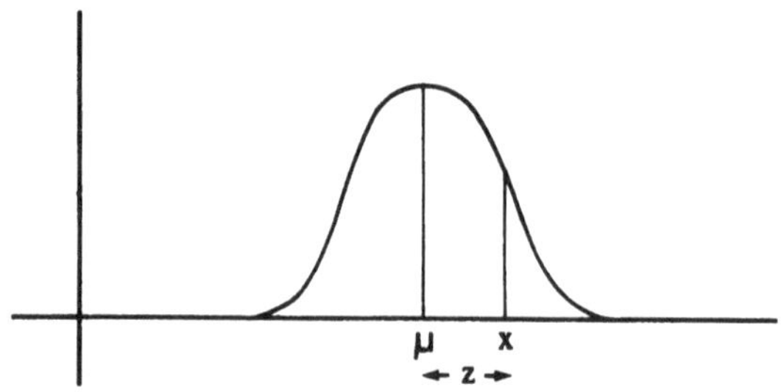

Fig. 5.4 (a)

z_1 will be associated with the distance of x_1 from the mean. Similarly z_2, z_3, will be associated with x_2, x_3.

Example 1: A normal distribution has mean 30 and standard deviation 5, find the z_1 which corresponds with (a) $x_1 = 35$ (b) $x_2 = 32{\cdot}5$ (c) $x_3 = 39{\cdot}95$.

Answer

The following diagram will be of assistance.

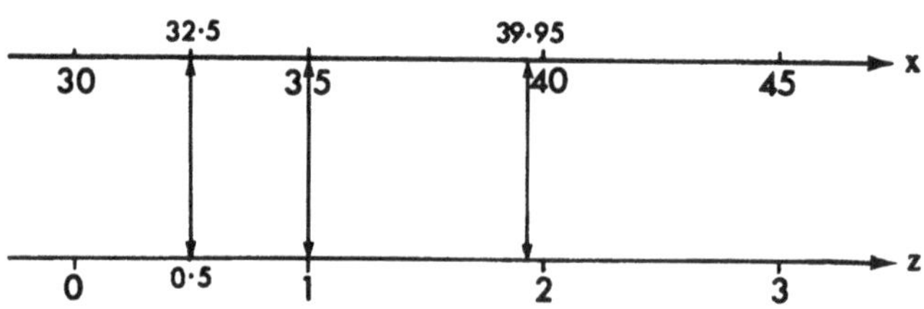

(a) $x_1 = 35$ is one standard deviation from the mean, so $z_1 = 1$

(b) $x_2 = 32{\cdot}5$ is half way between 30 and 35 and will be half a standard deviation from the mean, hence $z_2 = 0{\cdot}5$

(c) $x_3 = 39{\cdot}95$ is between 35 and 40 and so z_3 will be between 1 and 2. x_3 is 4·95 of the way between 35 and 40 and so z_3 will be proportionally the same distance from 1. Expressed as a fraction 4·95 is $\frac{4\cdot95}{5}$ of the way between 35 and 40, that is 0·99. z_3 will thus be 0·99 of the distance between 1 and 2, and so $z_3 = 1{\cdot}99$.

Example 2: Find the area under the curve and between the mean and x_2, and the mean and x_3 for the last example.

Answer

$x_2 = 32{\cdot}5$ gives $z_2 = 0{\cdot}5$. Look down the first column, headed z, of the table until 0·5 is reached, then look in the column headed 0·00. Here we find 0·1915 which is the required area.

$x_3 = 39{\cdot}95$ gives $z_3 = 1{\cdot}99$. Again look down the first column, of Appendix 3 headed z, until 1·9 is reached, then look across until the column headed 0·09 is reached, this gives 0·4767 and is the required area.

Because of the symmetry of the normal curve it is only necessary to tabulate the areas for one side of the curve. Areas which straddle the mean can be found as in the following example.

Example 3: Find the area between $z = 0$ and $z = -1{\cdot}13$.

Answer

As the distribution is symmetrical the area between $z = 0$ and $z = -1{\cdot}13$ will be the same as the area between $z = 0$ and $z = +1{\cdot}13$. Looking this up in the table in the way already described gives 0·3708

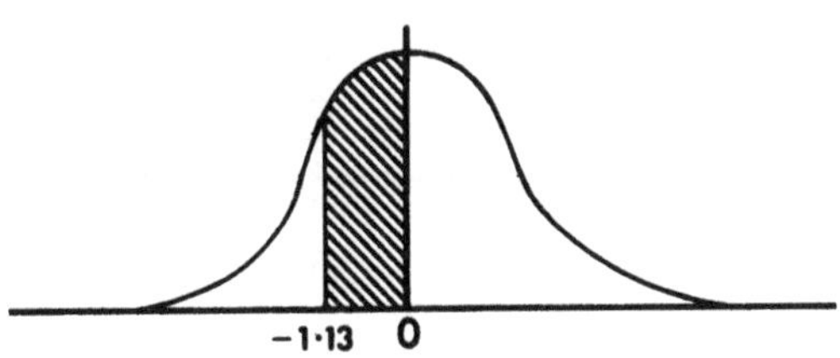

Fig. 5.4 (b)

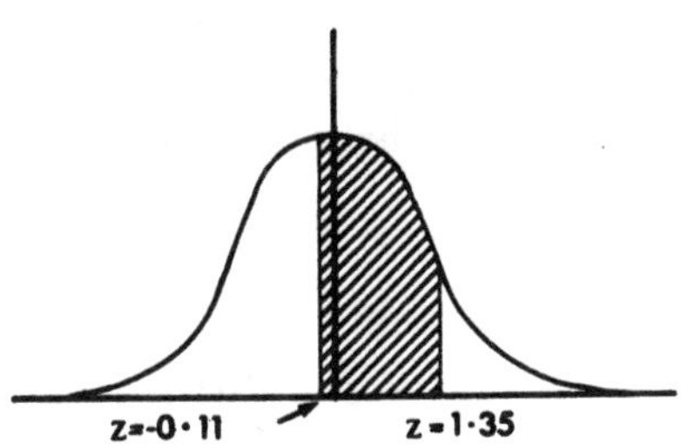

Fig. 5.4 (c)

Example 4: Find the area between $z = -0{\cdot}11$ and $z = 1{\cdot}35$

Answer

We find the area in two parts. First the area between $z = 0$ and $z = 1{\cdot}35$, and secondly the area between $z = -0{\cdot}11$ and $z = 0$. From the previous example we know the second area is equivalent to the area between $z = 0$ and $z = 0{\cdot}11$. Looking up $z = 1{\cdot}35$ gives 0·4115. Looking up $z = 0{\cdot}11$ gives 0·0438. Total area therefore is 0·4553.

Example 5: Find the area between $z = 1{\cdot}1$ and $z = 2{\cdot}31$.

Answer

This is found by first finding the area for $z = 2{\cdot}31$, then finding the area for $z = 1{\cdot}1$ and subtracting the second from the first. $z = 2{\cdot}31$ gives 0·4896 $z = 1{\cdot}1$ gives 0·3643. Therefore the area is 0·1253. Warning: it is not possible to first subtract $z = 1{\cdot}1$ from $z = 2{\cdot}31$ to get 1·2, and then look up 1·2 in the table. Why not?

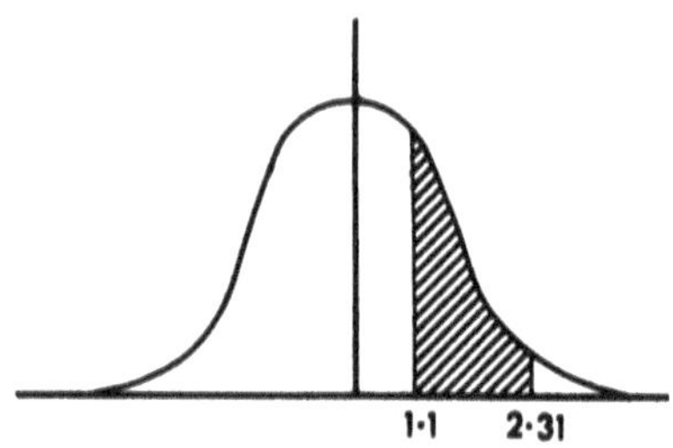

Fig. 5.4 (d)

The student should now by the application of the addition and subtraction methods shown, be able to find any area given either x or z values.

A quick way of finding z given x is to use the formula $z = \frac{x-\mu}{\sigma}$. The reader should examine this formula and ensure that he understands how it expresses the distance between x and μ in terms if σ.

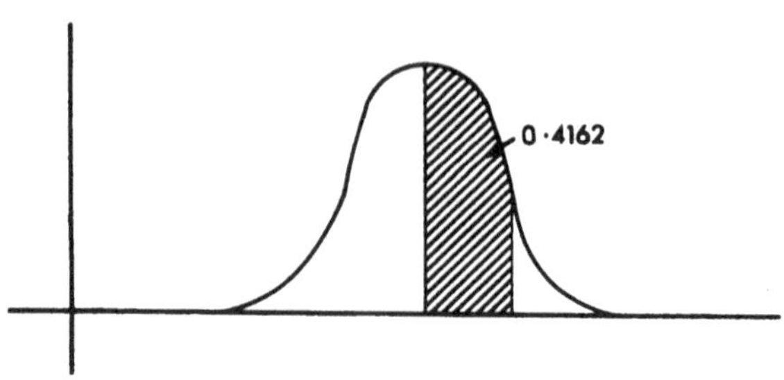

Fig. 5.4 (e)

Example 6: A distribution has mean 15 and standard deviation 3. Assuming it is normal find x if the area between 15 and x is 0·4162.

Answer

This is just the reverse process of the process given above. To reverse the process we first look for 0·4162 in the body of the table. Reading backwards gives the z value as 1·38. We now require the point x which corresponds to this value of z.

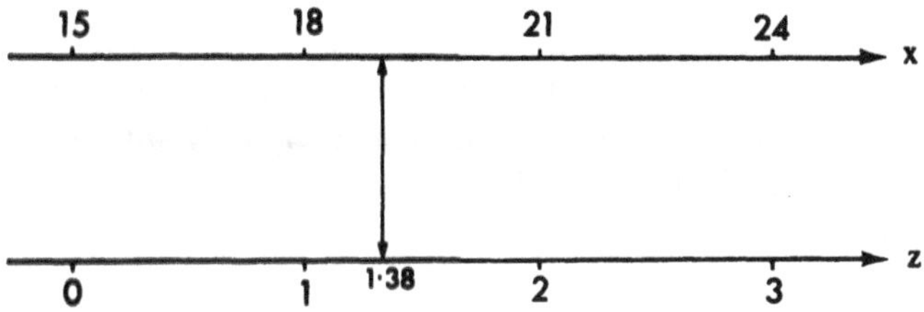

x will be between 18 and 21 and will be 0·38 of the distance from 18. The distance between 18 and 21 is 3 so x will be $0{\cdot}38 \times 3$ from 18, that is 1·14. Thus $x = 18 + 1{\cdot}14 = 19{\cdot}14$. Alternatively we may use the formula $z = \frac{x-\mu}{\sigma}$ Substituting the known figures gives,

$$1{\cdot}38 = \frac{x-15}{3} \quad \text{therefore} \quad x = 3 \times 1{\cdot}38 + 15$$

giving $\quad x = 4{\cdot}14 + 15 = 19{\cdot}14,\quad$ as before.

5.5 Standard Form of the Normal Curve

The idea of the distance of a point x from the mean can be used in the following situation.

Example 1: A boy took an examination in History and scored 42 out of a possible 109. All the students taking this examination had an average score of 51 and the standard deviation of the distribution of scores was 12·3. A girl took an examination in English and scored 24 out of a possible 50, and all the students taking this examination had an average score of 25·2 and the standard deviation of the distribution of scores was 7·2. Compare their performances.

Answer

Although the boy's score was higher than the girl's the possible score was also much higher and so comparison of actual marks will be of no value. To compare their performances we must see where they lie in relation to other students who took the examination, and the one who has the highest position *relative to their own group* will be adjudged to have the better performance. To find their relative positions we must find their z scores.

$$\text{(a) Boy.} \quad z = \frac{42 - 51}{12{\cdot}3} = -0{\cdot}73$$

$$\text{(b) Girl.} \quad z = \frac{24 - 25{\cdot}2}{7{\cdot}2} = -0{\cdot}16$$

Comparing $-0{\cdot}73$ with $-0{\cdot}16$ we see that $-0{\cdot}16$ is closer to zero than $-0{\cdot}73$. Therefore a score of 24 is closer to a mean of 25·2 where the standard deviation is 7·2, than 42 is to a mean of 51 with a standard deviation of 12·3. We therefore judge the girl's performance to be the better one.

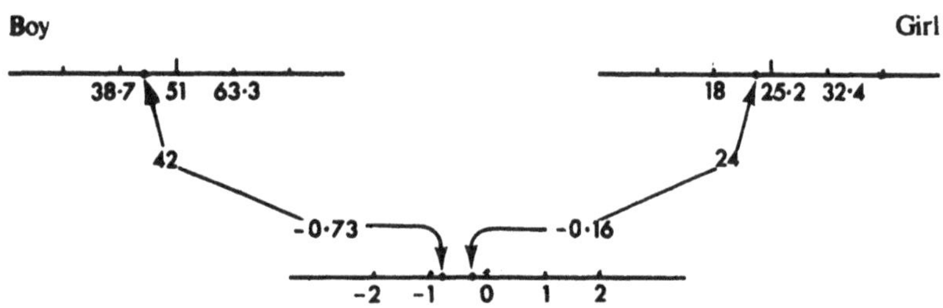

Fig. 5.5 (a)

This idea of judging relative merit by reference to distance from the mean in terms of standard deviations leads on to the notion of putting a variable $\underset{\sim}{x}$, normally distributed $N(\mu,\sigma^2)$, into its so called *standard form.*

If we take the normal curve

$$f(x) = \frac{1}{\sigma\sqrt{2\pi}}\, e^{-\frac{(x-\mu)}{2\sigma^2}}$$

and compare it with

$$g(z) = \frac{1}{\sqrt{2\pi}}\, e^{-\frac{z^2}{2}}$$

we note that there is a one to one correspondence between points in the outcome spaces, Fig. 5.5 (b).

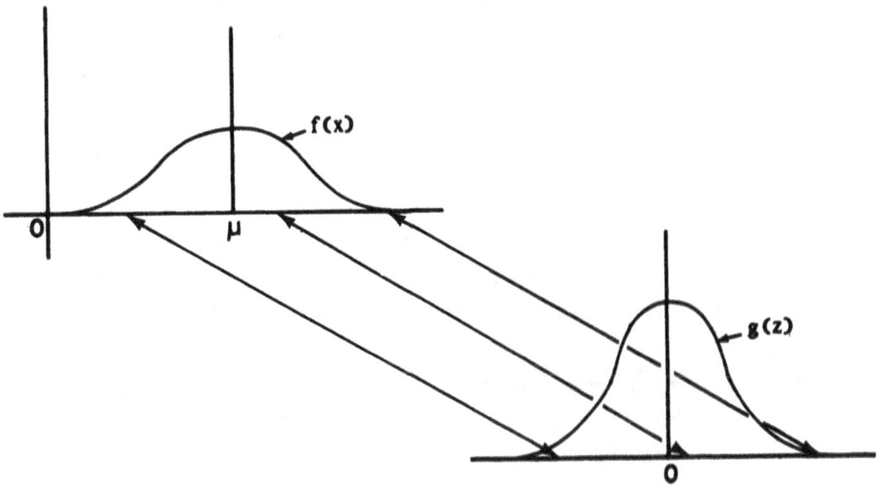

Fig. 5.5 (b)

For every point in the outcome space of z there is one, and only one, point in the outcome space of x, and corresponding points are related by the formula

$$z = \frac{x - \mu}{\sigma}.$$

Furthermore it can be seen that z is distributed normally with mean zero and standard deviation one, that is $N(0,1)$.

We now take the variable x and form the associated variable

$$z = \frac{x - \mu}{\sigma}.$$

and this simple transformation enables us to study any feature of the variable x in its simpler form. As we have already seen the area between a normal curve and two variates in the outcome space is the same as the area between the curve in its standard form and the corresponding z scores of the two variates. A similar advantage holds in connection with the values of $f(x)$ for a variate x and the value of $g(z)$ for the point z corresponding to x.

Putting any variable x, $N(\mu,\sigma^2)$ into the form $N(0,1)$ by means of

$$z = \frac{x - \mu}{\sigma}$$

is called putting $\underset{\sim}{x}$ into its standard form. Finding a z score of an individual value x of $\underset{\sim}{x}$, is called finding the standard score of x.

Standardising scores is a frequent practice in educational spheres as the following example shows.

Example 2: An examination standard allows the top 10% to be classified as A; the next 20% to be classified as B; the next 40% to be classified as C; the next 20% to be classified as D; and the remaining 10% to be classified as E. If 350 students take this examination and the results are distributed normally $N(70,21)$ find the boundary scores for these divisions and how many students were graded A.

Answer

The following diagram shows the various areas together with the z scores of the boundaries. These z scores were found in the usual way with the normal probability table.

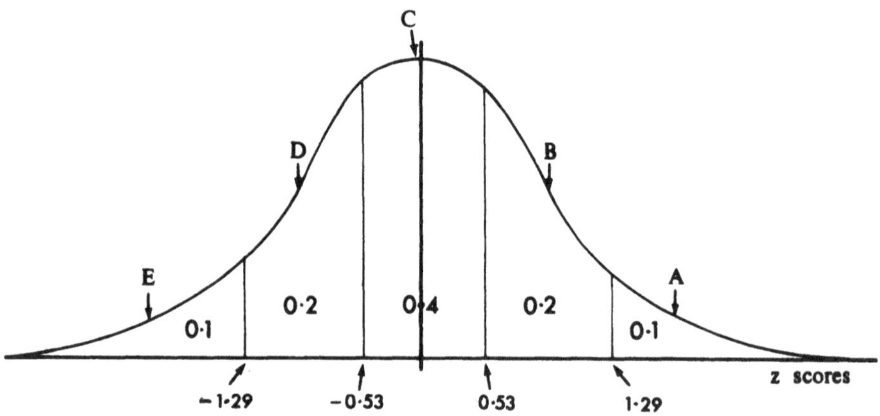

Fig. 5.5(c)

The score corresponding to $z = 1{\cdot}29$ is given by $1{\cdot}29 = \frac{x-70}{21}$, which gives $x = 21 \times 1{\cdot}29 + 70 = 97{\cdot}09$. Thus the boundary mark A/B is approximately 97. The score corresponding to $z = 0{\cdot}53$ is given by $0{\cdot}53 = \frac{x-70}{21}$, which gives $x = 21 \times 0{\cdot}53 + 70 = 91{\cdot}53$. Thus the B/C boundary mark is approximately 92. The remaining boundary marks were calculated in the same way and the following table compiled.

	z score	Boundary score	Marking scheme
10% *A*	1·29	97·09	98 and above
20% *B*	0·53	81·13	82 up to 97
40% *C*	-0·53	58·87	59 up to 81
20% *D*	-1·29	42·91	43 up to 58
10% *E*			42 and below

5.6 Fitting a Theoretical Curve to Data

Just as with the binomial and Poisson distributions it is possible to fit a theoretical curve to a given set of numerical data which is normally distributed. Essentially this involves the comparison of the areas of each class interval in the histogram of the data with the corresponding area of a normal curve which has the same mean and standard deviation as the data.

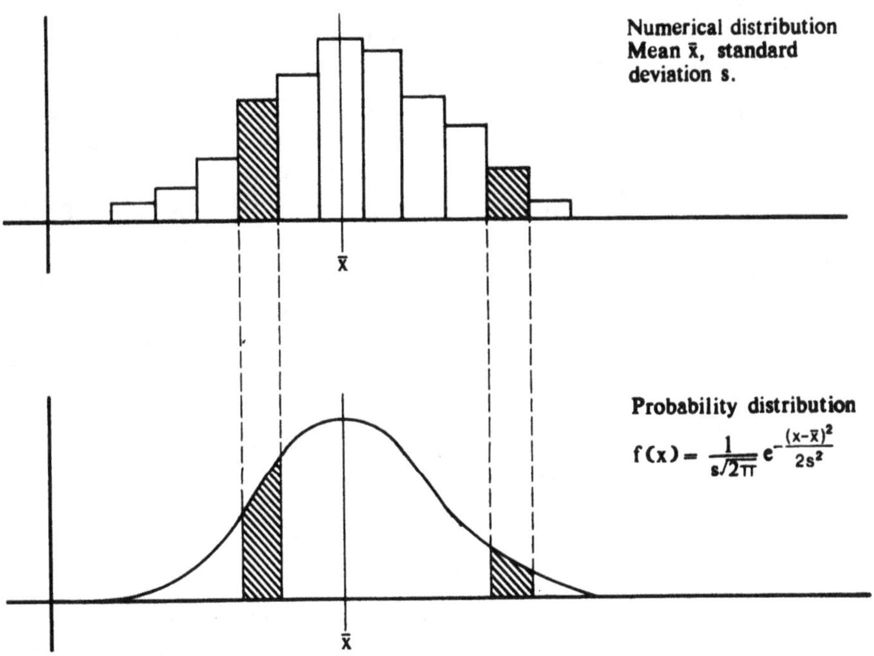

Fig. 5.6 (a)

The sequence of operations is as follows:

1. If given raw data select class intervals and construct frequency table.
2. Calculate the mean $\bar{x}$, and standard deviation s of the data.
3. Form the probability distribution

$$f(x) = \frac{1}{s\sqrt{2\pi}}e^{-\frac{(x-\bar{x})^2}{2s^2}}$$

4. Find the area under the probability distribution curve and between the class boundaries of the given data as indicated in the above diagram.
5. Calculate from the probability distribution the expected number of variates for each class interval.
6. Compare the actual with the expected results.

The following example will make the above clear.

Example 1: 50 male students were measured and their heights were recorded as in the first three columns of the following table. Fit a normal curve to the data and comment on the result.

Height Class Boundaries	Class Mid Point	No. of Students	z scores of class Boundaries	Area for each interval	Expected number per class
59·5 –	61	3	−2·73	0·0936	4·68 → 5
62·5 –	64	10	−1·30	0·1909	9·55 → 10
65·5 –	67	23	−0·56	0·4246	21·23 → 20
68·5 –	70	12	0·56	0·1909	9·55 → 10
71·5 to 74·5	73	2	1·30	0·0948	4·74 → 5

Explanation

First the mean and standard deviation werd calculated, $\bar{x} = 67$ and $s = 2{\cdot}75$, Then we compare the curve

$$f(x) = \frac{1}{2.75\sqrt{2\pi}}e^{-\frac{(x-67)^2}{15\cdot 12}}$$

with the histogram of the above data. We work in detail the class interval 62·5 – 65·5. We wish to know what area there is between these two figures and the probability curve $f(x)$. To find the area between these two figures we find the area between the corresponding z scores.

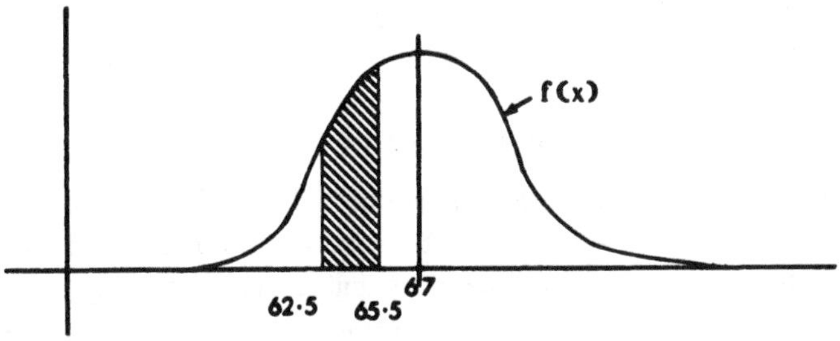

Fig. 5.6 (b)

$$z_1 = \frac{62{\cdot}5 - 67}{2{\cdot}75} = -1{\cdot}30 \qquad z_2 = \frac{65{\cdot}5 - 67}{2{\cdot}75} = -0{\cdot}56$$

The area between 0 and –1·30 is the same as the area between 0 and +1·30 = 0·4032.
The area between 0 and –0·56 is the same as the area between 0 and +0·56 = 0·2123.
The area between these two z scores is therefore 0·1909, and this is the area between the two figures 62·5 and 65·5 and $f(x)$. This is entered in the fifth column of the table.

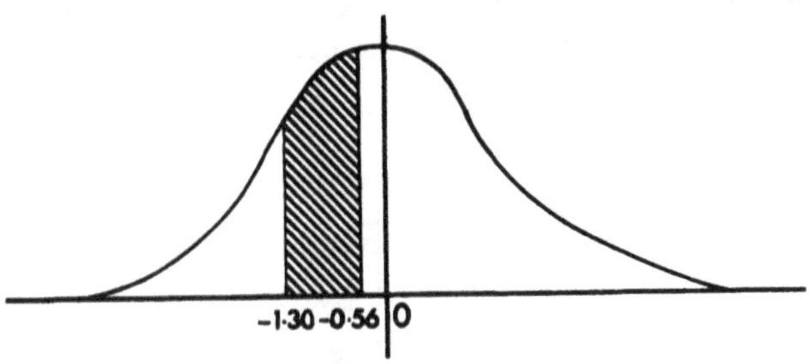

Fig. 5.6 (c)

To find now the expected number of students in the probable distribution we use the same argument as in previous chapters and get 50 × 0·1909 = 9·55 which gives 10 students and these figures are in the final column of the table.

The remaining figures were calculated in a like manner.

Comment

For such a small sample the fit is quite good. It should be noted that the area for the class interval 71·5 to 74·5 includes some area which would be more accurately associated with an interval 74·5 and above, consequently the estimated figure for this interval is rather high. A similar remark applies to the lowest class interval.

5.7 The Binomial and the Normal Distribution

We argued in Section 4.10 that if two probability distributions have very similar graphs then one may be used to approximate to the other, and we showed how the Poisson distribution is used to approximate to to the binomial. We now recall that when $p = \frac{1}{2}$ the graph of the binomial distribution is symmetrical and is, in shape, very similar to a normal curve. Under these circumstances, and again because the binomial probabilities are difficult to calculate, we can use the normal distribution as an approximation to the binomial distribution. Again the idea of comparison of areas under graphs is used. The histogram of the binomial distribution $B(x;\, n,p)$ is compared with the graph of the normal distribution $N(\mu,\sigma^2)$ where $\mu = np$ and $\sigma^2 = npq$.

Since the binomial distribution is a discrete distribution and the normal distribution is a continuous distribution there is some difficulty in connection with the approximation of a discrete distribution by a continuous distribution but first a rather tricky point must be explained. We saw in Section 5.2 that the area under a curve and between two points, a and b, represents the probability associated with all the points between a and b. To find an area in this sort of case we need to use the calculus, and if $f(x)$ is the curve, then the area between a and b is given by $\int_a^b f(x)dx$.

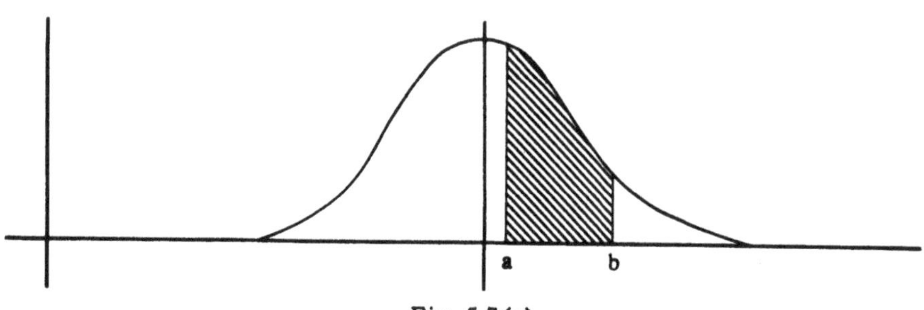

Fig. 5.7 (a)

But how can we find the probability associated with a *single point* in the outcome space of a continuous distribution? If we consider $\int_a^a f(x)dx$ we see that this is obviously zero, and we are led to the rather strange result that for a continuous variable the probability associated with a single point x is zero. This is not quite so paradoxical as it first appears and might be explained in simpler terms as follows. If you were measuring the heights of individuals selected at random, what would be the probability that the next individual selected would be exactly six feet tall? Not 6·000 000 000 000 1 feet tall, but exactly six feet tall. The chances of this happening are rather remote and you might well be inclined to associate a probability of zero with this particular event, This is just what the above mathematics says.

It might now be asked, 'What is the probability that the next individual measured will be between 5ft 11 inches and 6ft 1 inches tall?' Because we now have a certain amount of leeway we would be inclined to associate a figure higher than zero with this particular event. If we keep expanding this interval we would be inclined to increase the probability until we finally arrived at the stage where we would say that the probability that the next person measured being between 2 feet and 10 feet tall is a certainty and so ascribe a probability of unity. This argument shows that for a continuous variable probabilities are assigned not to individual points in the outcome space but to *intervals* in the outcome space.

The main point then is that for any x in the outcome space of a continuous variable $P(x) = 0$ and probabilities are assigned only to intervals.

To return now to the binomial distribution. This distribution being a discrete distribution has probabilities assigned *only* to single individual isolated points, that is 0, 1, 2, 3, . . . , n. There is no probability assigned to 1·35 since this point does not even come into the outcome space. How then are we to approximate a discrete distribution with a continuous distribution if in a discrete distribution probabilities are assigned *only* to single points and yet in a continuous distribution the probability of any single point is zero? The answer is that we take the probability of a *point* in a discrete outcome space, say $P(3)$, and compare it with the *interval* of unit width which has the point at its *centre*, in a comparable continuous distribution: that is for the point 3 in the discrete distribution we take the interval 2·5 – 3·5 in the associated continuous distribution. For the point 0 we use the interval –0·5 to 0·5, for the point 36 we take 35·5 to 36·5 and so on.

We now state that the normal distribution can approximate to the binomial distribution when

1. p is not small and
2. n is fairly large.

In practice the approximation is good if np is bigger than 5, and the closer p is to $\frac{1}{2}$ the better will be the approximation even in cases where n is fairly small. The mathematical justification for this will be given in a later chapter.

Example 1: A fair coin is tossed 12 times. Find the probability of getting (a) 9 heads, (b) between 4 heads and 6 heads inclusive. Use a normal approximation to the binomial for the same figures and see how the results compare.

Answer

(a) Prob of 9 heads $= B(9;12,\frac{1}{2}) = 12C9(\frac{1}{2})^3(\frac{1}{2})^9 = 0{\cdot}0537$

(b) Prob of 4 to 6 heads $= \sum_{x=4}^{6} 12Cx(\frac{1}{2})^{12-x}(\frac{1}{2})^x$

$= 0{\cdot}1208 + 0{\cdot}1934 + 0{\cdot}2256 = 0{\cdot}5398$

Using a normal approximation we use the distribution

$$f(x) = \frac{1}{\sqrt{6\pi}} e^{-\frac{(x-6)^2}{6}}$$

where we have put $\mu = np = 6$ and $\sigma^2 = npq = 3$.

(a) The probability of 9 heads is considered as 8·5 to 9·5 and we therefore require the area between these two figures and $f(x)$ above.

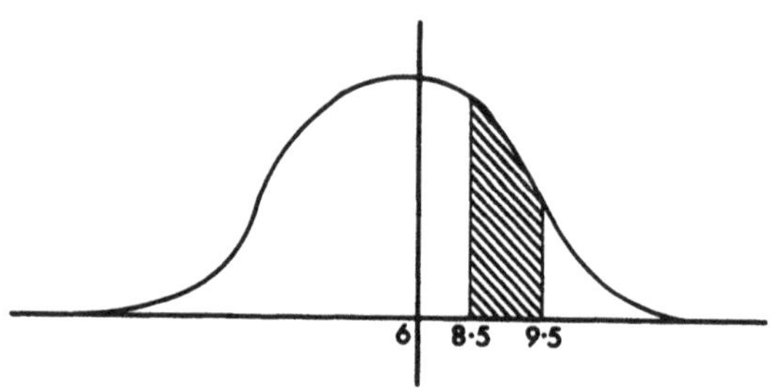

Fig. 5.7 (b)

This is found as before by using z scores.

$$z = \frac{8{\cdot}5 - 6}{3} = 1{\cdot}443 \qquad z = \frac{9{\cdot}5 - 6}{3} = 2{\cdot}02$$

The area between 1·443 and 2·02 is 0·4783 − 0·4251 = 0·0532

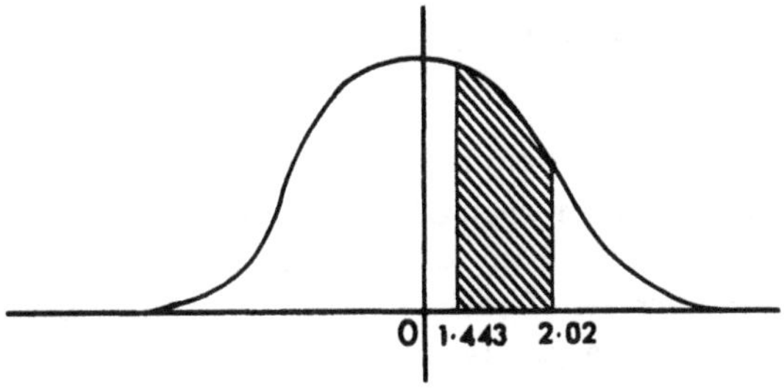

Fig. 5.7 (c)

(b) The probability of 4 to 6 heads is considered as 3·5 to 6·5 heads. As before

$$z = \frac{3{\cdot}5 - 6}{3} = -1{\cdot}443 \qquad z = \frac{6{\cdot}5 - 6}{3} = 0{\cdot}29$$

The area between −1·443 and 0·29 is 0·4251 + 0·1141 = 0·5392.

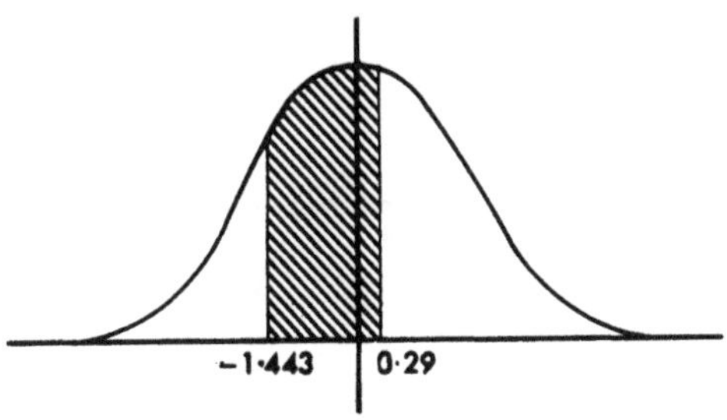

Fig. 5.7 (d)

It will be seen that the approximation is very good in both cases even though n is not large.

Having explained the method of using a continuous normal distribution to approximate a discrete distribution we can now consider further this notion of *correction for continuity*.

When we are concerned in measuring a variable which is continuous we are forced by practical considerations to round off measurements. this means we measure to the nearest inch or half-inch or quarter-inch and so on. If we measure to the nearest centimetre then any item which lies in the interval 3·5 to 4·5 will be counted as 4 cm. Thus *in practical terms* we turn a continuous variable into a discrete one and only count measurements at certain fixed points. In order to compensate for this we have to subsequently *correct for continuity*. An example will make this clear.

Example 2: 200 children were measured and the resulting figures were distributed normally with mean 68 cm and standard deviation 3 cm. Assuming measurements were to (a) the nearest cm (b) to the nearest half-cm, find the number of children (i) taller than 72 cm (ii) between 65 and 71 cm exclusive (iii) less than 63 cm.

Answer

(a) (i) Since recording is to the nearest centimetre taller than 72 cm means, when corrected for continuity, in excess of 72·5 cm. We therefore require the area shown in Fig. 5.7 (a). Finding the z score of 72·5 we get

$$z(72{\cdot}5) = \frac{72{\cdot}5 - 68}{3} = 1{\cdot}66$$

From normal tables the area is 0·5000 – 0·4521 (using interpolation) which is 0·0479. Multiplying this by 200 we get 9·58 or, rounding up, 10 children.

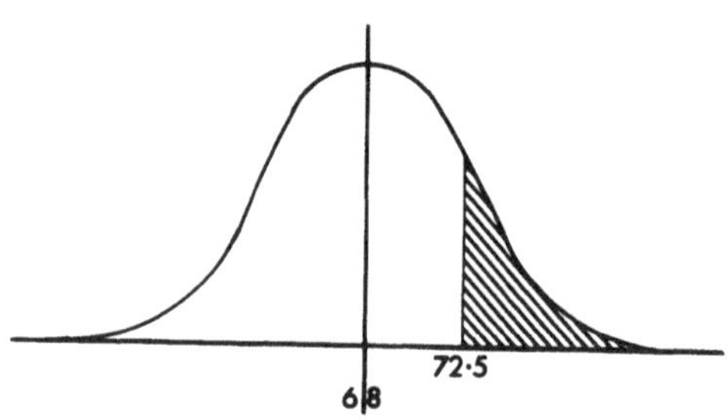

Fig. 5.7 (e)

(ii) Between 65 and 71 cm exclusive means between 65·5 and 70·5 cm when correcting for continuity. We therefore require the area shown in Fig. 5.7 (f). Since these scores are symmetrical about the mean we need only find the area on one side of the mean. Finding the z score of 70·5 we get

$$z(70{\cdot}5) = \frac{70{\cdot}5 - 68}{3} = 0{\cdot}833.$$

From normal tables the area is 0·2976. Doubling this for the total area required we get 0·5952. Multiplying this by 200 gives 119·14 or 119 children.

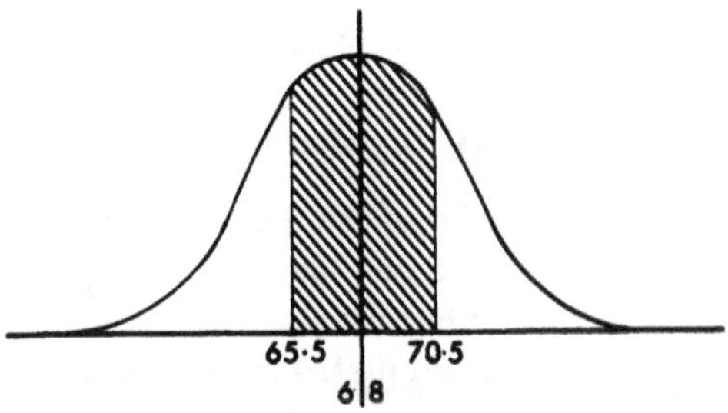

Fig. 5.7 (f)

(iii) Less than 63 cm means 62·5 and less when correcting for continuity, Fig. 5.7 (g). Arguing as in (i) and (ii) we find

$$z(62{\cdot}5) = \frac{62{\cdot}5 - 68}{3} = -1{\cdot}833$$

and the required area is 0·5000 − 0·4666 = 0·0734. Multiplying by 200 we get 14·68 or 15 children.

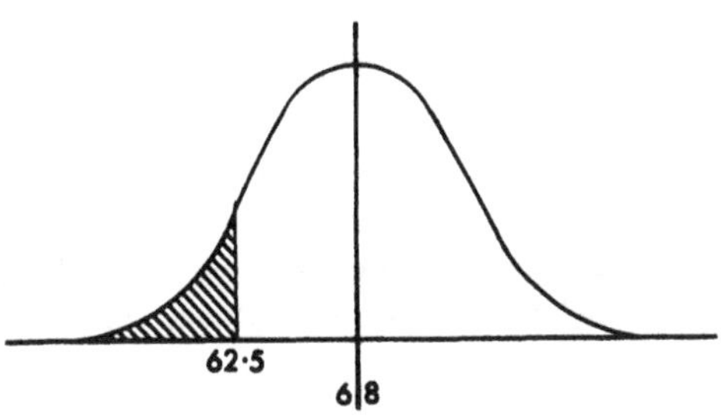

Fig. 5.7 (g)

(b) The ideas of (a) are repeated but this time the measurements are to the nearest half-centimetre and so we have to use corrected figures as follows:

(i) Taller than 72 cm means 72·25 and over.

(ii) Between 65 and 71 exclusive, means between 65·25 and 70·75 cm.

(iii) Less than 63 cm means 62·75 and below.

The remainder of the working is left as an exercise.

Example 3: If in the previous example there had been no correction for continuity find the difference in the result for (a) (ii).

Answer

If the figures 65 and 71 cms are used then the resulting figure is 137 children, so the difference is 18 children.

5.8 The Poisson and the Normal Distribution

The student who drew the graphs of the Poisson distributions as indicated in Section 4.4 will have noticed that when a gets larger the graph loses its skew appearance and becomes more symmetrical. It thus becomes closer in shape to a normal distribution $N(a,a)$. Since, like the binomial, the Poisson distribution is a discrete variable we apply a similar argument to that used in the last section in the finding of corresponding probabilities. We now state that the normal distribution $N(a,a)$ can be used to approximate to the Poisson distribution $P(x;a)$ when a is large. The mathematical justification for this will again be deferred until a later chapter.

Example 1: A Poisson distribution has mean and variance 1·9. Find the probability of getting (a) 2 successes and (b) more than 4 successes in one trial. Find the equivalent probabilities by using a normal approximation.

Answer

(a) Probability of 2 successes $= P(2,1{\cdot}9)$

$$= e^{-1\cdot 9}\frac{(1{\cdot}9)^2}{2!} = 0{\cdot}27$$

(b) Probability of more than 4 successes = the probability of 5 or more successes = 0·0441 to four decimal places. Using a normal approximation

$$f(x) = \frac{1}{\sqrt{3{\cdot}8\pi}}e^{-\frac{(x-1\cdot 9)^2}{3\cdot 8}}$$

arrived at by putting $\mu = a = 1{\cdot}9$ and $\sigma^2 = a = 1{\cdot}9$

(a) The probability of 2 successes is considered correcting for continuity as 1·5 to 2·5. We therefore require the area between these two figures and $f(x)$ above. Again we use z scores.

$$z = \frac{1{\cdot}5 - 1{\cdot}9}{1{\cdot}378} = -0{\cdot}2902 \qquad z = \frac{2{\cdot}5 - 1{\cdot}9}{1{\cdot}378} = 0{\cdot}4353$$

Area between these two figures is 0·1141 + 0·1700 = 0·2841.

(b) The probability of getting more than 4 successes is considered as 4·5 and upwards.

$$z = \frac{4{\cdot}5 - 1{\cdot}9}{1{\cdot}378} = 1{\cdot}886$$

Area above 1·886 = 0·5 − area below 1·886

= 0·5 − 0·4703 = 0·0297

Comment

In (a) the approximation is quite good but in (b) it is less satisfactory. In practice the Poisson probabilities are easy to compute with the aid of Poisson probability charts and so there is no pressing need to find alternative methods of computation and so normal approximations are not used a great deal. The higher the value of a the better the approximation will be, and since here the value of a is quite small a good approximation could not be expected.

5.9 Distribution Function 1

We saw in Section 3.12 the distribution function for a discrete variable. The equivalent definition for a continuous variable makes use of the integral sign as distinct from the sigma sign and is given next.

Definition

For a continuous random variable $\underset{\sim}{x}$, with probability finction $f(x)$ the function

$$F(s) = P(x \leqslant s) = \int_{-\infty}^{s} f(x)dx$$

is called the distribution function. $F(s)$ represents the probability that a random variable $\underset{\sim}{x}$ assumes a value less than or equal to s. Again the domain of $F(s)$ is $-\infty$ to ∞ and the range is zero to one.

Example 1: Let $\underset{\sim}{x}$ be normally distributed $N(0,1)$. If $F(s)$ is the distribution function find values for $F(-2)$, $F(-1)$, $F(0)$, $F(1)$ and $F(2)$. Compare the graphs of the two functions

Fig. 5.9(a)

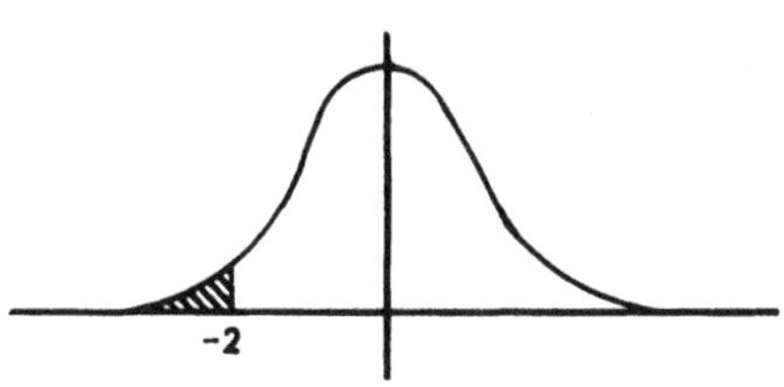

$$F(-2) = \int_{-\infty}^{-2} f(x)dx = \frac{1}{\sqrt{2\pi}}\int_{-\infty}^{-2} e^{-\frac{x^2}{2}} dx$$

$$= 0{\cdot}0228 \text{ using normal probability tables.}$$

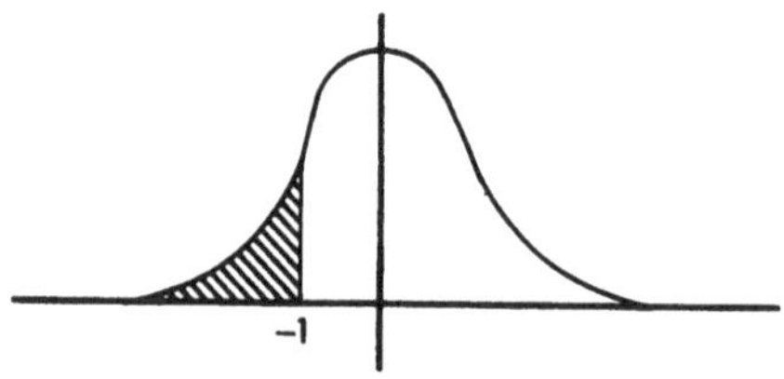

Fig. 5.9 (b)

$$F(-1) = \frac{1}{\sqrt{2\pi}}\int_{-\infty}^{-1} e^{-\frac{x^2}{2}} dx = 0{\cdot}1587$$

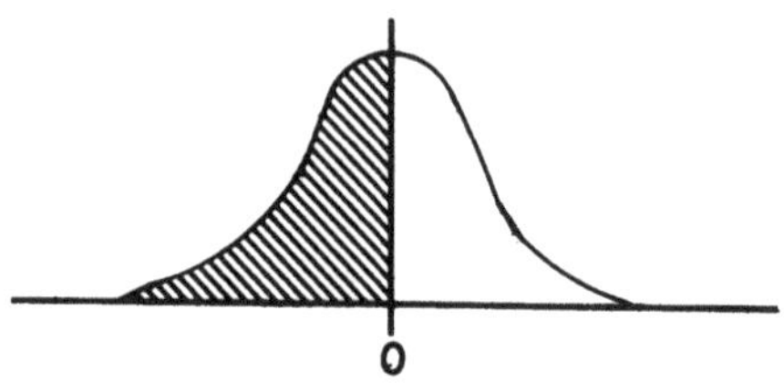

Fig. 5.9 (c)

$$F(0) = \frac{1}{\sqrt{2\pi}}\int_{-\infty}^{0} e^{-\frac{x^2}{2}} dx = 0{\cdot}5$$

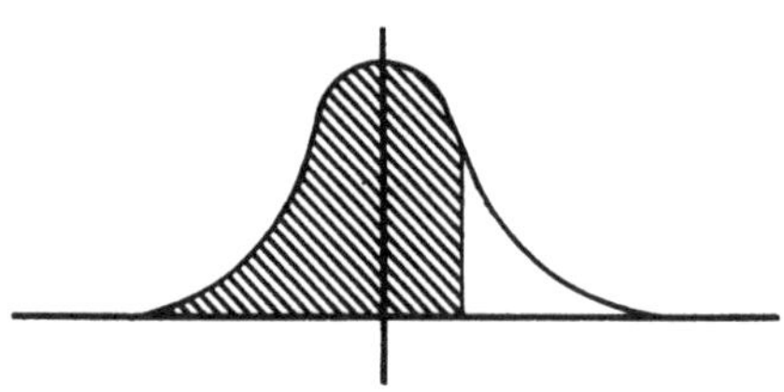

Fig. 5.9 (d)

$$F(1) = \frac{1}{\sqrt{2\pi}}\int_{-\infty}^{1} e^{-\frac{x^2}{2}} dx = 0{\cdot}8413$$

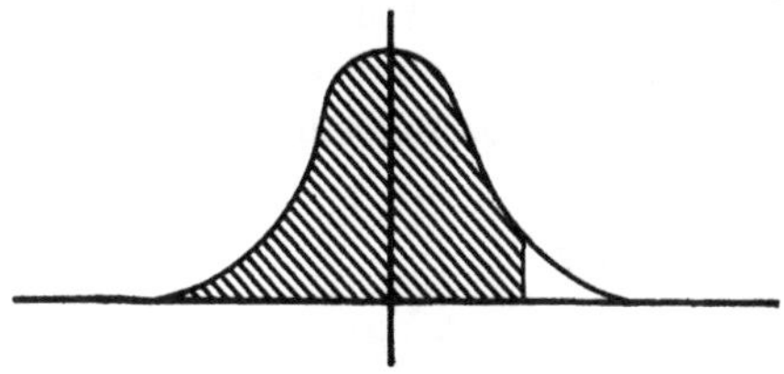

Fig. 5.9(e)

$$F(2) = \frac{1}{\sqrt{2\pi}}\int_{-\infty}^{2} e^{-\frac{x^2}{2}}\,dx = 0{\cdot}9772$$

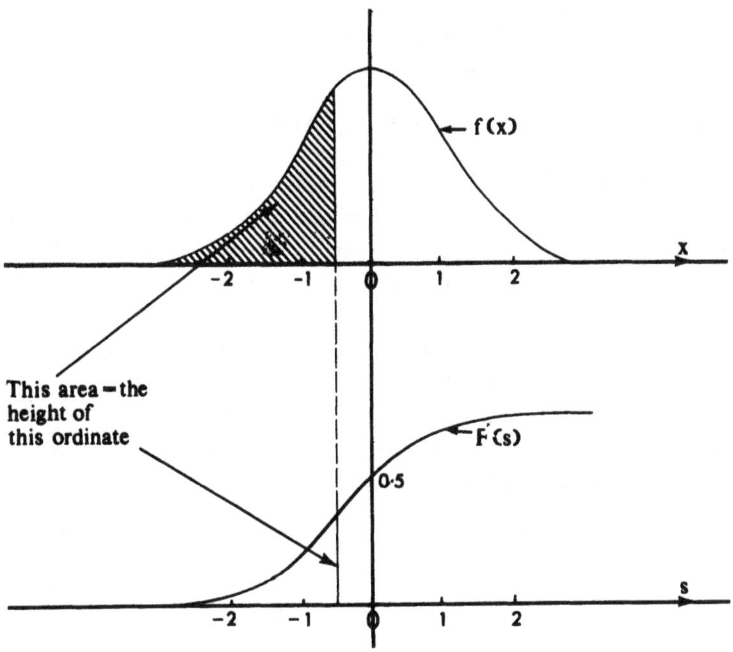

Fig. 5.9(f)

The student should compare this with Example 2 of Section 1.12, of *Descriptive Statistics and Probability Theory*, where a cumulative and relative cumulative frequency curve is shown for a continuous variable. It is also of interest that just as we arrived at a continuous curve to represent a set of data by taking smaller and smaller class intervals in the histogram of that data, then the same idea can be applied to the cumulative frequency diagram of a set of data. By taking smaller and smaller intervals the distribution function can be obtained.

5.10 Distribution Function 2

From the definition we see that any distribution function satisfies the following,

(1) $F(-\infty) = 0$

(2) $F(\infty) = 1$

(3) $F(s)$ is either constant or increasing, that is $F(a) \leqslant F(b)$ for $a<b$.

These properties are quite simply deduced from the definition and are left as exercises for the reader.

Let us now look at the probability that $\underset{\sim}{x}$ assumes a value bigger than a but less than or equal to b.

$$P(a<x\leqslant b) = F(b) - F(a) = \int_{-\infty}^{b} f(x)dx - \int_{-\infty}^{a} f(x)dx = \int_{a}^{b} f(x)dx$$

which is what we had before. We have also seen that in the continuous case the probability that $\underset{\sim}{x}$ assumes one particular value in its outcome space is zero, and so the above integral represents the probability that $\underset{\sim}{x}$ assumes a value between a and b *including or excluding either* end point.

Since $\underset{\sim}{x}$ is continuous then $F(s)$ is non decreasing and differentiating $F(s) = \int_{-\infty}^{s} f(x)dx$ yields $F'(s) = f(s)$ at every point where $f(x)$ is continuous. This shows that given a distribution function it is possible to determine a probability function just as it is possible to determine a distribution function given a probability function.

Example 2: Given the following distribution function determine the probability function.

$$F(s) = \begin{cases} 1 - e^{-s} & \text{for } s>0 \\ 0 & \text{for } s\leqslant 0 \end{cases}$$

Note first that $F(s)$ is a distribution function since $F(-\infty) = 0$, $F(\infty) = 1$, and $F(s)$ is non decreasing. Differentiating gives

$$f(x) = \begin{cases} e^{-x} & \text{for } x>0 \\ 0 & \text{for } x\leqslant 0 \end{cases}$$

The two graphs are shown below

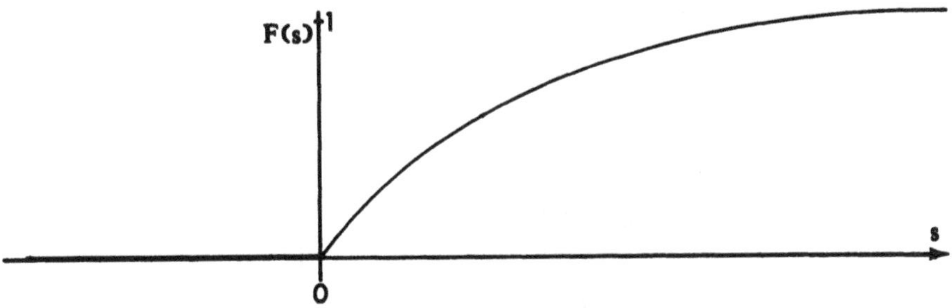

Fig. 5.10(a)

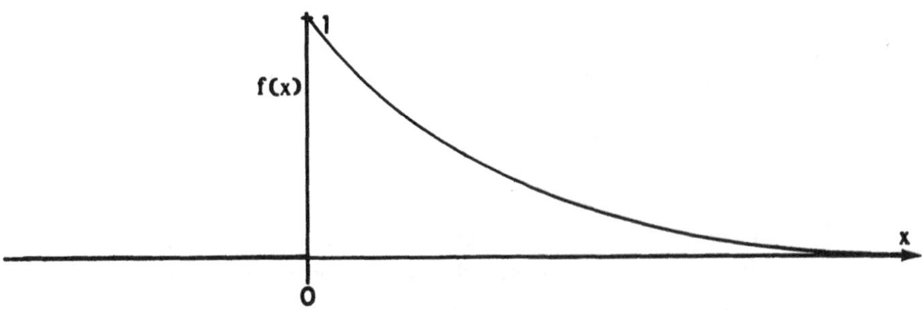

Fig. 5.10(b)

5.11 Moments

Using notation analogous to that for a discrete variable the r'th moment about an arbitrary number k, of a continuous random variable $\underset{\sim}{x}$, is defined as

$$m_r(k) = E[(\underset{\sim}{x} - k)^r] = \int_a^b (x - k)^r f(x)dx$$

where $f(x)$ is the probability function of $\underset{\sim}{x}$, and a and b are again the lowest and highest values of the outcome space.

As before $m_1(0)$ is the mean and $m_2(\mu)$ is the variance of a distribution and all the theorems proved in Chapter 2 hold for a continuous variable.

Example 1: Prove that $E(\underset{\sim}{x} + k) = E(\underset{\sim}{x}) + k$, for any continuous variable.

Answer

$$\begin{aligned} E(\underset{\sim}{x} + k) &= \int_a^b (x + k)f(x)dx \\ &= \int_a^b xf(x)dx + k\int_a^b f(x)dx \\ &= E(x) + k \end{aligned}$$

The remainder of the theorems of Chapter 2 are left as an exercise. Let us now look at the mean and variance of the random variable

$$z = \frac{x - \mu}{\sigma},$$

where x has mean μ and variance σ^2.

$$E(z) = E\left[\frac{x - \mu}{\sigma}\right] = E\left[\frac{x}{\sigma} - \frac{\mu}{\sigma}\right] = E\left[\frac{x}{\sigma}\right] - E\left[\frac{\mu}{\sigma}\right]$$

$$= \frac{\mu}{\sigma} - \frac{\mu}{\sigma} = 0$$

This shows that the mean of z is 0.

$$\text{Var}(z) = \text{Var}\left[\frac{x - \mu}{\sigma}\right] = \text{Var}\left[\frac{x}{\sigma} - \frac{\mu}{\sigma}\right] = \text{Var}\left[\frac{x}{\sigma}\right]$$

$$= \frac{1}{\sigma^2}\text{Var}[x] = \frac{\sigma^2}{\sigma^2} = 1$$

This shows that the variance of z is unity. Now this last piece of work has been done without regard to how x is distributed and so we see that *any* random variable x may be converted to standard form by forming the related random variable

$$\frac{x - \mu}{\sigma}$$

where μ and σ^2 are the mean and variance of x.

The application of this definition of moments to the case of the normal curve yields the results that $m_1(0) = \mu$ and $m_2(\mu) = \text{Var}(x) = \sigma^2$. The details of this are mathematically rather difficult and, as we have already assumed knowledge of μ and σ^2, unnecessary here.

5.12 Confidence Intervals and Confidence Limits

The area under the normal curve can help to introduce another important idea in statistics. We have seen that 0·6827 of the area under a normal curve is within one standard deviation of the mean and this can be utilised as follows. If a population is normally distributed then 68·27% of the population will lie within one standard deviation of the mean and thus we may say that we are 68·27% confident that any item selected from the population will lie within one standard deviation of the mean, that is $P(\mu - \sigma \leqslant x \leqslant \mu + \sigma) = 68{\cdot}27\%$.

We can also work in the reverse way. We can specify a degree of confidence and then work back to the interval around the mean. For instance if we wish to be 90% certain then we are looking for a number k such that $P(\mu - k\sigma \leqslant x \leqslant \mu + k\sigma) = 90\%$. Using the normal probability tables we see that $k = 1{\cdot}645$, so $P(\mu - 1{\cdot}645\sigma \leqslant x \leqslant \mu + 1{\cdot}645\sigma) = 90\%$.

The two most frequently used confidence limits are the 95% and the 99% confidence limits. They are for the normal curve.

$$P(\mu - 1{\cdot}96\sigma \leqslant x \leqslant \mu + 1{\cdot}96\sigma) = 95\%$$
$$P(\mu - 2{\cdot}58\sigma \leqslant x \leqslant \mu + 2{\cdot}58\sigma) = 99\%$$

We can now state the following. If an interval is given such that a variate will fall in this interval with a certain probability, then this interval is called a *confidence interval*, and the probability *associated with this interval* is the *degree of confidence*. The least and highest figures in the interval are called the *lower* and *upper confidence limits*.

Although confidence intervals and limits have been introduced through the normal curve they are not exclusively associated with this curve but apply to many other distributions and situations.

Example 1: A normal population has a mean of 100 and a standard deviation of 10. Find the 90% and 95% confidence intervals for an item selected at random.

Answer

The 90% confidence interval is given by

$$P(\mu - 1{\cdot}645\sigma \leqslant x \leqslant \mu + 1{\cdot}645\sigma) = 90\%$$

Now $\quad \mu - 1{\cdot}645\sigma = 100 - 1{\cdot}645 \times 10 = 83{\cdot}55$

and $\quad \mu + 1{\cdot}645\sigma = 100 + 1{\cdot}645 \times 10 = 116{\cdot}45$

so $\quad P(83{\cdot}55 \leqslant x \leqslant 116{\cdot}45) = 90\%$,

that is we can be sure that 90% of the items of the population will lie in the interval 83·55 to 116·45.

A similar argument gives the 95% confidence interval as 80·4 to 119·6, therefore $P(80{\cdot}4 \leqslant x \leqslant 119{\cdot}6) = 95\%$.

Exercise 5

1. Measure the height or weight of 150 persons in three lots of 50. Take the first lot of 50 and draw a histogram using (a) 4 (b) 6 (c) 8 (d) 10 classes. Comment on the graphs you get. Add a second lot of 50 to the

first lot and repeat. Again comment. Finally add the third lot of 50 and repeat with comments. Compare your results with Section 5.1.

2. Explain in your own words the difference between a discrete and a continuous variable.

3. Explain in your own words what a histogram is and why it is necessary to use a histogram to graph continuous data.

4. Draw the graphs of the following normal curves.

mean	2	3	10	2	2	2	3
standard deviation	1	1	1	3	4	5	2

5. A normal distribution has mean 37 cms and standard deviation 4·5 cms. Find the z scores of (a) 37 cms (b) 42·5 cms (c) 50·5 cms (d) 30 cms.

Answer

(a) 0 (c) 3

6. A normal distribution has mean 0 seconds and standard deviation 1·5 seconds. If the area between 0 and x is (a) 0·3212 (b) 0·4265 (c) 0·4932 (d) 0·4783, find x.

Answer

(a) ±1·38 (c) ±3·71

7. An examination allows the top 35% only to proceed to the next stage. If the scores of 450 students are normally distributed $N(55,9)$, what score must a candidate get to proceed to the next stage?

Answer

59 or more

8. A set is normally distributed with mean 50. If 17% of the set lie between the mean and 60, what is the standard deviation?

Answer

22·7

9. If a population has a mean of 21 and a standard deviation of 3, find the probability that an element selected at random will be (a) less than 18 (b) less than 17 (c) more than 20 (d) more than 23 (e) less than 17 or more than 23 (f) between 17 and 23. Assume a normal distribution.

Answer

(a) 0·1587 (c) 0·63 (e) 0·444

10. Light bulbs have a mean life of 4,500 hours and a standard deviation

of 900 hours. Assuming the lifetimes follow a normal distribution, what percentage of the bulbs would last (a) between 4,000 and 5,000 hours (b) between 3,000 and 5,500 hours (c) less than 2,500 hours?

Answer

(a) 0·421 (c) 0·0132

11. In a normal population the mean is 25 and the probability that a variate selected at random is over 29 is 0·05. Find the standard deviation.

Answer

2·43

12. The mean length of nails produced by a machine is 1″ and the standard deviation is 0·05″. For a lot of 200 nails how many will be (a) less than 0·9″ (b) bigger than 1·05″?

Answer

(a) approximately 5

13. A manufacturer produses on average 13% defective items. Use a normal approximation to find the probability that a lot of 50 will contain (a) 1 (b) 2 (c) 3 (d) 4 defectives.

Answer

(a) 0·0003 (c) 0·0173

14. A manufacturer produces on average 13% defective items. Use a normal approximation to find the probability that lots of (a) 50 (b) 100 (c) 150 (d) 200 will contain exactly 5 defectives.

Answer

(a) 0·1613 (c) zero

15. A manufacturer's batteries have a mean life of 150 hours. A customer wishes to replace all his batteries after 140 hours and to have had not more than 15% failures. What is the maximum standard deviation the manufacturer must work to to satisfy his customer?

Answer

9·6 hours

16. A coin is tossed 100 times. Find the probability that (a) exactly 50 heads (b) 40 heads or less will be obtained. Use the binomial distribution and a normal approximation.

Answer

	Binomial	Normal
(a)	0·08	0·08
(b)	0·028	0·029

17. 125 students sit an exam and their results are normally distributed with mean 80 and standard deviation 6. How many students scored between 74 and 86.

Answer

85

18. A screw manufacturer produces on average 2% defectives. What is the probability that a lot of 2000 will contain $1\frac{1}{2}$% or more defectives?

Answer

0·893

19. A certain species of apple has a mean weight of 4 oz with a standard deviation of 0·6 oz. Find what percentage of apples lie between (a) 4 oz and 5 oz (b) 5 oz and 6 oz (c) over 6 oz (d) 3 oz and $5\frac{1}{2}$ oz. Assume the weights to be normally distributed.

20. Television tubes had the lives indicated in the following table

Length of life in hours	Percentage of tubes
210 –	6%
213 –	17%
216 –	42%
219 –	26%
222 – 225	9%

Fit a theoretical normal curve to the data and find the expected frequencies to the nearest 1%.

Answer

4%, 20%, 40%, 28%, 8%.

21. In a normal distribution with mean 60 and standard deviation 2·92, it is known that 70 variates exceed 64·05. What is the total number of variates in the distribution?

Answer

200

22. A teacher assigns 10% A's, 20% B's, 40% C's, 20% D's and 10% E's. An examination gives a mean of 70 and a standard deviation of 19. Assuming they are normally distributed, find the borderline mark between the B's and C's.

Answer

79

23. Find the distribution functions, $F(s)$, for the following continuous distributions.

(a) $f(x) = \begin{cases} 1 & 0 \leqslant x \leqslant 1 \\ 0 & \text{elsewhere} \end{cases}$ (b) $f(x) = \begin{cases} 1 & 1 \leqslant x \leqslant 2 \\ 0 & \text{elsewhere} \end{cases}$

(c) $f(x) = \begin{cases} 1 & 12 \leqslant x \leqslant 13 \\ 0 & \text{elsewhere} \end{cases}$ (d) $f(x) = \begin{cases} \frac{1}{2} & 1 \leqslant x \leqslant 3 \\ 0 & \text{elsewhere} \end{cases}$

(e) $f(x) = \begin{cases} \frac{1}{3} & 1 \leqslant x \leqslant 4 \\ 0 & \text{elsewhere} \end{cases}$ (f) $f(x) = \begin{cases} \frac{1}{6} & 1 \leqslant x \leqslant 7 \\ 0 & \text{elsewhere} \end{cases}$

24. Given the continuous function

$$f(x) = \begin{cases} 2e^{-2} & x \geqslant 0 \\ 0 & x < 0 \end{cases}$$

prove that this function may be used as a probability function, and find its distribution function. Given a population distributed in this way what is the probability that an item selected at random will be less than or equal to 1?

Answer

$1 - e^{-2}$

25. Given the following function

$$f(x) = \begin{cases} 1 - \frac{1}{2}x & 0 \leqslant x \leqslant 2 \\ 0 & \text{elsewhere} \end{cases}$$

find its distribution function. Given a population distributed in this way what is the probability that an item selected at random will be bigger than 1.

Answer

$\frac{1}{4}$.

26. Books were selected at random in a library and their thickness measured. The results are shown in the following table:

Number of books	3	6	13	18	15	7	4	1
Thickness of books (inches)	0·5 –	1·0 –	1·5 –	2·0 –	2·5 –	3·0 –	3·5 –	4·0 – 4·5

Answer

Expected figures (rounded off) 3, 7, 13, 17, 15, 8, 4, 1.

27. Try to fit a normal curve to a set of data which is obviously not normal. Discuss your attempt.

28. Fit a normal distribution to number 16, Exercise 4. Compare your results with the poisson figures and comment.

29. Prove that if x is a continuous variable then

(a) $E(ax) = aE(x)$ (b) $E(ax + b) = aE(x) + b$

(c) $\text{Var}(x + b) = \text{Var}(x)$ (d) $\text{Var}(ax) = a^2\text{Var}(x)$

(e) $\text{Var}(ax + b) = a^2\text{Var}(x)$.

30. A population has mean 75 and a standard deviation of 10. Find (a) the 90% and (b) the 95% confidence intervals for an item selected at random.

Answer

(a) 58·55 to 91·45 (b) 55·4 to 94·6

31. Given a variable x, which has mean μ and standard deviation σ, has a 90% confidence interval of $\mu + k\sigma$, (a) show that the variable $x + b$ as a 90% confidence interval of $(\mu + b) \pm k\sigma$, and (b) show that the variable ax has a 90% confidence interval of $a(\mu \pm k\sigma)$.

6 Some Less Common Distributions

6.1 Introduction

The binomial, Poisson and normal are without doubt the most commonly used models in statistics, but many others have been developed to cope with situations that are beyond the scope of these three. In order to give the reader some idea of what other distributions there are, some of them are given in outline below.

6.2 The Discrete Uniform Dirtribution

If a random variable with n element in its outcome space has equal probabilities assigned to each element then it is called a *discrete uniform distribution*. Thus if the outcome space of $\underset{\sim}{x}$ is $\{x_1, x_2, \ldots, x_n\}$ and

$$P(x_i) = \frac{1}{n} \quad \text{for } i = 1, 2, 3, \ldots, n$$

then the probability distribution of $\underset{\sim}{x}$ is a *discrete uniform distribution.* The rolling of a normal dice is an example of a random variable with a discrete uniform distribution.

Example 1: A discrete random variable $\underset{\sim}{x}$ distributed uniformly has outcome space $\{-3, -2, -1, 0, 1, 2, 3\}$. Draw the graph and find the probabilities that (a) $\underset{\sim}{x}$ assumes a value bigger than 0, and (b) $\underset{\sim}{x}$ assumes a value between -2 and $+2$ inclusive.

Answer

Since there are 7 elements in the outcome space $P(x_i) = \frac{1}{7}$. The graph is

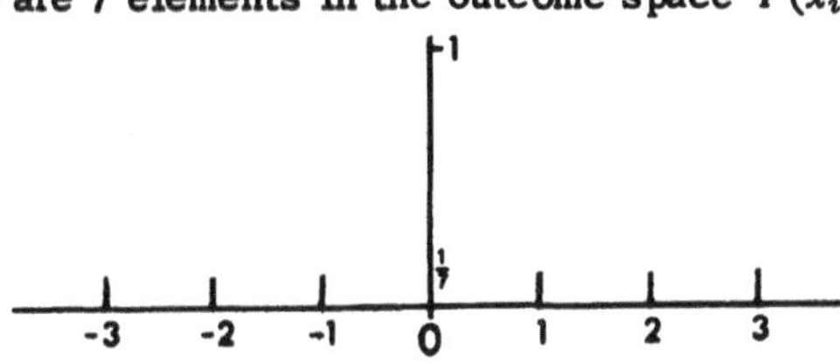

(a) The probability that $\underset{\sim}{x}$ assumes a value bigger than $0 = P(1) + P(2) + P(3) = \frac{1}{7} + \frac{1}{7} + \frac{1}{7} = \frac{3}{7}$

(b) The probability that $\underset{\sim}{x}$ assumes a value between -2 and $+2$ inclusive $= P(-2) + P(-1) + P(0) + P(1) + P(2) = \frac{5}{7}$

6.3 The Continuous Uniform Distribution

Analogous to the discrete uniform distribution is the continuous uniform distribution. It is defined as

$$f(x) = \begin{cases} \dfrac{1}{b-a} & \text{for } a \leqslant x \leqslant b \\ 0 & \text{elsewhere} \end{cases}$$

where a and b are the least and highest values in the outcome space of $\underset{\sim}{x}$.

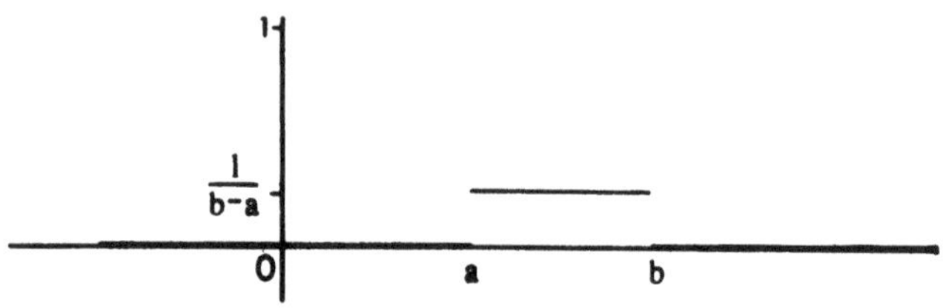

Fig. 6.3 (a)

Example 1: Show that $f(x)$ defined above satisfies the conditions necessary for a function to be a probability distribution.

Answer

(i) $f(x) \geqslant 0$ for all x between a and b, that is positive probabilities are associated with the elements of the outcome space of x.

(ii) $$\int_a^b f(x)dx = \int_a^b \frac{dx}{(b-a)} = \left[\frac{x}{b-a}\right]_a^b = \frac{b-a}{b-a} = 1$$

Therefore $f(x)$ is a probability distribution.

6.4 The Multinomial Distribution

Analogous to the binomial theorem $(a + b)^n$ there is the multinomial theorem $(a + b + c + \ldots + k)^n$, and just as the binomial distribution can act as a model for a situation involving two outcomes the multinomial distribution can act as a model for situations involving more than two outcomes. All that is necessary is that each outcome can be associated with one, and only one, of the individual elements of the multinomial $(a + b + c + \dots + k)$. The probabilities associated with each outcome must be constant from trial to trial and the sum of the probabilities must be unity.

Definition

If one trial in an experiment has k outcomes $e_1, e_2, \dots, e_k$, and associated with these outcomes are probabilities $p_1, p_2, \dots, p_k$, respectively, then the probability that $e_1, e_2, \dots, e_k$, occur $x_1, x_2, \dots, x_k$ times in n trials is

$$P(x_1, x_2, \dots, x_k) = \frac{n!}{x_1!x_2! \dots x_k!} p_1^{x_1} \cdot p_2^{x_2} \cdot p_3^{x_3} \dots p_k^{x_k}$$

where $0 \leqslant x_i \leqslant n$ and $x_1 + x_2 + x_3 + \dots + x_k = n$

Example 1: A cube has painted on the six faces the numbers 1, 1, 2, 2, 3, 4. Find the probability that in 5 rolls of this cube the number 1 appears twice, number 2 appears once, number 3 appears twice, and number 4 does not appear.

Answer

$P(1) = \frac{1}{3}$, $P(2) = \frac{1}{3}$, $P(3) = \frac{1}{6}$, $P(4) = \frac{1}{6}$. The probabilities required are given by the expansion of $(\frac{1}{3} + \frac{1}{3} + \frac{1}{6} + \frac{1}{6})^5$ and

$$P(2, 1, 2, 0) = \frac{5!}{2!1!2!0!} (\tfrac{1}{3})^2 (\tfrac{1}{3})^1 (\tfrac{1}{6})^2 (\tfrac{1}{6})^0 = 0{\cdot}03086$$

N.B. $\Sigma x_i = n$ and $\Sigma p_i = 1$. The multinomial is a discrete distribution.

6.5 The Geometric Distribution

If a series of trials which satisfy the assumption of the binomial situation are concerned not with the number of successes in n trials but with the number of the trial which is the first successful one, then, clearly, n is not fixed. The model for this situation is the so called *geometric distribution*. If p is the probability of success and q is the probability of failure for any one trial and x is the number of the trial when the first success occurs then the geometric distribution is defined as

$$G(x;p) = pq^{x-1} \text{ for } x = 1, 2, 3, \dots, n$$

Example 1: A rifleman fires as many shots as he needs to hit the bull. If the probability that he will hit the bull with any one shot is $\frac{3}{5}$ find the probability that he will take (a) exactly 4 shots, (b) at most 4 shots, to hit the bull.

Answer

(a)
$$G(4;\tfrac{3}{5}) = (\tfrac{3}{5})(\tfrac{2}{5})^{4-1} = (\tfrac{3}{5})(\tfrac{2}{5})^{3} = \tfrac{24}{625}$$
$$= 0{\cdot}0384$$

(b) At most 4 shots means 4 or less, that is

$$G(1;\tfrac{3}{5}) + G(2;\tfrac{3}{5}) + G(3;\tfrac{3}{5}) + G(4;\tfrac{3}{5}).$$

$$\left.\begin{aligned} G(1;\tfrac{3}{5}) &= (\tfrac{3}{5})(\tfrac{2}{5})^{0} = \tfrac{3}{5} \\ G(2;\tfrac{3}{5}) &= (\tfrac{3}{5})(\tfrac{2}{5})^{1} = \tfrac{6}{25} \\ G(3;\tfrac{3}{5}) &= (\tfrac{3}{5})(\tfrac{2}{5})^{2} = \tfrac{12}{125} \\ G(4;\tfrac{3}{5}) &= (\tfrac{3}{5})(\tfrac{2}{5})^{3} = \tfrac{24}{625} \end{aligned}\right\}$$

adding these gives $\tfrac{609}{625}$ which is the required probability.

The geometric distribution is so called because – as will be clearly seen from the last example – the successive terms form a geometric progression. This is another discrete distribution.

6.6 The Hypergeometric Distribution

The binomial distribution applies to situations where p remains constant from trial to trial. If it is applied to sampling problems where so many are selected from a population, then in order to ensure that p remains constant the sample will have to be replaced into the population. Therefore the binomial distribution applies to sampling with replacement. If the population is sufficiently large to enable a sample to be taken and not replaced without altering p then the binomial may be used for sampling without replacement. Let us for the moment confine ourselves to populations which are not this large. There are situations where it is not possible to replace a sample back into the population from which it was taken because examination of the sample necessarily involves some alteration or even destruction of the members of the sample. In order to deal with this situation, known as sampling without replacement, the hypergeometric distribution has been developed. We approach the general case through an example.

If we have a population of 10 balls in a jar, 3 of which are labelled 'success' and 7 of which are labelled 'failure' and we are going to select a sample of 2, then we are interested in the probability of getting either 0 successes and 2 failures, 1 success and 1 failure, or 2 successes and 0 failures. Each of the 10 balls has an equal chance of being selected so there are $10C2$ ways of selecting different samples of 2. Thus the probability of selecting any particular sample of 2 is $\frac{1}{10C2}$

Now each sample of 2 will consist of x successes and $2 - x$ failures, where $x = 0, 1$ or 2. There are $3Cx$ ways of selecting x of the 3 balls labelled 'success' and $7C(2 - x)$ ways of selecting $2 - x$ balls from the 7 balls labelled 'failure'. By the multiplication rule, for a fixed x, the number of ways of selecting x successes and $2 - x$ failures will be the product of $3Cx$ and $7C(2 - x)$. It now follows that the probability consisting of 3 successes and 7 failures is

$$P(x) = \frac{[3Cx] \times [7C(2-x)]}{10C2}, \quad x = 0, 1 \text{ or } 2.$$

$$P(0) = \frac{3C0 \times 7C2}{10C2} = \frac{21}{45}$$

$$P(1) = \frac{3C1 \times 7C1}{10C2} = \frac{21}{45}$$

$$P(2) = \frac{3C2 \times 7C0}{10C2} = \frac{3}{45}$$

We now define the hypergeometric distribution. If a population consists of $s + f$ ('s' can be thought of as standing for success and 'f' for failure) elements and a sample of n is taken without replacement, then the probability of getting x successes and $n - x$ failures in this sample is

$$H(x;n,s,f) = \frac{[sCx] \times [fC(n-x)]}{(s+f)Cn} \quad \text{for } x = 0, 1, 2, \ldots, n.$$

This probability distribution is called the *hypergeometric distribution* and the notation $H(x;n,s,f)$ is self explanatory.

Example 1: An inspection process involves taking a sample of 2 from a box of 10. If either of these 2 are defective the box of 10 is rejected. What is the probability that a box of 10 which in fact contains 3 defective items will be passed as correct.

Answer

From the above working, the probability of getting 0 successes from 10 items which include 3 successes is $\frac{21}{45}$. Here the finding of a defective item counts as a success so the probability that 0 defectives will be found in a sample of 2 taken from a box of 10 which includes 3 defectives is $\frac{21}{45}$. Thus the probability that such a box would be passed as correct is $\frac{21}{45}$.

When n is small compared with $s + f$ then the binomial distribution can be used to approximate to the hypergeometric distribution. The hypergeometric is a discrete distribution.

6.7 The Triangular Distribution

A random variable $\underset{\sim}{x}$ with probability distribution $f(x)$ defined as

$$f(x) = \begin{cases} \dfrac{1}{a^2}(a + x) & -a \leqslant x \leqslant 0 \\ \dfrac{1}{a^2}(a - x) & 0 \leqslant x \leqslant a \\ 0 & \text{elsewhere} \end{cases}$$

has a triangular distribution. Its graph is as follows:

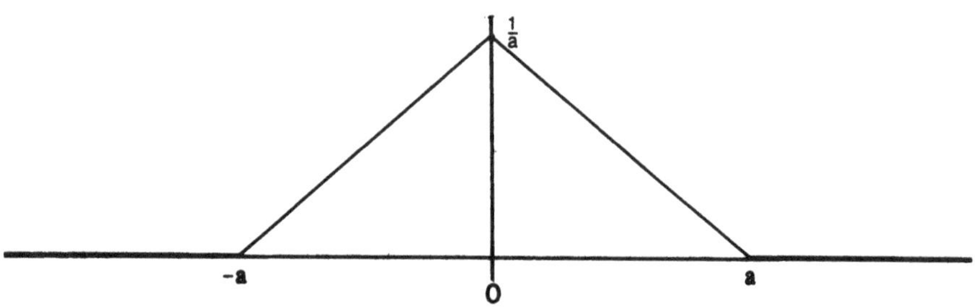

Fig. 6.7 (a)

The triangular distribution is a continuous distribution, and the shape of its graph is the reason for its name.

Example 1: Show that the area under the graph in the above diagram is unity.

Answer

The area of a triangle $= \frac{1}{2}$ base $\times$ height

$$= \tfrac{1}{2} \times 2a \times \tfrac{1}{a} = 1.$$

6.8 The Cauchy Distribution

The *Cauchy distribution* is defined as

$$f(x) = \frac{1}{\pi} \cdot \frac{a}{(a^2 + x^2)} \qquad -\infty < x < \infty$$

where $a > 0$.

Its graph is

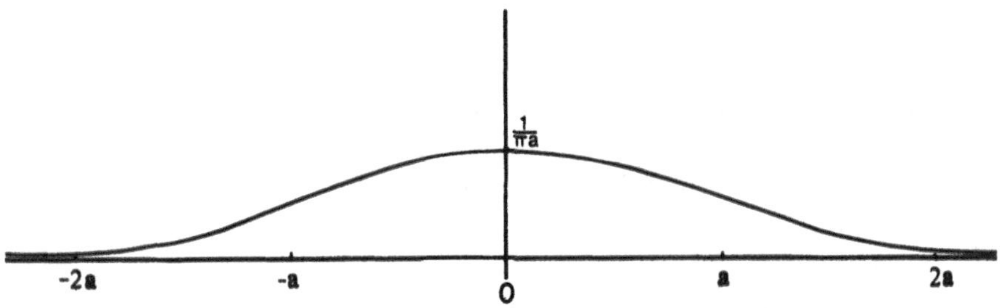

Fig. 6.8 (a)

which is very much like the graph of a normal distribution but the properties of the Cauchy distribution differ markedly from the properties of the normal distribution. The Cauchy distribution is a continuous distribution.

Exercise 6

1. A mechanic called out to cars which will not start notes that one quarter of them have battery trouble, one third have mechanical trouble and the remainder have electrical trouble apart from the battery. He is called out to six cars in one day. What is the probability that one car had battery trouble, 2 cars had mechanical trouble and the remainder had electrical trouble apart from the battery?

Answer

$\frac{625}{5184}$

2. A red die and a white die are thrown and the number appearing on the red die is subtracted from the number appearing on the white die. Find the probability distribution for the resulting number.

3. Two dice are thrown and the numbers added. Seven is then subtracted from this total. Show that the probability distribution for the resulting number is the same as the probability distribution in the previous question.

4. The probability that a soldier goes through a campaign without injury is $\frac{4}{9}$, the probability that he will receive a minor injury is $\frac{3}{9}$ and the probability that he will receive a major injury is $\frac{2}{9}$. What is the probability that four brothers in a regiment will go through a campaign and have two injured, one with a minor injury and one with a major injury?

Answer

$\frac{128}{729}$

5. A holiday resort claims that during their summer season the probability of a bright sunny day is $\frac{4}{10}$, the probability of a bright but sunless day is $\frac{3}{10}$, the probability of a dull day is $\frac{2}{10}$, and the probability of rain is $\frac{1}{10}$. A family takes a 10 day holiday at this resort. Calculate the probability that they will get 4 bright sunny days, 3 bright but sunless days, 2 dull days and 1 day of rain.

Answer

0·00035

6. A penny is tossed until a head appears. Find the probability function for this experiment.

7. Given a continuous rectangular distribution over the interval, 0,1, show that

$$m_k(0) = \frac{1}{k+1} \quad \text{and} \quad m_k(\mu) = \frac{1}{k+1}\{\tfrac{1}{2}^{k+1} - (-\tfrac{1}{2})^{k+1}\}$$

8. Given a continuous rectangular distribution over the interval a to b show that

$$m_k(0) = \frac{b^{k+1} - a^{k+1}}{(b-a)(k+1)}$$

9. Find the distributions which form models for the following situations:

(a) spinning a pointer and measuring round the circumference the distance from a fixed point on the circumference to where the pointer stops.

(b) repeat (a) but instead of measuring round the circumference measure directly.

(c) spinning a pointer and measuring the angle it makes with a fixed line through the centre of rotation when it comes to rest.

(d) a Roulette wheel.

10. Draw the graph of the geometric distribution of Example 1, Section 6.5. Draw also the graph of number 6, Exercise 6. Compare these two graphs. What conclusions do you draw?

11. A man needs 'double 14' to win a game of darts. If his probability of hitting this part of the dartboard with a single dart is $\frac{1}{4}$, what is his probability of winning the game?

Answer

$\frac{37}{64}$

12. Construct a question involving a billiards player. Write out clearly any assumptions you make concerning his probability of a successful shot. How closely to the real situation are your assumptions?

13. Find $P(0)$, $P(1)$ and $P(2)$ for the hypergeometric distribution $H(x;3,6,44)$.

Answer

0·68, 0·29, 0·03

14. A delivery of 50 items is accepted if an examination of 3 of them reveals no more than 1 defective. How 'safe' is this inspection if there are 6 defectives in the delivery?

Answer

Probability of wrong acceptance is 0·035.

15. Find the mean and variance of the hypergeometric distribution.

Answer

$$\bar{x} = \frac{ns}{s+f} \qquad s^2 = \frac{nsf(s+f-n)}{(s+f)^2(s+f-1)}$$

16. Given $\underset{\sim}{x}$ and $\underset{\sim}{y}$ are random variables denoting the rolling of an eight sided die, find experimentally the graph of the random variables (a) $\underset{\sim}{z} = \underset{\sim}{x} + \underset{\sim}{y}$ (b) $\underset{\sim}{w} = \underset{\sim}{x} - \underset{\sim}{y}$.

7 Moment Generating Functions

7.1 Introduction

It has been seen that the various lower moments of a distribution are of importance in characterising it. Since they are so important, and because statisticians when concerned with statistical theory wish to study not only the lower moments but the higher ones as well, there has been developed a method of generating *all* the moments of a distribution. The method is to use the so called *moment generating function* and we examine these in this chapter. For brevity we shall refer to them as m.g.f.'s. The use of a m.g.f. not only generates all the moments of a given distribution, it usually supplies a simpler method than the somewhat tedious ones met with so far.

Before defining the m.g.f. we extend the notation of the expectation of a related random variable as used in chapter 2.

If $\underset{\sim}{x}$ is a random variable and $g(\underset{\sim}{x})$ is any function of $\underset{\sim}{x}$, the expectation of $g(\underset{\sim}{x})$ is given by

(i) $E[g(\underset{\sim}{x})] = \sum_i g(x_i)P(x_i)$

(ii) $E[g(\underset{\sim}{x})] = \int_{-\infty}^{\infty} g(x)f(x)dx$

for the discrete and continuous cases. $g(x_i)$ is the value of $g(\underset{\sim}{x})$ at x_i and $P(x_i)$ is the probability that $\underset{\sim}{x}$ assumes the value x_i. A similar remark applies for the continuous case.

Example 1: $E[c.g(\underset{\sim}{x})] = \sum_i c.g(x_i)P(x_i) = c\sum_i g(x_i)P(x_i)$

$$= c.E[g(\underset{\sim}{x})]$$

Example 2: $E[g_1(\underset{\sim}{x}) + g_2(\underset{\sim}{x})] = \sum_i [g_1(x_i) + g_2(x_i)]P(x_i)$

$$= \sum_i g_1(x_i)P(x_i) + \sum_i g_2(x_i)P(x_i)$$

$$= E[g_1(x)] + E[g_2(x)]$$

Example 3: Prove

$$E\left[\sum_{k=1}^{n} g_k(x)\right] = \sum_{k=1}^{n} E[g_k(x)]$$

The proof of this follows the same lines as Example 2 and is left for the reader.

7.2 Definition of Moment Generating Functions

In what follows we will work variously in either discrete or continuous variables and it will be left to the reader to work for himself the corresponding part omitted.

Definition

If $\underset{\sim}{x}$ is a discrete random variable with probability function $P(x_i)$ the expectation of the related function $e^{t\underset{\sim}{x}}$ gives the moment generation function for the variable $\underset{\sim}{x}$,

$$M_{\underset{\sim}{x}}(t) = E(e^{t\underset{\sim}{x}}) = \sum_i e^{tx_i} P(x_i)$$

The m.g.f. of $\underset{\sim}{x}$ is a function of t, where t is a real number. For certain values of t the summation may diverge to ∞ and consequently for those values of t the m.g.f. does not exist. The notation $M_{\underset{\sim}{x}}(t)$ is used to show that it is the m.g.f. of the variable $\underset{\sim}{x}$, with t as an independent variable.

Recalling the expansion of e to any power, we get,

$$M_{\underset{\sim}{x}}(t) = \sum_i \left[1 + tx_i + \frac{t^2 x_i^2}{2!} + \frac{t^3 x_i^3}{3!} + \ldots + \frac{t^r x_i^r}{r!} \ldots\right] P(x_i)$$

$$= \sum_i P(x_i) + t\sum_i x_i P(x_i) + \frac{t^2}{2!}\sum_i x_i^2 P(x_i) + \ldots + \frac{t^r}{r!}\sum_i x_i^r P(x_i)$$

$$= 1 + m_1(0)t + m_2(0)\frac{t^2}{2!} + m_3(0)\frac{t^3}{3!} + \ldots + m_r(0)\frac{t^r}{r!}$$

The fact that the coefficient of $\frac{t^r}{r!}$ is $m_r(0)$ shows clearly why this is called the m.g.f.

Example 1: Find the m.g.f. of the random variable $\underset{\sim}{x}$, associated with the rolling of a die.

Answer

$$M_{\underset{\sim}{x}}(t) = E(e^{t\underset{\sim}{x}}) = \sum_{x=1}^{6} e^{tx}P(x)$$

$$= \frac{1}{6}e^{t} + \frac{1}{6}e^{2t} + \frac{1}{6}e^{3t} + \frac{1}{6}e^{4t} + \frac{1}{6}e^{5t} + \frac{1}{6}e^{6t}$$

$$= \frac{1}{6}\sum_{k=1}^{6} e^{kt}$$

Example 2: If $\underset{\sim}{x}$ is a binomial distribution, $B(x;1,p)$, find the m.g.f. of $\underset{\sim}{x}$.

Answer

$$M_{\underset{\sim}{x}}(t) = E(e^{t\underset{\sim}{x}}) = \sum_{x=0}^{1} e^{tx}P(x) = \sum_{x=0}^{1} e^{tx}(1Cx)q^{1-x}p^{x}$$

$$= \sum_{x=0}^{1} (1Cx)q^{1-x}(e^{t}p)^{x}$$

$$= q + pe^{t}$$

Example 3: Plot the graphs of the m.g.f. of (a) $B(x;1,\frac{1}{10})$ and (b) $B(x;1,\frac{1}{2})$ on the same graph and compare.

Answer

(a) $B(x;1,\frac{1}{10})$; using the m.g.f. found above, we get,

$t = 0 \quad M_{\underset{\sim}{x}}(0) = (q + pe^{0}) = (q + p) = (\frac{9}{10} + \frac{1}{10}) = 1$

$t = 1 \quad M_{\underset{\sim}{x}}(1) = (q + pe^{1}) = (\frac{9}{10} + \frac{e}{10}) = 1{\cdot}1718$

$t = 2 \quad M_{\underset{\sim}{x}}(2) = (q + pe^{2}) = (\frac{9}{10} + \frac{e^2}{10}) = 8{\cdot}323$

(b) $B(x;1,\frac{1}{2})$; using the m.g.f. found above, we get,

$t = 0 \quad M_{\underset{\sim}{x}}(0) = (\frac{1}{2} + \frac{1}{2}) = 1$

$t = 1 \quad M_{\underset{\sim}{x}}(1) = (\frac{1}{2} + \frac{e}{2}) = 1{\cdot}859$

$t = 2 \quad M_{\underset{\sim}{x}}(2) = (\frac{1}{2} + \frac{e^2}{2}) = 4{\cdot}212$

Graphing these results gives:

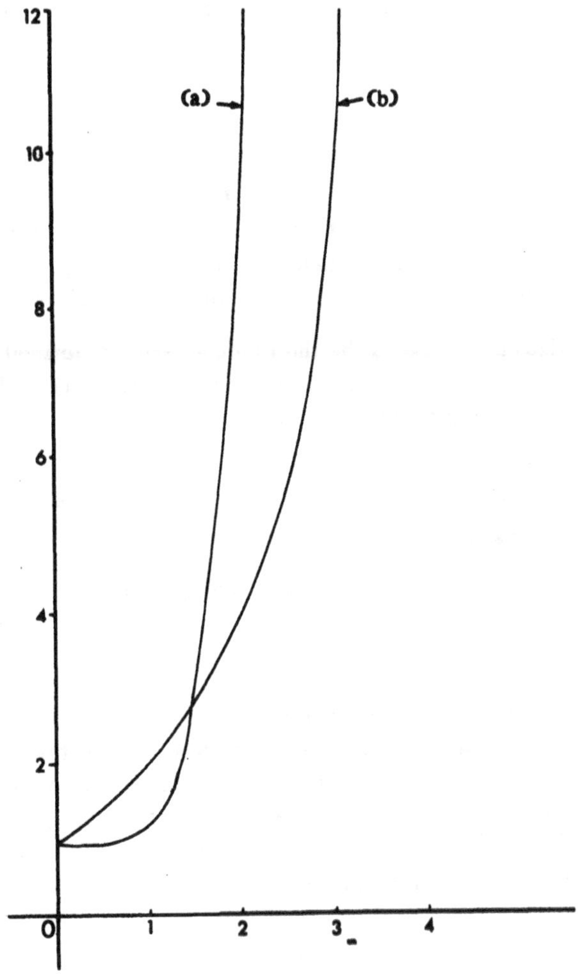

Fig. 7.2(a)

Example 4: For $\underset{\sim}{x}$ binomially distributed, $B(x;n,p)$, $M_{\underset{\sim}{x}}(t) = (q + pe^t)^n$. The proof of this follows just the same lines as the proof in Example 2 and is left for the reader.

7.3 Some Theorems on Moment Generating Functions

Since a m.g.f. is defined in terms of expectation it is to be expected that the theorems concerned with expectation will be applicable to a m.g.f. Let us assume that we are given the m.g.f. of a random variable $\underset{\sim}{x}$, $M_{\underset{\sim}{x}}(t)$, and consider the m.g.f. of the related random variable $\underset{\sim}{x} + b$.

$$
\begin{aligned}
M_{\underset{\sim}{x}+b}(t) &= E(e^{(\underset{\sim}{x}+b)t}) = \sum_i e^{(x_i+b)t} P(x_i) \\
&= \sum_i e^{x_i} e^{bt} P(x_i) = e^{bt} \sum_i e^{x_i} P(x_i) \\
&= e^{bt} M_{\underset{\sim}{x}}(t)
\end{aligned}
$$

This shows that if we know the moment generating function of a random variable $\underset{\sim}{x}$, then we can find the m.g.f. of a random variable related in the form $\underset{\sim}{x} + b$. We simply multiply $M_{\underset{\sim}{x}}(t)$ by e^{bt}.

Example 1: Let $\underset{\sim}{x}$ be the random variable defined by the rolling of a die. Find the m.g.f. of a random variable defined by 'rolling a die and adding 4 to the result'.

Answer

$M_{\underset{\sim}{x}}(t) = \frac{1}{6} \sum_{k=1}^{6} e^{kt}$; from Section 7.2. We require the m.g.f. of the random variable $\underset{\sim}{x} + 4$

$$
\begin{aligned}
M_{\underset{\sim}{x}+4}(t) &= e^{4t} M_{\underset{\sim}{x}}(t) = e^{4t} \frac{1}{6} \sum_{k=1}^{6} e^{kt} \\
&= \frac{1}{6} \sum_{k=1}^{6} e^{(4+k)t}
\end{aligned}
$$

and this is the required m.g.f.

This latter result now enables us to find the moments of a random variable about any point. If we wish to find the moments of a random variable, $\underset{\sim}{x}$, about the mean μ, we find the m.g.f. of the related random variable $\underset{\sim}{x} - \mu$ and this will give us a function producing $m_r(\mu)$ as the following working shows.

$$
\begin{aligned}
M_{\underset{\sim}{x}-\mu}(t) &= \sum_i \left[1 + t(x_i - \mu) + \frac{t^2(x_i - \mu)^2}{2!} + \ldots \right] P(x_i) \\
&= \sum_i P(x_i) + t \sum_i (x_i - \mu) P(x_i) + \frac{t^2}{2!} \sum_i (x_i - \mu)^2 P(x_i) + \ldots \\
&= 1 + m_1(\mu)t + m_2(\mu)\frac{t^2}{2!}
\end{aligned}
$$

and here the coefficient of $\frac{t^r}{r!}$ is the rth moment of x about the mean μ, $m_r(\mu)$.

Let us now consider the m.g.f. of a related random variable, $a\underset{\sim}{x}$.

$$M_{a\underset{\sim}{x}}(t) = E(e^{at\underset{\sim}{x}}) = \int_{-\infty}^{\infty} e^{atx} f(x)dx$$

$$= \int_{-\infty}^{\infty} e^{(at)x} f(x)dx = M_{\underset{\sim}{x}}(at)$$

which shows that the m.g.f. of the related random variable, $a\underset{\sim}{x}$, is found from the m.g.f. of $\underset{\sim}{x}$ by simply multiplying t by a.

If we now combine these two last results we can prove that

$$M_{a\underset{\sim}{x}+b}(t) = e^{bt} M_{\underset{\sim}{x}}(at)$$

and the reader should formulate in words the meaning of this equality, as well as working through the proof which follows the lines as shown above.

Example 2: If the m.g.f. of the random variable $\underset{\sim}{x}$ is K^{t^2-1}, find the m.g.f. of the variable $2\underset{\sim}{x} - 5$.

Answer

$$M_{2\underset{\sim}{x}-5}(t) = e^{-5t} M_{\underset{\sim}{x}}(2t) = e^{-5t} K^{4t^2-1}$$

7.4 Moment Generating Functions of Particular Distributions

We have seen the m.g.f. of the binomial distribution in Example 4 of Section 7.2 and now we look at the m.g.f. of some other distributions.

(1) *Poisson Distribution*

If $\underset{\sim}{x}$ has a Poisson distribution, $P(x;a)$ then,

$$M_{\underset{\sim}{x}}(t) = E(e^{t\underset{\sim}{x}}) = \sum_{x=0}^{\infty} e^{tx} P(x) = \sum_{x=0}^{\infty} e^{tx} \frac{e^{-a} a^x}{x!}$$

$$= e^{-a} \sum_{x=0}^{\infty} \frac{(ae^t)^x}{x!}$$

and this last summation is the expansion of $e^{(ae^t)}$, so

$$M_{\underset{\sim}{x}}(t) = e^{-a} e^{ae^t} = e^{a(e^t-1)}$$

(2) *Normal Distribution*

If $\underset{\sim}{x}$ is distributed normally, $N(\mu,\sigma^2)$

$$M_{\underset{\sim}{x}}(t) = E(e^{t\underset{\sim}{x}}) = \int_{-\infty}^{\infty} e^{tx} . \frac{1}{\sigma\sqrt{2\pi}} e^{-\frac{(x-\mu)^2}{2\sigma^2}} dx$$

$$= \frac{1}{\sigma\sqrt{2\pi}} \int_{-\infty}^{\infty} e^{tx - \frac{(x-\mu)^2}{2\sigma^2}} dx$$

Consider the exponent,

$$tx - \frac{(x-\mu)^2}{2\sigma^2} = \frac{2tx\sigma^2 - (x-\mu)^2}{2\sigma^2}$$

$$= -\left[\frac{(x-\mu)^2 - 2tx\sigma^2}{2\sigma^2}\right]$$

Now by completing the square

$$= -\left[\frac{\{x-(\mu+t\sigma^2)\}^2 - 2\mu t\sigma^2 - t^2\sigma^4}{2\sigma^2}\right]$$

$$= -\left[\frac{\{x-(\mu+t\sigma^2)\}^2}{2\sigma^2} - \mu t - \frac{t^2\sigma^2}{2}\right]$$

$$= -\left[\frac{\{x-(\mu+t\sigma^2)\}^2}{2\sigma^2}\right] + \mu t + \frac{t^2\sigma^2}{2}$$

We can now write

$$M_x(t) = \frac{1}{\sigma\sqrt{2\pi}}\int_{-\infty}^{\infty} e^{-\left[\frac{x-(\mu+t\sigma^2)^2}{2\sigma^2} + \mu t + \frac{t^2\sigma^2}{2}\right]}dx$$

$$= \frac{e^{\mu t + \frac{t^2\sigma^2}{2}}}{\sigma\sqrt{2\pi}}\int_{-\infty}^{\infty} e^{-\frac{(x-(\mu+t\sigma^2)^2}{2\sigma^2}}dx$$

The exponent of e in the integrand is now that of a normal distribution with mean $\mu + t\sigma^2$ and variance σ^2. This integral, together with $\frac{1}{\sigma\sqrt{2\pi}}$ outside, will represent the area under this latter normal distribution and will reduce to 1.

Thus we get

$$M_x(t) = e^{\mu t + \frac{t^2\sigma^2}{2}}$$

If x is distributed normally $N(0,1)$, then the m.g.f. will be $e^{\frac{t^2}{2}}$

(3) *Rectangular Distribution*

If x is a continuous rectangular distribution as given in Section 6.3, then

$$M_{\underset{\sim}{x}}(t) = E(e^{t\underset{\sim}{x}}) = \int_{-\infty}^{\infty} \frac{e^{tx}}{b-a} dx = \frac{1}{(b-a)}\left[\frac{1}{t}e^{tx}\right]_a^b$$

$$= \frac{1}{(b-a)}\left[\frac{1}{t}(e^{bt} - e^{at})\right] = \frac{1}{t(b-a)}(e^{bt} - e^{at})$$

(4) *Geometric Distribution*

If $\underset{\sim}{x}$ is a geometric distribution, then,

$$M_{\underset{\sim}{x}}(t) = E(e^{t\underset{\sim}{x}}) = \sum_{x=1}^{\infty} e^{tx} pq^{x-1}$$

$$= \frac{p}{q}\sum_{x=1}^{\infty} (e^t q)^x$$

$$= \frac{p}{q}\left[e^t q + e^{2t} q^2 + e^{3t} q^3 \quad + \ldots\right]$$

$$= \frac{p}{q}\left[-1 + 1 + e^t q + e^{2t} q^2 + e^{3t} q^3 \quad + \ldots\right]$$

just bringing in $-1 + 1$.

Now it can be shown by the usual binomial laws that

$$(1 - x)^{-1} = 1 + x + x^2 + x^3 + x^4 + \ldots + x^n + \ldots$$

so if we regard x as being $e^t q$ then we can say

$$(1 - e^t q)^{-1} = 1 + e^t q + e^{2t} q^2 + e^{3t} q^3 + \ldots + e^{nt} q^n + \ldots$$

and we can now say that

$$M_{\underset{\sim}{x}}(t) = \frac{p}{q}\left[-1 + (1 - e^t q)^{-1}\right]$$

Now k^{-1} is another way of writing $\frac{1}{k}$ so we get

$$M_{\underset{\sim}{x}}(t) = \frac{p}{q}\left[-1 + \frac{1}{(1 - e^t q)}\right]$$

$$= \frac{p}{q}\left[\frac{-1(1 - e^t q) + 1}{(1 - e^t q)}\right] \quad \text{by the usual fraction laws}$$

$$= \frac{p}{q}\left[\frac{e^t q}{(1 - e^t q)}\right]$$

$$= \frac{e^t p}{(1 - e^t q)}$$

7.5 Differentiation of $M_{x}(t)$

Since the m.g.f. of any random variable x is a continuous function of t it may be differentiated with respect to t.
Differentiating

$$M_{x}(t) = 1 + m_1(0)t + m_2(0)\frac{t^2}{2!} + \ldots + m_r(0)\frac{t^r}{r!} + \ldots$$

we get

$$\frac{d}{dt}[M_{x}(t)] = m_1(0) + m_2(0)t + \ldots + m_r(0)\frac{t^{r-1}}{(r-1)!} + \ldots$$

and we can see that $m_1(0)$ is the only term on the right hand side independent of t, so if we put $t = 0$ we get

$$\frac{d}{dt}[M_{x}(0)] = m_1(0)$$

and we know $m_1(0)$ is the mean of x.

This result tells us that if we take the m.g.f. of a random variable x, differentiate it and put $t = 0$ in the resulting expression we will get the mean of x.

Example 1: If x is distributed binomially, $B(x;n,p)$ find the mean.

Answer

We know $M_{x}(t) = (q + pe^t)^n$, so differentiating,

$$\frac{d}{dt}[M_{x}(t)] = n(q + pe^t)^{n-1}pe^t$$

applying the usual rules for differentiating a function of a function.
Putting $t = 0$.

$$\frac{d}{dt}[M_{x}(0)] = n(q + p)^{n-1}p = np,$$

as expected.

If we now differentiate $M_{x}(t)$ a second time, we get

$$\frac{d^2}{dt^2}[M_{x}(t)] = m_2(0) + m_3(0)t + m_4(0)\frac{t^2}{2!} + \ldots + m_r(0)\frac{t^{r-2}}{(r-2)!} + \ldots$$

and this time the only term on the right hand side independent of t is $m_2(0)$. Again putting $t = 0$ we get

$$\frac{d^2}{dt^2}[M_{x}(0)] = m_2(0)$$

This result tells us that if we take the m.g.f. of a random variable

$\underset{\sim}{x}$; differentiate it twice and put $t = 0$ in the resulting expression we will get $m_2(0)$. that is the second moment of $\underset{\sim}{x}$ about zero.

Example 2: A random variable is defined by the rolling of a dice. Find $m_2(0)$.

Answer

We have $M_{\underset{\sim}{x}}(t) = \frac{1}{6}\sum_{k=1}^{6} e^{kt}$

$$\frac{d}{dt}[M_{\underset{\sim}{x}}(t)] = \frac{1}{6}\sum_{k=1}^{6} ke^{kt}$$

$$\frac{d^2}{dt^2}[M_{\underset{\sim}{x}}(t)] = \frac{1}{6}\sum_{k=1}^{6} k^2e^{kt}$$ Now putting $t = 0$,

$$\frac{d^2}{dt^2}[M_{\underset{\sim}{x}}(0)] = \frac{1}{6}\sum_{k=1}^{6} k^2$$

$$= \frac{1}{6}\{1 + 4 + 9 + 16 + 25 + 36\}$$

$$= \frac{91}{6} = 15\tfrac{1}{6}$$

Therefore, $m_2(0) = 15\frac{1}{6}$.

The arguments of the preceeding work now enable us to state the following result

$$\frac{d^r}{dt^r}[M_{\underset{\sim}{x}}(t)]_{t=0} = m_r(0),$$

which reads 'the rth differential of $M_{\underset{\sim}{x}}(t)$ at $t = 0$ gives the rth moment about 0'.

The above method enables us to find the moments of any order about the point zero. We now look at the way to find moments of any order about *any* point.

We can find the moments of a distribution about any point by using a method which the previous work suggests. We take the m.g.f. of the necessary related variable, differentiate the required number of times, and then put $t = 0$ in the result. We know for instance that the moments about the mean are frequently required so let us look at moments about this point.

If $\underset{\sim}{x}$ is the random variable, we take the related random variable $\underset{\sim}{x} - \mu$, where μ is the mean of $\underset{\sim}{x}$, and form $M_{\underset{\sim}{x}-\mu}(t)$. We know from Section 7.3 that

$$M_{\underset{\sim}{x}-\mu}(t) = 1 + m_1(\mu)t + m_2(\mu)\frac{t^2}{2!} + m_3(\mu)\frac{t^3}{3!} + \ldots$$

Differentiating we get,

$$\frac{d}{dt}[M_{x-\mu}(t)] = m_1(\mu) + m_2(\mu)t + m_3(\mu)\frac{t^2}{}$$

Now put $t = 0$, and

$$\frac{d}{dt}[M_{x-\mu}(0)] = m_1(\mu).$$

Arguing along the lines indicated we can arrive at the general result

$$\frac{d^r}{dt^r}[M_{x-\mu}(t)]_{t=0} = m_r(\mu).$$

Example 3: Show that

$$\frac{d}{dt}[M_{x-\mu}(t)]_{t=0} = 0$$

for any random variable x with mean μ.

Answer

Let the m.g.f. of x be $M_x(t)$.
Then $M_{x-\mu}(t) = e^{-\mu t}M_x(t)$ by the theorem in Section 7.3.

$$\frac{d}{dt}[M_{x-\mu}(t)] = -\mu e^{-\mu t}M_x(t) + e^{-\mu t}\frac{d}{dt}[M_x(t)]$$

using the usual for differentiation of a function of a function. Now put $t = 0$, and

$$\frac{d}{dt}[M_{x-\mu}(0)] = -\mu M_x(0) + \frac{d}{dt}[M_x(0)]$$

Now we know that for all m.g.f.'s $M_x(0) = 1$, and

$$\frac{d}{dt}[M_x(0)] = \mu,$$

so the right hand side of the above becomes $-\mu + \mu = 0$, as required.

Example 4: Find $m_2(\mu)$ for a random variable x distributed normally $N(0,1)$.

Answer

We know the m.g.f. of this distribution is

$$M_x(t) = e^{\frac{t^2}{2}}$$

Differentiating we get

$$\frac{d}{dt}[M_x(t)] = te^{\frac{t^2}{2}}$$

and

$$\frac{d^2}{dt^2}[M_x(t)] = e^{\frac{t^2}{2}} + t^2e^{\frac{t^2}{2}}$$

Putting $t = 0$ in this last expression makes the right hand side $1 + 0 = 1$, as expected.

7.6 Moment Generating Functions of Standardised Variables

The theorem $M_{ax+b}(t) = e^{bt}M_x(at)$ is used most when $a = \frac{1}{\sigma}$ and $b = -\frac{\mu}{\sigma}$. This gives

$$M_{\frac{x-\mu}{\sigma}}(t) = e^{-\frac{\mu}{\sigma}t}M_x\left(\frac{t}{\sigma}\right)$$

and enables us to find the m.g.f. of a random variable when it has been standardised.

If x is distributed normally, $N(\mu,\sigma^2)$, then we have

$$M_x(t) = e^{\mu t + \frac{t^2\sigma^2}{2}}$$

The m.g.f. of the standardised random variable $\frac{x-\mu}{\sigma}$ is

$$M_{\frac{x-\mu}{\sigma}}(t) = e^{-\frac{\mu}{\sigma}t}M_x\frac{t}{\sigma} = e^{-\frac{\mu}{\sigma}t}e^{\frac{\mu t}{\sigma}+\frac{t^2\sigma^2}{\sigma^2 2}}$$

$$= e^{-\frac{\mu}{\sigma}t+\frac{\mu}{\sigma}t+\frac{t^2}{2}} = e^{\frac{t^2}{2}}$$

It was promised in Sections 5.7 and 5.8 to give a mathematical justification for approximating with a normal distribution the binomial and Poisson distributions. We now come to that justification.

First we must consider the question of the uniqueness of moment generating functions. Is it possible for two random variables to have the same m.g.f.? It is possible to prove – although the proof is beyond the scope of this book – that the m.g.f. of a given random variable is in fact unique, that is there is a one-one correspondence between the set of random variables and the set of their moment generating functions. This uniqueness will be required in the justification in hand,

We work the case of the normal approximation to the Poisson distribution in detail.

If x is a poisson distribution with mean and variance a, $P(x;a)$, then we know

$$M_x(t) = e^{a(e^t - 1)}$$

Consider now the m.g.f. of the standardised random variable,

$$\frac{x - a}{\sqrt{a}}$$

which is the standardised poisson distribution,

$$M_{\frac{x-a}{\sqrt{a}}}(t) = e^{-\frac{a}{\sqrt{a}}t} M_x\left(\frac{t}{\sqrt{a}}\right) = e^{-\sqrt{a}t} e^{a(e^{\frac{t}{\sqrt{a}}}-1)}$$

$$= e^{-\sqrt{a}t + ae^{\frac{t}{\sqrt{a}}} - a} \quad = e^{a(e^{\frac{t}{\sqrt{a}}}-1-\frac{t}{\sqrt{a}})}$$

Consider now the exponent

$$a(e^{\frac{t}{\sqrt{a}}} - 1 - \frac{t}{\sqrt{a}}), \quad \text{and expand} \quad e^{\frac{t}{\sqrt{a}}}.$$

This gives

$$a\left\{1 + \frac{t}{\sqrt{a}} + \left(\frac{t}{\sqrt{a}}\right)^2 \frac{1}{2!} + \left(\frac{t}{\sqrt{a}}\right)^3 \frac{1}{3!} + \left(\frac{t}{\sqrt{a}}\right)^4 \frac{1}{4!} + \dots - \frac{t}{\sqrt{a}}\right\}$$

$$= a\left\{\left(\frac{t}{\sqrt{a}}\right)^2 \frac{1}{2!} + \left(\frac{t}{\sqrt{a}}\right)^3 \frac{1}{3!} + \left(\frac{t}{\sqrt{a}}\right)^4 \frac{1}{4!} + \dots\right\}$$

We know that the normal approximation holds when a is large. We therefore chose a large enough, and t small enough to make $\frac{t}{\sqrt{a}}$ sufficiently small that third and higher powers of $\frac{t}{\sqrt{a}}$ may be neglected. This now makes the exponent $\frac{t^2}{2}$, and we can write

$$M_{\frac{x-a}{\sqrt{a}}}(t) = e^{\frac{t^2}{2}}$$

and we recognise this as the m.g.f. of a standard normal random variable.

Thus under the condition that a is sufficiently large the m.g.f. of the standardised Poisson distribution approaches the m.g.f. of a standard normal distribution.

By the uniqueness theorem quoted above we can affirm that the standardised Poisson distribution approaches that of a standard normal distribution. We now work back from this standard normal distribution to the Poisson distribution $P(x;a)$ and to the Normal distribution $N(a,a)$. Since the standardised distribution of $P(x;a)$ approaches the standardised distribution of $N(a,a)$, then $P(x;a)$ must approach $N(a,a)$, and then $N(a,a)$ can be used to approximate to $P(x;a)$.

It is, of course, possible to deduce this result directly without using m.g.f. but this use of the m.g.f. will give the reader a glimpse of some of the reasoning used in more advanced statistical theory. It is also possible by the use of m.g.f. and appeal to the uniqueness theorem to justify the Poisson approximation and the normal approximation to the binomial and the reader should try working through the proof. In each case the conditions under which the approximation will be valid will be needed in the course of the proofs, just as the condition that a must be large was used above to show the normal approximation to the Poisson distribution.

7.7 Characteristic Functions

A disadvantage of the m.g.f. is that for some values of t it diverges and hence does not exist for these values of t. If however we introduce $i = \sqrt{-1}$, and a little complex number theory, we can produce a m.g.f. which converges for all values of t. This m.g.f. is called the *characteristic function* of the random variable $\underset{\sim}{x}$, and is defined as

(i) $C_{\underset{\sim}{x}}(t) = E(e^{it\underset{\sim}{x}}) = \sum_i e^{itx_i}P(x_i)$

and (ii) $C_{\underset{\sim}{x}}(t) = E(e^{it\underset{\sim}{x}}) = \int_{-\infty}^{\infty} e^{itx}f(x)dx$

for the discrete and continuous cases.

To show that $C_{\underset{\sim}{x}}(t)$ always exists we use the fact that

$$e^{itx} = \text{Cos}\,(tx) + \sin(tx)$$

and so the modulus of e^{itx}, that is $|e^{itx}| = \{\cos^2(tx) + \sin^2(tx)\}^{\frac{1}{2}} = 1$

$$(\cos^2\theta + \sin^2\theta = 1, \text{ for all } \theta)$$

This allows us to look at the modulus of $C_{\underset{\sim}{x}}(t)$

$$\begin{aligned}|C_{x}(t)| &= |\sum_i e^{itx_i} P(x_i)| \leqslant \sum_i |e^{itx_i} P(x_i)| \\ &= \sum_i |e^{itx_i}|\ |P(x_i)| = \sum_i |P(x_i)| \\ &= \sum_i P(x_i) \quad \text{since all } P(x_i) \geqslant 0 \\ &= 1\end{aligned}$$

Therefore $C_x(t) \leqslant 1$ and so does not diverge for any value of t.

All the ideas and theorems of the m.g.f., $M_x(t)$, can be extended to the characteristic function $C_x(t)$ by the introduction of it for t and making the necessary algebraic alterations. The introduction of i makes the characteristic function of much more powerful weapon in statistical theory than the m.g.f. but it also introduces much more sophisticated ideas of more advanced mathematics. The reader hungry for more details is referred to more advanced texts in statistical theory.

Exercise 7

1. Given x is the random variable denoting the rolling of a die, find the expectation of the following related random variables:

(a) $g_1(x) = x^3$ (b) $g_2(x) = x^2 + 3$ (c) $g_3(x) = 5x$ (d) $g_4(x) = 7x^2 + 2x$

Answer

(a) 73·5 (c) 17·5 (d) 113·166

2. Prove (a) $E[ag_1(x) + bg_2(x)] = aE[g_1(x)] + bE[g_2(x)]$

(b) $E[\sum_i a_i g_i(x)] = \sum_i a_i E[g_i(x)]$

3. Define the m.g.f. for a continuous random variable. Expand your result as in Section 7.2 and compare.

4. Prove that the m.g.f. for $B(x,n,p)$ is $(q + pe^t)^n$.

5. Given x is the random variable denoting the rolling of a tetrahedron, find its m.g.f.. Find also the m.g.f.'s of the following related random variables:

(a) $g_1(x) = x + 5{\cdot}3$ (b) $g_2(x) = x - 2{\cdot}5$ (c) $g_3(x) = 4x$ (d) $g_4(x) = 5x - 2{\cdot}5$

Answer

$\frac{1}{4}\sum_{k=1}^{4} e^{kt}$ (b) $\frac{1}{4}\sum_{k=1}^{4} e^{t(k-2\cdot5)}$ (d) $\frac{1}{4}\sum_{k=1}^{4} e^{t(5k-2\cdot5)}$

6. Expand the m.g.f. of the random variable throwing a die in the form of a series where $m_r(0)$ is the coefficient of $\frac{t^r}{r}$.

Answer

$\frac{1}{6}(1 + 21t + 91\frac{t^2}{2} + 441\frac{t^3}{2} + \ldots)$

7. Prove that

$$M_{a\underset{\sim}{x}+b}(t) = e^{bt}M_{\underset{\sim}{x}}(at)$$

8. Find the value of the m.g.f. of $B(x;5,\frac{1}{2})$ at (a) $t = 0$ (b) $t = 1$ (c) $t = 2$

Answer

(a) 1 (c) 1300

9. Graph the following m.g.f.'s: (a) $P(x;\frac{1}{2})$ (b) $P(x;1)$ (c) $P(x;2)$ (d) $P(x;3)$ (e) $N(0,1)$ (f) $N(1,1)$ (g) $N(2,1)$ (g) $N(0,2)$. Comment on your results.

10. Given $\underset{\sim}{x}$ a continuous rectangular distribution over the interval 0,1, show that

$$M_{\underset{\sim}{x}}(t) = \frac{e^t - 1}{t}$$

11. Use moment generating functions to show that the sum or difference of 2 uniform distributions is a triangular distribution.

12. Given the triangular distribution

$$f(x) = \begin{cases} x & 0 \leqslant x \leqslant 1 \\ 2 - x & 1 \leqslant x \leqslant 2 \end{cases}$$

show that the moment generating function is

$$\frac{(e^t - 1)^2}{t^2}$$

13. Find the mean and variance of the geometric distribution (a) by expanding its m.g.f. and (b) by differentiation.

Answer

$\frac{1}{p}, \frac{q}{p^2}$

14. State in words the meaning of the following statement, and then prove the result:

Given $\underset{\sim}{x}$ and $\underset{\sim}{y}$ are independent random variables then $M_{\underset{\sim}{x}+\underset{\sim}{y}}(t) = M_{\underset{\sim}{x}}(t)M_{\underset{\sim}{y}}(t)$.

15. Find the first four moments about 0 of the standard normal distribution by differentiating its m.g.f.

Answer

0, 1, 0, 3.

16. Repeat number 15 for the Poisson, binomial and rectangular distributions.

17. Use m.g.f.'s to justify the normal approximation to the binomial distribution.

18. Prove that the characteristic function of a continuous random variable always exists.

19. Prove the following:

(a) If $\underset{\sim}{x}$ is distributed normally, $N(0,1)$ then $C_{\underset{\sim}{x}}(t) = e^{-\frac{t^2}{2}}$.

(b) If $\underset{\sim}{x}$ has characteristic function $C_{\underset{\sim}{x}}(t)$, then

$$C_{a\underset{\sim}{x}+b}(t) = e^{ibt}\, C_{\underset{\sim}{x}}(at).$$

(c) If $\underset{\sim}{x}$ is a binomial distribution $B(x;n,p)$ then

$$C_{\underset{\sim}{x}}(t) = (q + pe^{it})^n$$

(d) If $\underset{\sim}{x}_i$ are independent random variables then

$$C_{\Sigma \underset{\sim}{x}_i}(t) = \pi C_{\underset{\sim}{x}_i}(t)$$

20. Find the first three moments about the mean of a binomial distribution by differentiating (a) the m.g.f. and (b) the characteristic function.

8 Large Sampling Theory

8.1 Introduction

A statistician is rarely able to examine every member of a population and his investigation of this population must be carried out be means of samples. Samples are taken from the population and the information they provide is used to make assessments or predictions about the population. It will be realised that because of it's frequent use and because of the necessity to obtain accurate information about a population, sampling is one of the most important concepts in statistics. In this and the following chapters we study the basic ideas of sampling theory. Before we begin however, it will be useful to gather together some of the ideas used in previous chapters. This will keep them in mind and provide a useful section for reference. At the same time as collecting these ideas together other related ideas will be introduced.

The word 'population' is used by statisticians in a very general sense. It covers not only populations consisting of people but populations consisting of objects of any kind - 'books in a library', 'ants in a colony', and 'seeds in a seed box', are all considered by the statistician to be populations. Any characteristic of the individuals of the population may be investigated. If the characteristic is one that is usually recorded numerically, then the *random variable* associated with the characteristic will be clearly defined, for example 'the number of pages in each book in a library', 'the weight of boys in a school', and so on. If the characteristic is a non-numerical one, for example colour or opinion, then it can be coded to a numerical form. Individual measurements of the variable are called *variates.*

When selecting members of a population there is no need to record only one measurement for each member. We can, if we wish, measure more than one characteristic, for example we may be interested in both the age and the weight of a member of a population. This can be recorded as an ordered pair, (x, y) and variables of this sort are called *bi-variate,* as opposed to the univariate ones that we have met so far in earlier chapters. The idea can be extended to *tri-variate* and eventually to *multi-variate* variables. It is also common to use the phrase 'bivariate population' when investigating two different aspects of members of a population. Multi-variate variables give rise to the study of regression and correlation.

Little has been said to far about samples other than they are subsets of a population, but for a sample to be of any use to a statistician it must be representative of a population. For it to be representative of a population it must have the same characteristics as the population. If, for example, a population is split in some way, say 25% X's and 75% Y's, then a sample must be similarly constituted. It has been found by experience that the best way to get a good sample is to make a random selection from the population. A *random sample* or a *random selection* is a sample in which any individual member of the population is as likely to be included as any other. If there are some members of a population which are more likely to be included than any other in a sample then this sample is called a *biased sample.*

Having said that a random sample is the most desirable sample it is another thing to produce a method whereby a random sample will be selected. The literature of statistics contains many examples of sampling methods which were conceived as methods of getting unbiased samples but which in practice turned out very biased samples. One such example is that of sampling by letter. Letters are sent out to a random selection of houses and a reply asked for. In practice a very low proportion of people bother to return the questionnaire forms, and those that do frequently have an axe to grind, and the sample loses it's randomness. This goes to show that techniques which we know today are safe to use have been built up over a period of time, and techniques which have failed have been discarded. 'Trial and error' or 'trial and success' are well written into the history of statistics.

Many techniques for producing random samples are now used but none of them will be expounded here. We are content to point out this feature of statistics, assume that all the samples we deal with from now on are random, and develop the ideas associated with these random samples.

We saw in the earlier chapters that such numbers as the mean and standard deviation are calculated for samples, and such numbers are called *sample parameters.* Corresponding to these sample parameters are *population parameters* which are again numbers such as the mean of the population, the standard deviation of the population, and so on. Generally Greek letters are used to denote population parameters, μ, σ, $\mu_2(\mu)$ etc., and roman letters are used to denote the corresponding sample parameters, $\bar{x}$, s, $m_2(\bar{x})$ etc.

It is from the sample parameters that the population parameters are estimated. In making estimations about the population from samples it can never be *known* that the estimation is absolutely correct and so these estimations are couched in terms of probability. They will be accurate within a given range for a stated degree of certainty, for example it will be 95% certain that μ will lie between a and b.

The relationship that a sample bears to a population, the inferences made about the population from the sample, indications of accuracy in terms of probability all go to make up the general study of *statistical inference*. Statistics concerned solely with the details of the samples without reference to the population from which they are taken is called *descriptive statistics*.

If a population consists of 100 members a random sample of 50 will be sure to give all the information that could be desired; but the same information could be obtained by using a much smaller sample. Sampling theory therefore also deals with *minimum* sized samples for *maximum* information.

Populations can be either *finite* or *infinite*.

Sampling is *with replacement* if each member of the population may be included *more than once* in *one* sample.

Sampling is *without replacement* if each member of the population may be included *only once* in *one* sample. An example will make clear this distinction. Suppose a population consists of the numbers 1. 2, 3, and 4, and samples of size three are taken. Possible samples for sampling with replacement are

$$\begin{array}{llll} (1, 1, 1), & (1, 1, 2), & (1, 2, 1), & (2, 1, 1). \\ (2, 2, 2), & (2, 2, 1), & (2, 1, 2), & (1, 2, 2), \\ (3, 3, 3), & \text{and so on} & & \end{array}$$

where the order in the triple indicates the order of the draw from the population. Possible samples for sampling without replacement are

$$(1, 2, 3) \quad (1, 2, 4) \quad (2, 3, 4) \quad (1, 3, 4)$$

and only these samples are possible. Since the items are taken out of the population at the same time (1, 2, 3) is considered the same as (1, 3, 2) or (3, 2, 1) and so on and no order is associated with the triple.

We thus have finite and infinite populations, and sampling with and without replacement. If the population is infinite it does not matter whether the sample is with or without replacement. For practical purposes a very large finite population may be considered as an infinite population. If samples are taken from a finite population with replacement, then obviously the process of taking samples can go on for an infinite length of time and ininitely many samples – not all different – may be selected; sampling under these circumstances may be considered as sampling from an infinite population.

finite population	with replacement	Equivalent to sampling from an infinite population
	without replacement	
infinite population	with replacement	Equivalent
	without replacement	

We thus have now two main divisions:

Sampling from an infinite population and sampling from a finite population with replacement

and

Sampling from a finite population without replacement.

8.2 Sampling Distributions of Statistics.

Consider a population with mean μ and variance σ^2. If we take a sample, of size n, from this population we can compute the mean $\bar{x}$. We can then take another sample, of size n, and again compute the mean $\bar{x}$. We can continue in this fashion until we have a set of numbers $K = \{\bar{x}_1, \bar{x}_2, \bar{x}_3, \ldots \bar{x}_k\}$, where $\bar{x}_i$ is the mean of the i'th sample. The numbers in K are not necessarily in the original sample space – for instance the original sample space may have been whole numbers and $\bar{x}_i$ may be a decimal for all i – but together they will form a distribution.

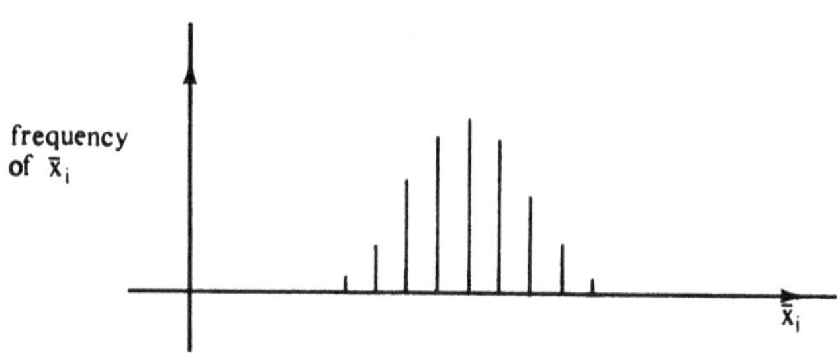

Fig. 8.2(a)

Since the $\bar{x}_i$ are numbers derived from samples and since they form a distribution this distribution is called the *sampling distribution of the mean.*

As a distribution in their own right this set of numbers will have a mean, a variance and a standard deviation, and all the other measures of characterisation that any distribution has.

From this same set of samples – or from others if wished – other statistics may be calculated. We can for example, form the set of standard deviations, $L = \{s_1, s_2, \ldots, s_l\}$ where s_i is the standard deviation of the i'th sample. Again a distribution will be formed

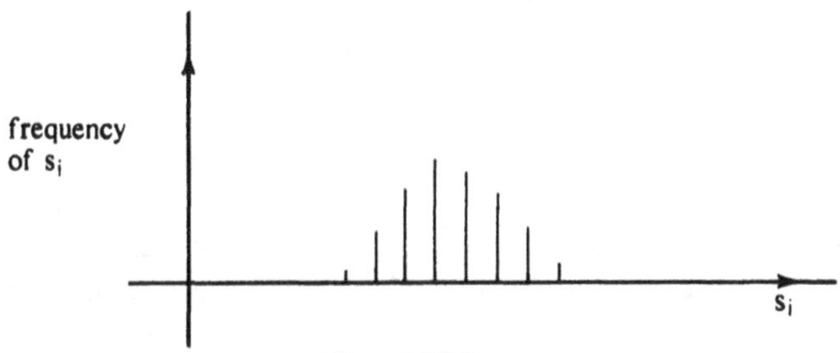

Fig. 8.2(b)

and by a similar argument this will be called the *sampling distribution of standard deviations.*

Similarly we can form the

$$\text{sampling distribution of the} \left\{ \begin{array}{l} \text{variances} \\ \text{medians} \\ \text{modes} \\ \text{etc.} \end{array} \right.$$

If T is any statistic taken from a sample and if the set $M = \{T_1, T_2, \ldots, T_m\}$ is formed, then the T_i will form a distribution. Such a distribution is called the *sampling distribution of the statistic T.*

To return to the sampling distribution of the means. As a distribution in their own right the set of numbers $\bar{x}_i$ will have a mean, standard deviation, and so on and these will be denoted by $\bar{x}_{\bar{x}}$, $s^2_{\bar{x}}$, $s_{\bar{x}}$, and $\bar{x}_{\bar{x}}$ is read as the 'mean of the sampling distribution of the mean', $s^2_{\bar{x}}$ will be read as the 'variance of the sampling distribution of the mean' and any other statistic taken from this sampling distribution will be put into similar notation. Likewise the sampling distribution of the variance will have a mean, variance and standard deviation, etc., and these will be denoted by, $\bar{x}_s$, s_s^2, s_s.

The following table may be useful

of the Sampling Distribution of the	mean	variance	standard deviation	median	mode
mean	$\bar{x}_{\bar{x}}$	$s^2_{\bar{x}}$	$s_{\bar{x}}$	$\text{med}_{\bar{x}}$	$\text{mode}_{\bar{x}}$
variance	$\bar{x}_{s^2}$	$s^2_{s^2}$	s_{s^2}	med_{s^2}	mode_{s^2}
standard deviation	$\bar{x}_s$	s^2_s	s_s	med_s	mode_s
median	$\bar{x}_{\text{med}}$	$s^2{}_{\text{med}}$	s_{med}	med_{med}	mode_{med}
mode	$\bar{x}_{\text{mode}}$	$s^2{}_{\text{mode}}$	s_{mode}	med_{mode}	$\text{mode}_{\text{mode}}$

It should be noted that some of these are never used – the table is put in so that the reader may see the whole pattern.

It will soon be seen that it is from these statistics, computed from the sampling distributions, that the population parameters are estimated.

Now the most remarkable point about all these sampling distributions of statistics is that, for n large enough, they are all very nearly normally distributed, *regardless of the way the population is distributed.* And this is a very important point in sampling theory since it enables us to apply all the usual normal distribution theory.

Note that the phrase 'for n large enough' – it is *only* if n is large – bigger than 30 in most cases – that these sampling distributions are normally distributed and for this reason sampling theory falls into two groups, Large Sample Theory and Small Sample Theory. For large samples the normal distribution holds but for small samples other distributions have to be used.

The proof that these sampling distributions are normally distributed is one of the most important in statistical theory. It is known as the Central Limit Theorem (sometimes CLT for short) and because it has been the subject of so much investigation it appears in slightly differing (but essentially the same) forms. The proof itself is beyond the scope of this book but many versions are available in more advanced books on statistical theory.

8.3 The Mean and Variance of the Sampling Distribution of the Mean.

For the first time a departure will be made from the practice of drawing general conclusions from ideas suggested by examples. We have enough theory to go straight to the general case, and we are interested in the mean and the variance of the sampling distribution of the mean.

Let $\underset{\sim}{x}$ be a random variable having probability distribution $f(x)$ with mean μ and variance σ^2. Now let us consider the mean of a sample. For convenience we consider this as sampling either from an infinite population or from a finite population with replacement. We know

$$\bar{x} = \frac{\sum_i x_i}{n}$$

where n is the size of the sample.

Now $x_1, x_2, \ldots, x_n$, will be the values of the variable $\underset{\sim}{x}$, where x_1 is the value of the first item drawn from the population, x_2 the value of the second, and so on. (Remember that sampling with replacement induces order upon the n'tuple of the sample $(x_1, x_2, \ldots, x_n)$)

A second sample of size n will produce a different ordered n'tuple $(x_{12}, x_{22}, x_{32}, \ldots, x_{n2})$, where the second subscript refers to the number of the sample. Thus the 'first member of a sample' will be a random variable $\underset{\sim}{x}_1$, the 'second member of the sample' will be a random variable $\underset{\sim}{x}_2$, and so on for all $\underset{\sim}{x}_i$. Since each x_i refers to the original population $\underset{\sim}{x}$, then $\underset{\sim}{x}_1 = \underset{\sim}{x}_2 = \underset{\sim}{x}_i = \underset{\sim}{x}$.

We can now consider the random variable $\underset{\sim}{\bar{x}}$ made up as follows

$$\underset{\sim}{\bar{x}} = \frac{\underset{\sim}{x}_1 + \underset{\sim}{x}_2 + \underset{\sim}{x}_3 + \ldots + \underset{\sim}{x}_n}{n}$$

$\underset{\sim}{\bar{x}}$ will vary as $\underset{\sim}{x}_1, \underset{\sim}{x}_2, \ldots, \underset{\sim}{x}_n$ assumes the different values $x_1, x_2, \ldots, x_n$, where each x_i is taken from the population.

If we rewrite this as

$$\underset{\sim}{\bar{x}} = \frac{\underset{\sim}{x}_1}{n} + \frac{\underset{\sim}{x}_2}{n} + \ldots + \frac{\underset{\sim}{x}_n}{n}$$

we see that $\underset{\sim}{\bar{x}}$ is made up of the sum of several random variables each of which is multiplied by the constant $1/n$.

We now refer to the various theorems in Expectation and Variance concerning random variables related in this way, and look at the mean of the sampling distribution of the mean, for instance $E(\underset{\sim}{\bar{x}})$.

Now
$$E(\underset{\sim}{\bar{x}}) = E\left(\frac{\underset{\sim}{x}_1}{n} + \frac{\underset{\sim}{x}_2}{n} + \ldots + \frac{\underset{\sim}{x}_n}{n}\right)$$

$$= E\left(\frac{\underset{\sim}{x}_1}{n}\right) + E\left(\frac{\underset{\sim}{x}_2}{n}\right) + \ldots + E\left(\frac{\underset{\sim}{x}_n}{n}\right)$$

$$= \frac{E(\underset{\sim}{x}_1)}{n} + \frac{E(\underset{\sim}{x}_2)}{n} + \ldots + \frac{E(\underset{\sim}{x}_n)}{n}$$

where we have used the theorem that $E(a\underset{\sim}{x} + b\underset{\sim}{y}) = aE(\underset{\sim}{x}) + bE(\underset{\sim}{y})$.
Now since $\underset{\sim}{x}_i = \underset{\sim}{x}$, $E(\underset{\sim}{x}_i) = E(\underset{\sim}{x}) = \mu$
and so

$$
\begin{aligned}
E(\underset{\sim}{\bar{x}}) &= \frac{\mu}{n} + \frac{\mu}{n} + \ldots + \frac{\mu}{n} \\
&= n \cdot \frac{\mu}{n} = \mu.
\end{aligned}
$$

Thus we see that the mean of the sampling distribution of the mean is the mean of the population from which the samples are drawn – a not altogether unexpected result.

Now let us consider the variance of the sampling distribution of the mean.

$$
\begin{aligned}
\text{Var}(\underset{\sim}{\bar{x}}) &= \text{Var}\left(\frac{\underset{\sim}{x}_1}{n} + \frac{\underset{\sim}{x}_2}{n} + \ldots + \frac{\underset{\sim}{x}_n}{n}\right) \\
&= \text{Var}\left(\frac{\underset{\sim}{x}_1}{n}\right) + \text{Var}\left(\frac{\underset{\sim}{x}_2}{n}\right) + \ldots + \text{Var}\left(\frac{\underset{\sim}{x}_n}{n}\right) \\
&= \frac{\text{Var}(\underset{\sim}{x}_1)}{n^2} + \frac{\text{Var}(\underset{\sim}{x}_2)}{n^2} + \ldots + \frac{\text{Var}(\underset{\sim}{x}_n)}{n^2}
\end{aligned}
$$

Where we have used the theorem $\text{Var}(a\underset{\sim}{x} + b\underset{\sim}{y}) = a^2\text{Var}(\underset{\sim}{x}) + b^2(\underset{\sim}{y})$.
Again since $\underset{\sim}{x}_i = \underset{\sim}{x}$, $\text{Var}(\underset{\sim}{x}_i) = \text{Var}(\underset{\sim}{x}) = \sigma^2$, so

$$
\begin{aligned}
\text{Var}(\underset{\sim}{\bar{x}}) &= \frac{\sigma^2}{n^2} + \frac{\sigma^2}{n^2} + \ldots + \frac{\sigma^2}{n^2} \\
&= n \cdot \frac{\sigma^2}{n^2} = \frac{\sigma^2}{n}
\end{aligned}
$$

This shows us that the variance of the sampling distribution of the mean is much smaller than the variance of the population. This is not altogether surprising, as a little reflection will show. We would expect the sample means to vary less than the variates of the population, and for them to vary even less when n increases in value. In other words, the larger the sample, the more reliable the mean $\bar{x}$ will be as an estimate of the population mean.

A point which has been tacitly assumed in the above working must now be made explicitly. Since this working is based on sampling from infinite populations or from a finite population with replacement, we know that each x_i selected in $(x_1, x_2, \ldots, x_n)$ will be independent of the others. If, in the case of the finite population, x_1 is replaced before x_2 is drawn then the drawing of x_2 will be independent of x_1. Thus the random variable $\underset{\sim}{x}_1$ will be independent of the random variable $\underset{\sim}{x}_2$, and the random variable $\underset{\sim}{x}_2$ will be independent of the random variable $\underset{\sim}{x}_3$, and so on. Thus all the $\underset{\sim}{x}_i$ will be independent. This point has to be made because the above working assumes that the $\underset{\sim}{x}_i$'s are independent, and if they were dependent, then this dependency would have to be allowed for in the theorems concerning the variance of the random variables. In fact what happens is that if the random variables are dependent what is called the *covariance* of two random variables has to be introduced. This covariance is a measure of the way two variables vary together. If two variables are independent then their covariance is zero and this fact was assumed in the above working.

Now if sampling from a finite population is *without* replacement then the $\underset{\sim}{x}_i$'s in

$$\bar{\underset{\sim}{x}} = \frac{\sum_i \underset{\sim}{x}_i}{n}$$

will not be independent and the above results will be modified in the following way. The mean of the sampling distribution of the mean, that is $E(\bar{\underset{\sim}{x}})$, is still μ, but the variance becomes

$$\text{Var}(\bar{\underset{\sim}{x}}) = \frac{\sigma^2}{n}\frac{(N-n)}{(N-1)}$$

where N is the size of the population and n is the size of the sample. We said earlier that if N is very large then sampling from a finite population is equivalent to sampling from an infinite population and now if the above expression is examined for the case when N is large $\frac{N-n}{N-1}$ is approximately equal to 1 and so $\text{Var}(\bar{\underset{\sim}{x}}) \simeq \frac{\sigma^2}{n}$, the same as we deduced for sampling from an infinite population.

We have now dealt with the mean and variance of the sampling distribution of the mean for samples from an infinite population or from a finite population with replacement, and for samples from a finite population without replacement.

We summarise the results of this section in the following two theorems.

Theorem 1. If $\underset{\sim}{x}_1, \underset{\sim}{x}_2, \ldots, \underset{\sim}{x}_n$ are independent random variables having the same probability distribution with mean μ and variance σ^2 then if

$$\bar{\underset{\sim}{x}} = \frac{\sum_i \underset{\sim}{x}_i}{n},$$

$$E(\bar{\underset{\sim}{x}}) = \mu \qquad \text{and} \qquad \text{Var}(\bar{\underset{\sim}{x}}) = \frac{\sigma^2}{n}$$

Theorem 2. If $\underset{\sim}{x}_1, \underset{\sim}{x}_2, \ldots, \underset{\sim}{x}_n$, are not independent random variables having the same probability distribution with mean μ and variance σ^2, then if,

$$\bar{\underset{\sim}{x}} = \frac{\sum_i \underset{\sim}{x}_i}{n},$$

$$E(\bar{\underset{\sim}{x}}) = \mu \qquad \text{and} \qquad \mathrm{Var}(\bar{\underset{\sim}{x}}) = \frac{\sigma^2}{n}\frac{(N-n)}{(N-1)}$$

Example 1. A population consists of the numbers 1, 2, 3, and 4. Take samples of 2, with replacement, from this population, find the set of means, draw graph of the sampling distribution of the means, calculate the mean and standard deviation of the sampling distribution of the means and compare with the population.

Answer

Population mean = 2·5. Population standard deviation = 1·12.

All possible samples of 2 are shown below together with their mean:

Sample	*Sample mean*	*Sample*	*Sample mean*
1, 1	1	3, 1	2
1, 2	1·5	3, 2	2·5
1, 3	2	3, 3	3
1, 4	2·5	3, 4	3·5
2, 1	1·5	4, 1	2·5
2, 2	2	4, 2	3
2, 3	2·5	4, 3	3·5
2, 4	3	4, 4	4

The set of means is therefore {1, 1·5, 2, 2·5, 1·5, 2, 2·5, 3, 2, 2·5, 3, 3·5, 2·5, 3, 3·5, 4}

The graph of the sampling distribution of the mean is given in Fig. 8.3 (a) Compare this with the original population, Fig. 8.3 (b)

Even with such a small population and with small samples the characteristic smaller variation of the sampling distribution of the mean compared with the population can be seen.

It can be clearly seen from the graph that $E(\bar{\underset{\sim}{x}}) = 2{\cdot}5 = E(\underset{\sim}{x})$.

The standard deviation of the sampling distribution of the mean is, after the usual calculations, 0·83. The above theory told us that $\mathrm{Var}(x) = (\sigma^2/n)$, and if the student works out the variance of both the population and the sampling distribution of the mean he will get the following results:

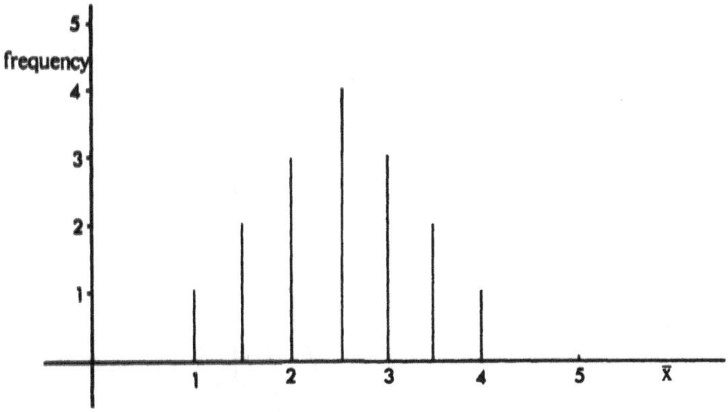

Fig. 8.3(a)

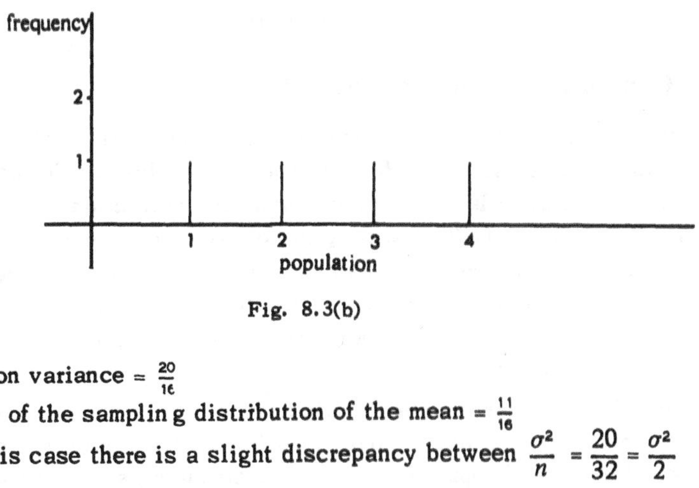

Fig. 8.3(b)

Population variance = $\frac{20}{16}$

Variance of the sampling distribution of the mean = $\frac{11}{16}$

and in this case there is a slight discrepancy between $\frac{\sigma^2}{n} = \frac{20}{32} = \frac{\sigma^2}{2}$ and Var(x). This slight discrepancy, $\frac{1}{16}$, is due to the small size of the sample – only 2 – and the small size of the population and this brings out the point that the above work is based upon large samples.

Example 2. It is left to the reader to repeat the above example but using sampling without replacement. Compare the results obtained with the population mean and variance, and see how accurate is the formula $\frac{\sigma^2}{2}\frac{(N-n)}{(N-1)}$.

Example 3. Draw the graphs of sampling distributions of the mean for increasing n, and compare with a population.

Answer

For convenience we pick a population which is normally distributed and the results are graphed below.

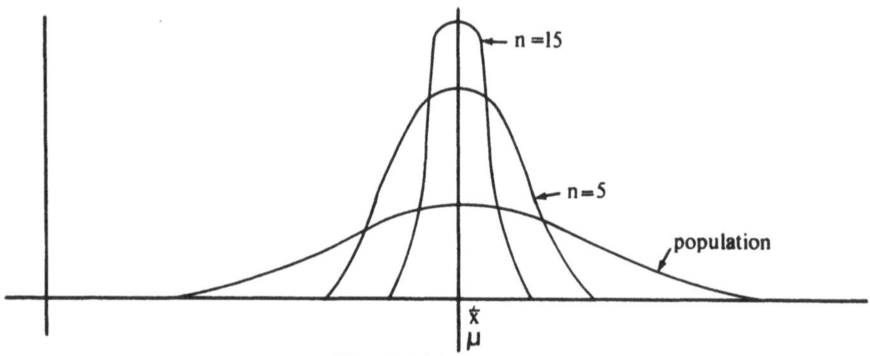

Fig. 8.3(c)

8.4 Sampling from a Normal Population

The previous section made no reference to the distribution of the population. The results apply for all populations. However it can be proved – as will be seen later – that *providing the population is normally distributed*, the distribution of $\bar{x}$ is normal *regardless of the size of the sample*. Thus even for small samples $\bar{x}$ is normally distributed if the parent population is normally distributed and since so many populations are normally distributed this can be very useful as the following example shows.

Example 1: A machine, when working properly, produces screws with a mean length of 2″ and a variance of 0·1″. If these screws may be looked upon as a population normally distributed, show how samples of 4 can be used to determine whether the machine is working accurately or not.

Answer

The population is the total number of the screws produced by the machine and will be large. The mean is 2″ and the standard deviation $= \sqrt{0{\cdot}1}'' = 0{\cdot}32''$. Samples of 4 will be distributed normally with mean 2″ and variance $= \frac{\sigma^2}{n} = \frac{0{\cdot}1}{4} = 0{\cdot}025$. Therefore the standard deviation of the sampling distribution of the mean will be $\sqrt{0{\cdot}025} = 0{\cdot}16$, and

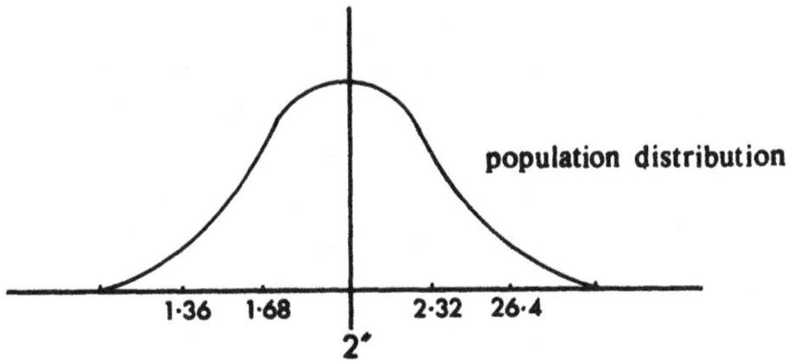

Fig. 8.4(a)

we get the distribution of $\bar{x}$ for samples of size 4 as

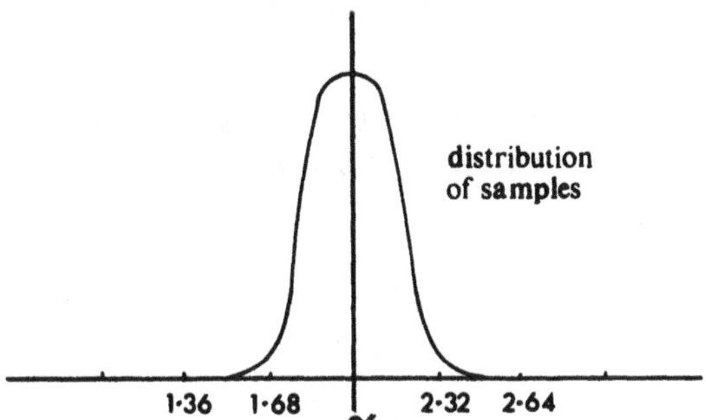

Fig. 8.4(b)

We refer now to Section 5.11 where details were given of confidence limits and confidence intervals. Since $\bar{x}$ in this case is normally distributed we may apply the results and figures given in Section 5.11. We know that just as we may be 95% sure that the mean of any sample will be within 1·96 standard deviations of the mean of the sampling distribution of the mean, but in this latter distribution the standard deviation is $\frac{\sigma}{\sqrt{n}}$.

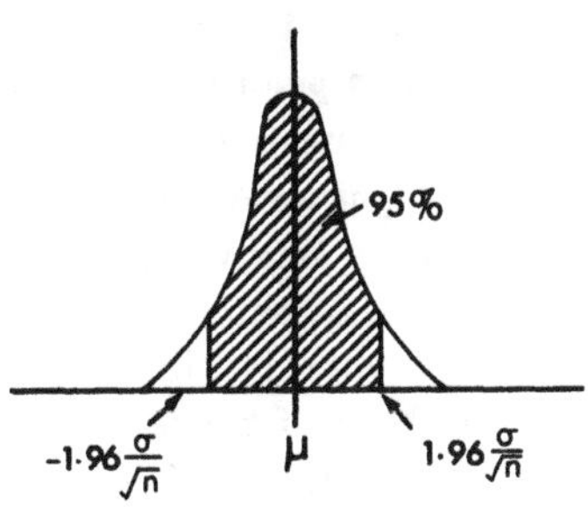

Fig. 8.4(c)

Thus if the machine is working accurately and samples are taken at regular intervals, 95% of the samples will have mean within 1·96 standard deviations of the mean of the sampling distribution of the mean.

For this production process then samples of 4 will be taken at regular intervals and the mean of the sample found. If it is within 1·96 standard deviations of the mean of the sampling distribution of the mean, that is $2 \pm 1{\cdot}96 \times 0{\cdot}16 = 2 \pm 0{\cdot}314$, that is the interval 1·786 to 2·314, then the machine will be regarded as being *under control* with a 95% degree of confidence.

Example 2: In Example 1, what is the probability that the machine will be working correctly but the sample will indicate that it is out of control?

Answer

We can expect that only 95% of the means of the samples taken will lie between the interval 1·786 to 2·314 so 5% will lie outside this interval.

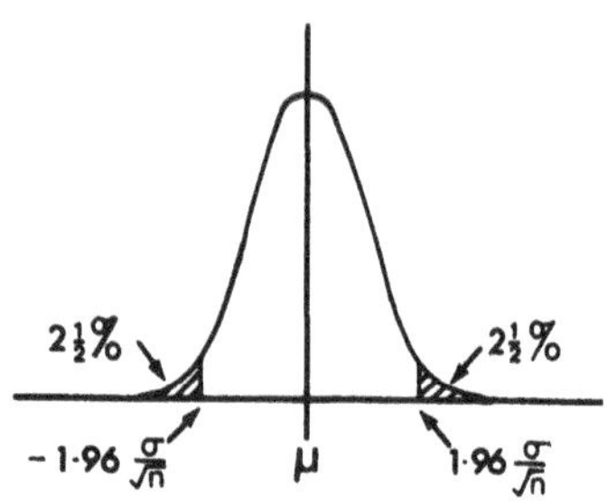

Fig. 8.4(d)

Thus when the machine is working normally 5% of the sample means will lie outside the given confidence interval, and so there is a 5% chance that a sample will indicate the machine is not working correctly when it is. What happens here in practice is, rather than stop a production process that may be running within the laid down limits, a further sample is taken straight away. If this second sample has a mean lying within the confidence interval then the machine is allowed to proceed without hinderence – it being realised that the first sample was one of the 5% outside the expected limits. If the second sample however does not lie within the confidence interval then it must be assumed that the machine has gone out of control and will have to be stopped and reset.

8.5 Estimating a Population Mean when the Population Variance is known

If it should happen that the variance σ^2 of a population is known then we can find the confidence limits for the unknown mean μ based upon a sample of size n. Using the notion of a confidence interval we know we can be 95% sure that any $\bar{x}$ will lie within 1·96 standard deviations of $E(\bar{x})$, that is

$$P[E(\bar{x}) - 1{\cdot}96 s.d. \leqslant \bar{x} \leqslant E(\bar{x}) + 1{\cdot}96 s.d.] = 95\%$$

We also know that $E(\bar{x}) = \mu$, and that $\text{Var}(\bar{x}) = \frac{\sigma^2}{n}$, so

$$P(\mu - 1{\cdot}96\frac{\sigma}{\sqrt{n}} \leqslant \bar{x} \leqslant \mu + 1{\cdot}96\frac{\sigma}{\sqrt{n}}) = 95\%$$

If we now take

$$\mu - 1{\cdot}96\frac{\sigma}{\sqrt{n}} \leqslant \bar{x}$$

we can write

$$\mu \leqslant \bar{x} + 1{\cdot}96\frac{\sigma}{\sqrt{n}}$$

Similarly taking

$$\bar{x} \leqslant \mu + 1{\cdot}96\frac{\sigma}{\sqrt{n}}$$

we can write

$$x - 1{\cdot}96\frac{\sigma}{\sqrt{n}} \leqslant \mu$$

Combining these two results we get

$$\bar{x} - 1{\cdot}96\frac{\sigma}{\sqrt{n}} \leqslant \mu \leqslant \bar{x} + 1{\cdot}96\frac{\sigma}{\sqrt{n}}$$

giving finally

$$P(\bar{x} - 1{\cdot}96\frac{\sigma}{\sqrt{n}} \leqslant \mu \leqslant \bar{x} + 1{\cdot}96\frac{\sigma}{\sqrt{n}}) = 95\%$$

which says that we can be 95% sure that a population mean lies within these two limits, and these limits give us our 95% confidence interval.

Example 1: A population has a variance of 225. A sample of size 900 produces a mean of 102. Estimate the population mean within a 95% confidence interval.

Answer

$\sigma^2 = 225$, so $\sigma = 15$.

The standard deviation of the sampling distribution of the mean $= \frac{\sigma}{\sqrt{n}} = \frac{15}{30} = \frac{1}{2}$. Substituting these figures in the above result gives,

$$P(102 - \tfrac{1\cdot96}{2} \leqslant \mu \leqslant 102 + \tfrac{1\cdot96}{2}) = 95\%$$

that is, $P(101\cdot02 \leqslant \mu \leqslant 102\cdot98) = 95\%$. Thus we can be 95% confident that the mean of the population lies between 101·02 and 102·98 – a confidence interval of nearly 2.

Example 2: Repeat Example 1 with samples of (a) 400 and (b) 100, assuming that these samples also give means of 102.

Answer

(a) If $n = 400$, then $\sqrt{n} = 20$ and we get

$$P(102 - 1\cdot96 \times \tfrac{15}{20} \leqslant \mu \leqslant 102 + 1\cdot96 \times \tfrac{15}{20}) = 95\%$$

giving $$P(100\cdot53 \leqslant \mu \leqslant 103\cdot47) = 95\%$$

that is, a confidence interval of 2·94.

(b) Similar calculations give

$$P\,(99\cdot06 \leqslant \mu \leqslant 105\cdot94) = 95\%$$

giving a confidence interval of 6·86.

Note

It is highly unlikely that three samples such as these would produce exactly the same mean. The point of the examples is that as n becomes smaller the confidence intervals become larger. We can therefore be less sure with small samples than with large samples – a fact we already know.

Example 3: Repeat Example 1 with a 99% degree of confidence.

Answer

For a 99% degree of confidence we get

$$P(\bar{x} - 2\cdot58 \frac{\sigma}{\sqrt{n}} \leqslant \mu \leqslant \bar{x} + 2\cdot58 \frac{\sigma}{\sqrt{n}}) = 99\%$$

which gives

$$P(102 - \tfrac{2\cdot58}{2} \leqslant \mu \leqslant 102 + \tfrac{2\cdot58}{2}) = 99\%$$

that is $$P(100\cdot71 \leqslant \mu \leqslant 103\cdot29) = 99\%$$

Thus we can say with 99% confidence that the mean of the population will lie between 100·71 and 103·29. Note that as we demand a higher degree of certainty the confidence interval becomes larger.

Example 4: Repeat Example 2 with a 99% degree of confidence and note the variation in the confidence interval.

Answer

(a) If $n = 400$, then $\sqrt{n} = 20$ and we get

$$P(102 - 2{\cdot}58 \times \tfrac{15}{20} \leqslant \mu \leqslant 102 + 2{\cdot}58 \times \tfrac{15}{20}) = 99\%$$

giving $$P(100{\cdot}06 \leqslant \mu \leqslant 103{\cdot}94) = 99\%$$

a confidence interval of 3·88

(b) Similar calculations give

$$P(95{\cdot}13 \leqslant \mu \leqslant 108{\cdot}87) = 99\%$$

giving a confidence interval of 13·64. Again note that as n becomes smaller the confidence interval widens. These four examples reveal clearly the two important factors involved – the degree of confidence required and the size of the sample taken. As the degree of confidence required increases the confidence interval must widen and as the sample size increases the confidence interval must narrow. One advantage of this situation is that a fixed degree of confidence can be taken together with a fixed confidence interval and then the size of the sample required to match these conditions can be calculated. Other combinations of these three conditions are obviously possible.

8.6 Estimating a Population Mean from Sample Information only

It is highly unlikely that a situation would arise where a population variance is known and the mean is not, so the previous section is somewhat artificial. The point of putting it in was to avoid introducing too many problems at once. Now we have seen the sort of manipulation used we can consider the more realistic situation of estimating a population mean when nothing is known about the mean or the variance. What is done is to use the variance, s^2, of the sample as an estimate of the population variance σ^2, and *if the sample is large* – bigger than 30 – this estimate of the population variance will be quite good. If n is smaller than 30 other methods have to be used and will be looked at later. It might be remarked in passing that since a population will in general contain more extreme data than a single sample s^2 will be slightly smaller than σ^2. A method for dealing with this discrepancy will be looked at later.

Using s^2 as an estimate of σ^2 the results of the last section become

$$P(\bar{x} - 1{\cdot}96\frac{s}{\sqrt{n}} \leqslant \mu \leqslant \bar{x} + 1{\cdot}96\frac{s}{\sqrt{n}}) = 95\%$$

and $$P(\bar{x} - 2{\cdot}58\frac{s}{\sqrt{n}} \leqslant \mu \leqslant \bar{x} + 2{\cdot}58\frac{s}{\sqrt{n}}) = 99\%$$

for the 95% and 99% confidence limits. Any other confidence limits can be found by altering the coefficient of $\frac{s}{\sqrt{n}}$ in accordance with the normal probability table.

Example 1: A sample of 36 has a mean of 25 and a variance of 25. Estimate the population mean with a 95% degree of confidence.

Answer

Using s as an estimate of σ we substitute the relevant values in the above result and get

$$P(25 - 1{\cdot}96 \times \tfrac{5}{6} \leqslant \mu \leqslant 25 + 1{\cdot}96 \times \tfrac{5}{6}) = 95\%$$

Performing the necessary calculations gives the following

$$P(23{\cdot}37 \leqslant \mu \leqslant 26{\cdot}63) = 95\%$$

Thus we may be 95% confident that the mean of the population lies between 23·37 and 26·63.

8.7 Standardised Random Variables

The work of Section 8.5 suggests that a standardised random variable may be used with slightly more facility.
If we take

$$\mu - 1{\cdot}96 \frac{\sigma}{\sqrt{n}} \leqslant \bar{x} \leqslant \mu + 1{\cdot}96 \frac{\sigma}{\sqrt{n}}$$

it can be rewritten as

$$-1{\cdot}96 \frac{\sigma}{\sqrt{n}} \leqslant \bar{x} - \mu \leqslant +1{\cdot}96 \frac{\sigma}{\sqrt{n}}$$

and by dividing by $\frac{\sigma}{\sqrt{n}}$ we get finally

$$-1{\cdot}96 \leqslant \frac{\bar{x} - \mu}{\frac{\sigma}{\sqrt{n}}} \leqslant +1{\cdot}96$$

As we know $\pm 1{\cdot}96$ are the z scores between which 95% of the area under a normal curve lies, we may write:

$$P\left(-1{\cdot}96 \leqslant \frac{\bar{x} - \mu}{\frac{\sigma}{\sqrt{n}}} \leqslant 1{\cdot}96\right) = 95\%$$

If we now consider the random variable

$$z = \frac{\bar{x} - \mu}{\frac{\sigma}{\sqrt{n}}}$$

we know that $\underset{\sim}{\bar{x}}$ is normally distributed if n is large. We know also μ is the mean of $\underset{\sim}{\bar{x}}$, and the standard deviation of $\underset{\sim}{\bar{x}}$ is $\frac{\sigma}{\sqrt{n}}$. Thus

$$\underset{\sim}{z} = \frac{\underset{\sim}{\bar{x}} - \mu}{\frac{\sigma}{\sqrt{n}}}$$

is the related standardised random variable and will be normally distributed, $N(0,1)$.

Thus we may consider $P(-z_k \leqslant z \leqslant z_k) = k$ where z is the z score of any particular $\bar{x}$ of $\underset{\sim}{\bar{x}}$, and k is the corresponding area under the normal curve. The reader should convince himself that the argument of Section 8.5 is equivalent to the argument used here.

Example 1: A population has a variance of 225. A sample of size 900 produced a mean of 102. Estimate the population mean within a 95% confidence interval (cf. Example 1, Section 8.5).

Answer

Consider the standardised random variable

$$\underset{\sim}{z} = \frac{\underset{\sim}{\bar{x}} - \mu}{\frac{\sigma}{\sqrt{n}}}$$

and put in the known values. Then

$$z = \frac{102 - \mu}{\frac{1}{2}} = 2(102 - \mu)$$

We now consider for the 95% degree of confidence interval

$$P(-1{\cdot}96 \leqslant 2(102 - \mu) \leqslant 1{\cdot}96) = 95\%$$

that is, $$P(-0{\cdot}98 \leqslant 102 - \mu \leqslant 0{\cdot}98) = 95\%$$

that is, $$P(-102{\cdot}98 \leqslant -\mu \leqslant -101{\cdot}02) = 95\%$$

that is, $$P(102{\cdot}98 \geqslant \mu \geqslant 101{\cdot}02) = 95\%$$

after multiplying through by –1 which necessitated the reversing of the inequality signs. We thus have the same result as before.

Another example using standardised random variables is now given.

Example 2: A population has mean 21 and variance 36. If 45 samples of size 49 were taken, how many of these samples would you expect to produce means between 20 and 22·5?

Answer

The sampling distribution of the mean for samples of 49 will have a mean of 21 and a standard deviation of $\frac{\sigma}{\sqrt{n}} = \frac{6}{7}$.

Consider now the standardised random variable

$$z = \frac{\bar{x} - \mu}{\frac{6}{7}}$$

The z score of $\bar{x} = 20$ is $\frac{20-21}{6/7} = -1{\cdot}16$. The z score of $\bar{x} = 22{\cdot}5$ is $\frac{22{\cdot}5}{6/7} = 1{\cdot}75$. The area under the normal curve $N(0,1)$ between $-1{\cdot}16$ and $1{\cdot}75 = 0{\cdot}3770 + 0{\cdot}4599 = 0{\cdot}8369$.

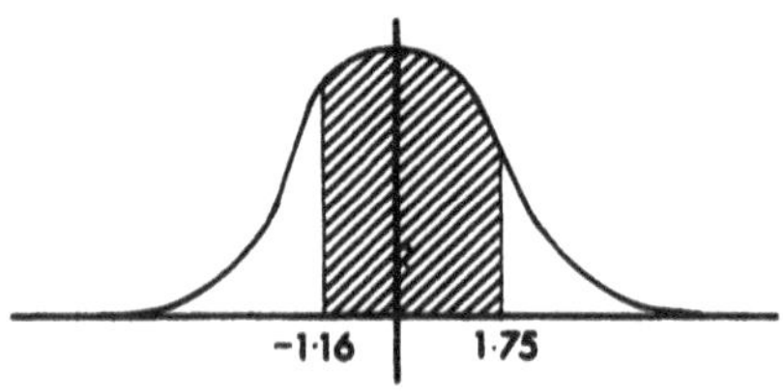

Fig. 8.7(a)

Therefore the number of samples with means between 21 and 22·5 will be $0{\cdot}8369 \times 45 = 37{\cdot}65 \simeq 38$.

8.8 Sampling from a Binomial Population

If a population is split into two groups, X's and not-X's, then the random selection of a member of that population will satisfy the assumptions of the binomial distribution. Such a population is called a binomial population. If π is the *proportion* of X's in the population then $1 - \pi$ is the proportion of not-X's and $\pi + (1 - \pi) = 1$. The probability of selecting an X will be π and π is the population parameter.

Example 1: If in a raffle 500 men have tickets and 600 women have tickets, what is the probability that a woman will win the first prize?

Answer

The population here is the set of ticket holders and if X denotes female the proportion of X's in this population is $\frac{600}{1100} = \frac{6}{11}$ and the probability that a woman will win the first prize is $\frac{6}{11}$.

If samples of size n are now taken from a population of X's and not-X's, that is a binomial population, for the purpose of determining what proportion π of the population are in fact X's, and if sampling is with replacement (or from a very large population) then each member of the sample will be selected in accordance with the binomial assumptions.

Again we use the convention that the drawing of an X will be counted a success and the drawing of a not-X will be counted a failure. If we also use the code that the drawing of a success will count 1 and the srawing of a failure will count 0, then the random variable $\underset{\sim}{x}$ associated with the selection of one item from the population will be binomially distributed $B(x;1,\pi)$.

If we now consider $\underset{\sim}{x}_1, \underset{\sim}{x}_2, \ldots, \underset{\sim}{x}_n$ as random variables each defined by the selection of one item from the population then each $\underset{\sim}{x}_i$, $i = 1, 2, \ldots, n$, will assume a value 0 or 1 and $\sum_i \underset{\sim}{x}_i$ will assume a value between 0 and n inclusive. If we now let

$$\bar{\underset{\sim}{x}} = \frac{\sum \underset{\sim}{x}_i}{n}$$

then $\bar{\underset{\sim}{x}}$ will represent the proportion of successes in the sample. For instance if a sample were of size 30 and 17 were successes then $\bar{x} = \frac{17}{30}$.

Since $\bar{\underset{\sim}{x}}$ will under these circumstances always produce a fraction representing the proportion of successes in the sample, the distribution of $\bar{\underset{\sim}{x}}$ is called the *sampling distribution of proportions*. We now find the mean and variance of this sampling distribution.

$$E(\bar{\underset{\sim}{x}}) = E\left(\frac{\sum \underset{\sim}{x}_i}{n}\right) = \frac{1}{n}E(\sum_i \underset{\sim}{x}_i) = \frac{1}{n}\sum_i E(\underset{\sim}{x}_i)$$

but $E(\underset{\sim}{x}_i) = n\pi$ for all i, so

$$E(\bar{\underset{\sim}{x}}) = \frac{1}{n}n\pi = \pi.$$

Thus for large n the mean of the sampling distribution of proportions will represent the proportion of successes in the population.

$$\text{Var}(\bar{\underset{\sim}{x}}) = \text{Var}\left(\frac{\sum \underset{\sim}{x}_i}{n}\right) = \frac{1}{n^2}\text{Var}(\sum_i \underset{\sim}{x}_i) = \frac{1}{n^2}\sum_i \text{Var}(\underset{\sim}{x}_i)$$

but $\text{Var}(\underset{\sim}{x}_i) = n\pi(1-\pi)$ for all i, so

$$\text{Var}(\bar{\underset{\sim}{x}}) = \frac{1}{n^2}n\pi(1-\pi) = \frac{\pi(1-\pi)}{n}$$

Note 1

These last two results could have been derived from the general case given in Section 8.3. The point of treating them separately here is to draw attention to their importance.

Note 2

For large n, $\underset{\sim}{x}$ will be normally distributed although the parent population is binomially distributed.

Example 2: In a university population of 2000, 500 are members of the Jazz club. If membership of the Jazz club is counted a success and non-membership a failure, then find the mean and variance of the sampling distribution of proportions for samples of size 25 taken with replacement.

Answer

$\pi = \frac{500}{2000} = \frac{1}{4}$, therefore $(1 - \pi) = \frac{3}{4}$.

$$E(\bar{\underset{\sim}{x}}) = \pi = \tfrac{1}{4}$$

$$\text{Var}(\bar{\underset{\sim}{x}}) = \frac{\pi(1-\pi)}{n} = \frac{\frac{3}{4} \times \frac{1}{4}}{25} = \frac{3}{400} = 0{\cdot}0075$$

Note the small variance and also that as the size of the sample increases the variance becomes smaller.

Example 3: If in Example 2, 35 samples of 25 are taken, how many of these would you expect to give π between $\frac{1}{8}$ and $\frac{3}{8}$.

Answer

Since $\bar{\underset{\sim}{x}}$ is normally distributed we may consider the standardised random variable

$$\frac{\underset{\sim}{x} - \mu}{\frac{\sigma}{\sqrt{n}}}$$

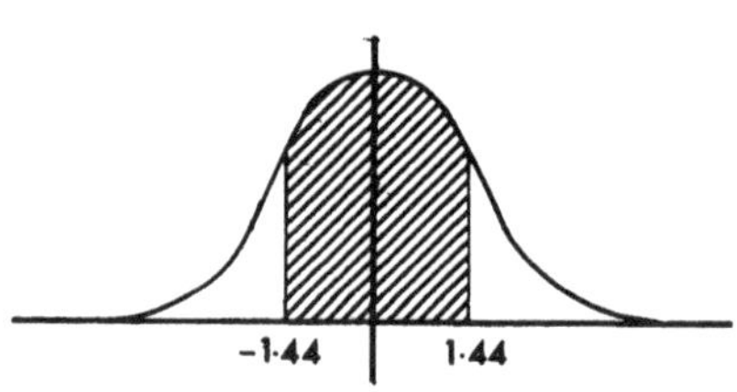

Fig. 8.8(a)

which for the binomial case becomes

$$\frac{\bar{x} - \pi}{\sqrt{\frac{\pi(1 - \pi)}{n}}}$$

$\frac{1}{8}$ in standard units is

$$\frac{\frac{1}{8} - \frac{1}{4}}{\frac{\sqrt{3}}{20}} = -1{\cdot}443$$

$\frac{3}{8}$ in standard units is

$$\frac{\frac{3}{8} - \frac{1}{4}}{\frac{\sqrt{3}}{20}} = 1{\cdot}443$$

Area between $-1{\cdot}44$ and $+1{\cdot}44$ is $0{\cdot}4251 + 0{\cdot}4251 = 0{\cdot}8502$. Therefore we would expect $0{\cdot}8502 \times 35 = 29{\cdot}76 \simeq 30$ samples to be between the limits $\frac{1}{8}$ and $\frac{3}{8}$.

We must now consider the case of sampling *without* replacement from a finite (and not large) population. Here the probability of success is not constant from trial to trial and so the binomial assumptions do not apply. In this case the hypergeometric assumptions apply. Now we know from number 15, Exercise 6, that the mean and variance of the hypergeometric distribution are

$$\bar{x} = \frac{ns}{s + f} \quad \text{and} \quad s^2 = \frac{nsf(s + f - n)}{(s + f)^2(s + f - 1)}$$

We also know that for a finite population the proportion of success is $\frac{s}{s+f}$ and this must be π.

If the population is of size N, then $s + f = N$, and the above formulae become

$$\bar{x} = n\pi \quad \text{and} \quad s^2 = \frac{n\pi(1 - \pi)(N - n)}{(N - 1)}$$

If we now calculate the mean and variance of $\bar{x}$, the sampling distribution of proportions, for the case of sampling without replacement from a finite population, the manipulation is identical with the case of sampling with replacement (given above), except for the factor

$$\frac{(N - n)}{(N - 1)},$$

and we get $E(\underset{\sim}{\bar{x}}) = \pi$ and

$$\text{Var}(\underset{\sim}{\bar{x}}) = \frac{\pi(1-\pi)(N-n)}{n(N-1)}$$

The reader will note the factor $\frac{(N-n)}{(N-1)}$ also appeared in variance of the sampling distribution of the mean in the similar case of sampling without replacement.

Example 4: If the samples of Example 2 are taken without replacement find the mean and variance of the sampling distribution of proportions.

Answer

$\pi = \frac{500}{2000} = \frac{1}{4}$ and $(1-\pi) = \frac{3}{4}$, and as before $E(\underset{\sim}{\bar{x}}) = \frac{1}{4}$.

$$\text{Var}(\underset{\sim}{\bar{x}}) = \frac{\pi(1-\pi)(N-n)}{n(N-1)} = \frac{1}{25}\cdot\frac{1}{4}\cdot\frac{1}{3}\cdot\frac{1975}{1999} = 0{\cdot}0074.$$

The final point to be considered in connection with the sampling distribution of proportions is the question of continuity. Suppose a sample of 10 is taken from a binomial population and the number of successes noted. There will be either 0, 1, 2, up to 10 successes, and this means that the sample proportion will be any one of 0·0, 0·1, 0·2, etc., up to 1·0, *and no other values will be possible*. Hence the sampling distribution of proportions will be a discrete distribution and, as we have seen before, when approximating a discrete distribution by a continuous one, in this case the normal distribution, a correction for continuity has to be made.

Example 5: An electronic tape process produces 2000 tapes per day. Each day a sample of 40 tapes is tested for defectives. If the process usually produces 8% defectives how many of 30 consecutive days' samples will show 2 to 6 defectives.

Answer

$\underset{\sim}{\bar{x}}$ will be normally distributed with $E(\underset{\sim}{\bar{x}}) = 0{\cdot}08$ and

$$\text{Var}(\underset{\sim}{\bar{x}}) = \frac{0{\cdot}08 \times 0{\cdot}92}{40} = 0{\cdot}00184.$$

We consider the standardised random variable

$$\underset{\sim}{z} = \frac{\underset{\sim}{\bar{x}} - \pi}{\sqrt{\dfrac{\pi(1-\pi)}{n}}} = \frac{\bar{x} - 0{\cdot}08}{\sqrt{0{\cdot}00184}}$$

The range of 2 to 6 defectives when corrected for continuity becomes 1·5 to 6·5 defectives. We therefore need the z score of $\frac{1\cdot5}{40}$ and $\frac{6\cdot5}{40}$.

$$z\left(\frac{1\cdot5}{40}\right) = \frac{\frac{1\cdot5}{40} - 0\cdot08}{\sqrt{0\cdot00184}} = -0\cdot983$$

$$z\left(\frac{6\cdot5}{40}\right) = \frac{\frac{6\cdot5}{40} - 0\cdot08}{\sqrt{0\cdot00184}} = 1\cdot92$$

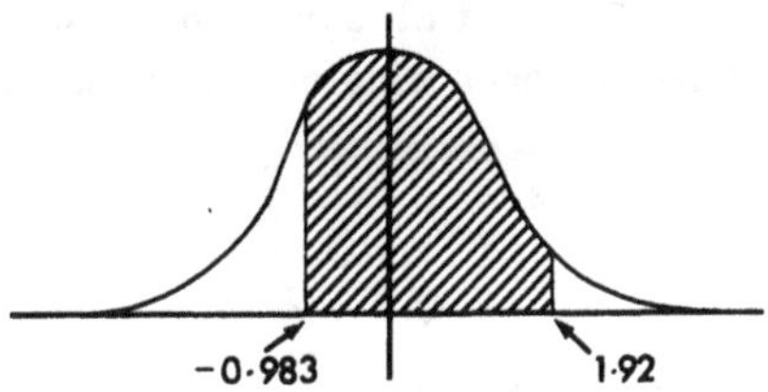

Fig. 8.8(b)

The area between these two z scores is $0\cdot3371 + 0\cdot4726 = 0\cdot8097$. Therefore out of 30 samples $30 \times 0\cdot8097 \simeq 24$ will have between 2 and 6 defectives.

8.9 Confidence Intervals for Proportions

We come now to the problem of estimating π, the proportion of successes in a population, from $\bar{x}$, the proportion of successes in a sample of size n.

The first method we look at is that of continuous sampling. If several samples can be taken a graph of the proportions obtained can be made and then π can be estimated from this graph. If we let p be the estimate of π from this graph, then

$$\sqrt{\frac{p(1-p)}{n}}$$

will be an estimate of the standard deviation of this sampling distribution and a confidence interval for π can be found by considering

$$z = \frac{p - \pi}{\sqrt{\frac{p(1-p)}{n}}}$$

The reader is urged to perform an experiment along the following lines.

Put a large number of marbles in a bag or box and then arrange for so many of them to be marked. If marbles are not readily available objects such as peas, beans, bolts and so on are just as good. The marking must obviously be such that any particular object does not become more liable to be selected in a sample than an unmarked one. Having thus set up the model take continuous samples with replacement and graph the results. Then estimate the proportion of marked objects – successes – in the population from the graph and check the result with the actual population.

Continuous sampling may not always be possible and so we look at a method of estimating π from a single sample. We know that

$$z = \frac{p - \pi}{\sqrt{\dfrac{\pi(1 - \pi)}{n}}}$$

will be normally distributed $N(0,1)$ and we use the value of p given by the sample to estimate $\pi(1 - \pi)$; that is we use

$$z = \frac{p - \pi}{\sqrt{\dfrac{pq}{n}}}$$

and apply the previous methods.

Example 1: Find a 95% confidence level for π if a sample of 100 contained 20 successes.

Answer

$$p = \tfrac{20}{100} = \tfrac{1}{5}$$

$$pq = \tfrac{1}{5} \times \tfrac{4}{5} = \tfrac{4}{25}$$

$$\frac{pq}{n} = \tfrac{4}{2500} \quad \text{so} \quad \sqrt{\frac{pq}{n}} = \tfrac{2}{50} = \tfrac{1}{25}$$

Substituting these results in the above formula gives

$$z = \frac{\tfrac{1}{5} - \pi}{\tfrac{1}{25}} \quad \text{and using}$$

$$P(-1{\cdot}96 \leqslant z \leqslant 1{\cdot}96) = 95\%, \quad \text{we get}$$

$$P(\tfrac{-1{\cdot}96}{25} \leqslant \tfrac{1}{5} - \pi \leqslant \tfrac{1{\cdot}96}{25}) = 95\%$$

$$P(-0{\cdot}0784 \leqslant 0{\cdot}2 - \pi \leqslant 0{\cdot}0784) = 95\%$$

$$P(0{\cdot}0784 + 0{\cdot}2 \leqslant \pi \leqslant 0{\cdot}2 - 0{\cdot}0784) = 95\%$$

$$P(0{\cdot}2784 \leqslant \pi \leqslant 0{\cdot}1216) = 95\%$$

that is we can be 95% sure that π lies in the interval 0·1216 and 0·2784.

Just as in the case of the mean of a population we can evaluate the sample size required to estimate π to a given degree of precision. Suppose we wish to work to a 95% limit, then

$$P(-1{\cdot}96 \leqslant z \leqslant {\cdot}196) = 95\%$$

where z is a value of

$$z = \frac{p - \pi}{\sqrt{\dfrac{\pi(1 - \pi)}{n}}}$$

Then

$$-1{\cdot}96 \leqslant \frac{p - \pi}{\sqrt{\dfrac{\pi(1 - \pi)}{n}}}$$

which rearranges to

$$\frac{-1{\cdot}96\sqrt{\pi(1 - \pi)}}{(p - \pi)} \leqslant \sqrt{n}$$

giving finally

$$\frac{(-1{\cdot}96)^2\pi(1 - \pi)}{(p - \pi)^2} \leqslant n$$

and this is the required sized sample.

Now an obvious snag to this result is that to use it we need to know π, a value we are trying to estimate. It is therefore necessary to try a pilot study first and get some estimate of π. Assuming this to have been done and a value of 0·3 obtained, then if we are to risk an error of 0·6% – that is the difference between our estimate of π and the true value of π – at a confidence level of 95% then we get

$$\frac{(-1{\cdot}96)^2(9{\cdot}3)(0{\cdot}7)}{(0{\cdot}06)^2} \leqslant n$$

giving

$$n \geqslant 225.$$

In general terms, if a sample produces p, an estimate of π, then if we are prepared to risk an error of $x\%$, that is $p - \pi = x$, then a further sample to estimate the true value of π will be of size

$$n \geqslant \frac{k^2 p(1 - p)}{x^2}$$

where k is related to the standardised normal curve so that the area between $-k$ and $+k$ is $c\%$, where c is the confidence level.

Example 2: The BBC knows from experience that a certain type of programme attracts about 10% of the listening audience. If they wish to find what proportion of their audience listened to a particular programme and they will risk a 5% error at a 90% level of confidence, how large should their sample be.

Answer

$p = 0{\cdot}1.\ c = 90\%$, so that $k = 1{\cdot}65.\ x = 0{\cdot}05$. Thus

$$n \geqslant \frac{(1{\cdot}65)^2(0{\cdot}1)(0{\cdot}9)}{(0{\cdot}05)^2}$$

giving $$n \geqslant 98.$$

8.10 Concluding Remarks

We have now looked at the sampling distributions of the mean and proportions. The sampling distributions of other statistics can be treated in exactly the same fashion. The following table shows the other sampling distributions commonly met.

Sampling distribution	mean	standard deviation	Notes
variances (normal population)	$\frac{\sigma^2(n-1)}{n}$	$\sigma^2\sqrt{\frac{2}{n}}$	When $n \geqslant 100$ the sampling distributions of s^2 and s are approximately normal. If the population moments $\mu_4(\mu)$ etc., are not known then a good approximation can be made to them by using the sample moments $m_4(\bar{x})$, and so on.
variances (non-normal population)	$\frac{\sigma^2(n-1)}{n}$	$\sqrt{\frac{\mu_4(\mu)-\mu_2^2(\mu)}{n}}$	
standard deviation (normal population)	very close to σ	$\frac{\sigma}{\sqrt{2n}}$	
standard deviation (non-normal population)	very close to σ	$\sqrt{\frac{\mu_4(\mu)-\mu_2^2(\mu)}{4n\mu_2^2(\mu)}}$	
median (normal or approximately normal population)	μ	$\frac{1{\cdot}25\sigma}{\sqrt{n}}$	When $n \geqslant 30$ the sampling distribution of the median is normally distributed.

The standard deviation of a sampling distribution is frequently called its *standard error*. Thus we get *the standard error of the mean* meaning the standard deviation of the sampling distribution of the mean. A similar interpretation is used for phrases such as *the standard error of proportions* and so on.

It is important to have some knowledge of the sampling distribution of a statistic because it is then possible to interpret an individual sample not only in relation to the population but in relation to other samples (actual and potential) from the population. It is possible to assign probability values to any range of values it might take just by using the figures given by the normal curve tables. It is important to remember that the sampling distribution of a statistic will vary for different values of n – in fact there will be a different sampling distribution for each value of n – since many of the parameters of the sampling distribution are calculated by using n at some stage.

It will be seen from the forgoing that some sampling distributions are normally distributed for $n \geqslant 30$ but others require $n \geqslant 100$ for a normal distribution; while on the other hand some sampling distributions are normal for values of n less than 30. These different figures tend to be confusing. It will help to clarify things if we consider exactly what is meant by large sampling theory. Generally this is concerned with situations where the sampling distribution of a statistic is normally distributed. Thus even small samples from a normal population can be treated under large sampling theory because their sampling distribution is normal. The theoretical justification for this is to be found in the *central limit theorem.*

Not all sampling distributions are normally distributed. In particular small samples are usually non-normal in their sampling distributions and so normal distribution theory cannot be applied to them. They have to be treated differently and the so called *small sampling theory* (a better terminology would be *exact sampling theory*) has been developed. This is looked at in the next chapter.

Exercise 8

1, A large population has mean 25 and standard deviation 4·5. Find the mean and standard deviation of the sampling distribution of the mean for samples of (a) 25 (b) 35 (c) 150 if sampling is without replacement.

Answer

(a) 25, 0·9 (c) 25, 0·037

2. If the population in the previous question is normal, find the mean

and standard deviation of the sampling distribution of the mean for samples of (a) 3 (b) 5 (c) 15.

Answer

(a) 25, 2·6 (c) 25, 1·16

3. A population has mean 40″ and standard deviation 9″. What size sample must be taken to ensure that the sample mean will be 99% sure of being within (a) 2″ of the population mean (b) 3″ of the population mean, sampling with replacement.

Answer

(a) $n \geqslant 135$.

4. If a normal population has mean 100 and standard deviation 15, what is the probability that the mean of a sample of 36 will be (a) above 105 (b) below 100 (c) between 99 and 101.

Answer

(a) 0·022 (c) 0·31.

5. If in the previous question the sample size is 16, between what two values would the mean of the sample lie, with probability of 95·44%.

Answer

92·5 to 107·5.

6. If a normal population has mean 90 and standard deviation 10, find n, the sample size, to be 95% sure that the mean of a sample will be (a) below 93 (b) above 86 (c) between 88 and 92.

Answer

(a) $n \geqslant 43$ (b) $n \geqslant 25$

7. If in question 6 you wish to be 95% sure that the mean of the sample lies between 98 and 102 what size sample would you take?

Answer

225.

8. A sample of 36 gives a mean of 15 and a standard deviation of 9. Find the 95% and 99% confidence intervals for the population mean.

Answer

95% interval 12·06 to 17·94.

9. Repeat the previous question if the sample size is 100 and the sample mean and variance are 71·5 and 10 respectively.

Answer

99% interval 70·63 to 72·32.

10. A normal population has a variance of 9. What size sample must be taken so that it is 90% sure that the sample mean will not differ from the true mean by more than 1?

Answer

$n \geqslant 24$

11. A normal population has a mean of 168 and a standard deviation of 3. Samples of 25 are taken. Find the mean and standard deviation of the sampling distribution of the mean.
If 70 samples of 25 are taken how many would you expect to give mean less than 166·8 or more than 169·2.

Answer

mean = 168, standard deviation = 0·6.

12. A machine produces 1″ nails and previous experience has shown that those nails may be considered as a normal population, with mean 1″ and standard deviation 0·05″. A sampling process selects 4 nails at random and calculates their mean. 40 samples are taken daily. How many of these would you expect to produce means between 1″ ± 0·05″?

Answer

38

13. A fair coin is tossed 200 times. Find the probability that (a) less than 80 will be heads and (b) between 86 and 114 will be tails.

Answer

(a) 0·002 (b) 0·96

14. The probability of passing a driving test at the first attempt is $\frac{6}{10}$. Fifty samples of 20 people just having taken their tests are taken. How many of these samples would you expect to contain (a) 12 passes and 8 failures (b) equal numbers of passes and failures?

Answer

(a) 9 (b) 6

15. A binomial population contains 40% successes. Samples of 20 are taken from this population. Find the mean and standard deviation of the sampling distribution of proportions. If fifty samples are taken how many would you expect to contain (a) 10 or more successes (b) exactly 12 successes?

Answer

p = 0·4. Standard deviation = 0·0346 (a) 12 (b) 2

16. The heights of 300 fifth formers are normally distributed with mean 65″ and standard deviation 3·2″. If samples of 20 were taken what would be the mean and standard deviation of the sampling distribution of the mean if sampling is (a) without replacement (b) with replacement?

Answer

(a) $\bar{x}_{\bar{x}} = 65''$ $s_{\bar{x}} = 0{\cdot}8''$ (b) $\bar{x}_{\bar{x}} = 65''$ $s_{\bar{x}} = 0{\cdot}72''$

17. A population of 500 contains 200 successes. Find the mean and standard deviation of the sampling distribution of proportions for samples of (a) 30 (b) 40 (c) 50

Answer

(b) 0·4, 0·0126

18. Perform the experiments as suggested at the beginning of 8.9. Vary (a) the proportion of successes in the population and (b) the size of the sample.

19. Select three dominoes, with replacement, from a set. Record the total number of spots on them. Repeat and record successively until you can estimate the average number of spots per dominoe. Then check your result by examing the full set. Try sampling without replacement – does it make any difference? Try samples of 2, 4, and so on, – do you arrive at a decision any quicker?

20. A sample of 500 had 80 successes in it. Find (a) 95% and (b) 99% confidence limits for π.

Answer

(b) 0·12 to 0·20

21. If in the previous question the sample had been 1,000 with 160 successes what would the difference in the confidence intervals be?

22. A manufacturing process habitually produces 12% defective items. If the manufacturer will only risk a 2% error at a 95% level of confidence what sample size must be taken to see if the process is working normally?

Answer

1522.

23. If the manufacturer of the previous question will risk a 5% error how will this affect the sample size?

Answer

n reduces to 244.

24. Explain in your own words the relationship between (a) the confidence interval (b) the degree of confidence (c) the sample size (d) the difference between the true value of π and an estimate.

9 Small Sampling Theory

9.1 Introduction

We have seen that the sampling distribution of the mean is distributed normally, $N(\mu,\frac{\sigma^2}{n})$ and that

$$z = \frac{\bar{x} - \mu}{\frac{\sigma}{\sqrt{n}}}$$

is distributed normally, $N(0,1)$. We have also seen that it is not usually the case that we know the variance of a population from which we take samples and so we used s^2 as an estimate of σ^2 and considered

$$z = \frac{\bar{x} - \mu}{\frac{s}{\sqrt{n}}}$$

Now as long as n is large s^2 is a fairly good estimate of σ^2 and this procedure is permissible. However when n is small s^2 is not a good estimate of σ^2 and so we have to consider what effect the substitution of s for σ will have in this case. What emerges is that

$$z = \frac{\bar{x} - \mu}{\frac{s}{\sqrt{n}}}$$

is no longer normally distributed but has a distribution which differs slightly. We examine this new distribution in the following sections.

9.2 Best estimate of σ^2

We have seen that it is possible to estimate the variance of a population by using s^2 from a sample where

$$s^2 = \frac{\sum_i f_i(x_i - \bar{x})^2}{n}$$

We also remarked earlier that a sample will not be expected to contain such extreme values as the population from which it is drawn so that s^2 will be expected to be slightly smaller than σ^2. A better estimate of σ^2 is obtained from a sample if

$$\hat{s}^2 = \frac{\sum f_i(x_i - \bar{x})^2}{n - 1} = \frac{n}{n-1} s^2$$

is used and $\hat{s}^2$ is called the 'best estimate' of σ^2. It should be noted that there may be particular cases where s^2 is closer to σ^2 than $\hat{s}^2$ – this is all part of the uncertainty of sampling – but in general $\hat{s}^2$ will be closer to σ^2 than s^2.

Since $\hat{s}^2$ is a better estimate of σ^2 than s^2 some statisticians prefer to define the variance initially as

$$\frac{\sum f_i(x_i - \bar{x})^2}{n - 1}$$

We do not adopt this approach and s^2 and $\hat{s}^2$ will be defined as above. Note that if n is large then $\frac{n}{n-1} \simeq 1$ and $\hat{s}^2$ approaches s^2. The reader should ensure that he understands the difference between σ^2, s^2 and $\hat{s}^2$.

9.3 Student's t Distribution

For small n $\hat{s}^2$ is the best estimate of σ^2, but because it will differ from σ^2 we can no longer use the related variable z which is distributed normally, $N(0,1)$. We therefore define the variable t

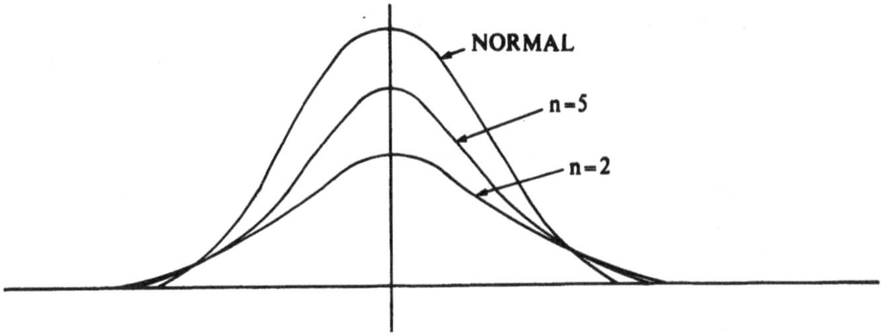

Fig. 9.3(a)

Distribution of t for $n = 5$ and $n = 2$, compared with a normal distribution.

$$t = \frac{\bar{x} - \mu}{\frac{\hat{s}}{\sqrt{n}}}$$

which will be seen to be analogous to z. The difference between the normal distribution, $N(0,1)$ of z and the distribution of t is shown, for different values of n, in Figure 9.3(a).

It will be seen from this diagram that the smaller value of n – the sample size – the wider the distribution of t. For higher values of n the t distribution approaches the normal distribution, and for large n, that is $n \gg 30$, the approximation is very good.

The area under the t-curve represents probabilities in just the same way as the area under the normal curve represents probabilities. Therefore to find the probability that any particular value t of t falls within any particular interval a similar procedure as was used for the z score is followed. There is one difference however and this involves the notion of 'degrees of freedom' which is now explained.

The notion of 'degrees of freedom' as used in statistics is a difficult one and is perhaps best approached by an example. Imagine a box with six compartments and six balls to be placed one to a compartment. The first ball may be placed in any of the six compartments, the second may be placed in any of the remaining five compartments, and so on until all the balls are placed. Now for the first five balls there will always be a choice of two or more compartments, but when the last ball is to be placed there will be no choice. Under these circumstances we say that five out of the six balls could be 'freely placed' so that there are five *degrees of freedom* in this exercise.

Thus we define the *number of degrees of freedom of a statistic* as the maximum number of variates that may be freely assigned in the calculation of this statistic. It is denoted by the greek letter ν and for any t score $\nu = 1$.

(If the reader finds this difficult he may be assured that continued familiarity with the idea will eventually produce understanding. In the meantime to calculate ν for any situation only a simple subtraction is required).

9.4 Equation of the t Distribution

The equation of the distribution of t is given by

$$g(t) = \frac{K}{\left(1 + \frac{t^2}{n-1}\right)^{\frac{n}{2}}} = K\left(1 + \frac{t^2}{n-1}\right)^{-\frac{n}{2}} = K\left(1 + \frac{t^2}{\nu}\right)^{-\frac{(\nu+1)}{2}} \quad -\infty < t < \infty$$

where K is a constant but depends on ν and is chosen in such a way as to make the total area under the curve equal to 1. It will be seen therefore that the distribution of t satisfies the conditions of a probability distribution.

When ν exceeds 30 $g(t)$ can be approximated with the standard normal distribution

$$f(t) = \frac{1}{\sqrt{2\pi}} e^{-\frac{t^2}{2}} \quad -\infty < t < \infty$$

It will be noted that the t distribution has a range $-\infty$ to $+\infty$, just as in the case of the normal distribution. It is also symmetrical about zero and whilst in shape it is similar to the normal distribution it has a wider dispersion than the latter, especially when the number of degrees of freedom is small. It is fortunately not necessary to fully understand the rather complex formula given above because tables have been produced which give the various required areas under the curve and between two limits; again, just as in the case of the normal distribution.

9.5 Area under the t-curve and use of t-tables

As previously stated the area under the t-curve represents probabilities in just the same way as the area under the z-curve.

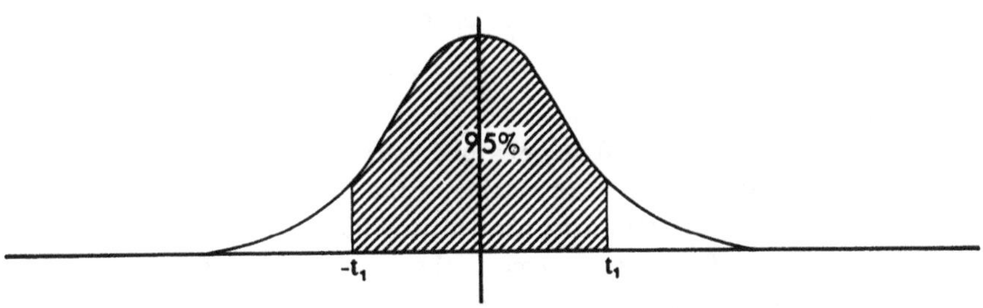

Fig. 9.5(a)

That is for a given value t_1, a certain percentage of the area will lie between $-t_1$ and $+t_1$ (with the necessary allowance for the number of degrees of freedom). If, for example, t_1 is such that 95% of the area under the curve lies between $-t_1$ and $+t_1$ then we can be 95% certain that any value of t obtained from a sample will lie between $-t_1$ and $+t_1$.

If t should lie outside these values then we say that it differs significantly at the 95% level of confidence.

In practice we are interested in values of t which are significant at various levels of confidence and so we are interested in the areas in the two tails of the distribution of t. Thus the table given in Appendix 4 is arranged so that it is the area in the two tails that is used.

Example 1: The t-curve for 10 degrees of freedom is shown in the diagram

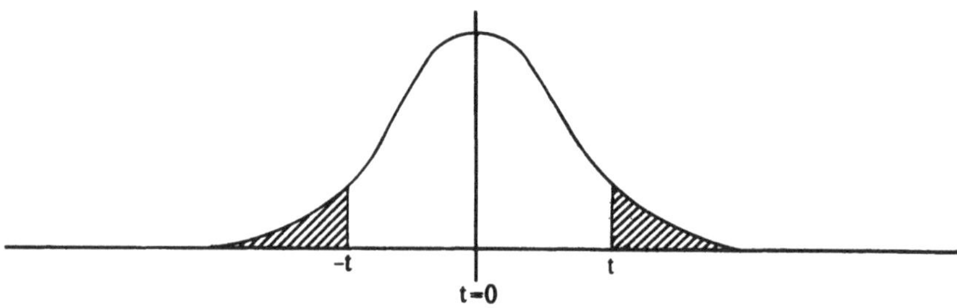

Fig. 9.5(b)

Find the values of t for which

(a) The total area shaded is 0·05

(b) The total area shaded is 10%

(c) The area shaded in the upper tail is 0·01

(d) The unshaded area between $-t$ and $t = 0$ is 0·45.

Answer

(a) Since there are 10 degrees of freedom (samples of size 11) we are concerned only with the entries in the horizontal line level with $\nu = 10$. Since the total area shaded is 0·05 we look down the column headed $A = 0{\cdot}05$ until we come to the $\nu = 10$ line. This gives the value 2·228 and so $t = 2{\cdot}228$ and $-t = -2{\cdot}228$.

(b) Since 10% of the area = 0·1 of the area, we look down the column headed $A = 0{\cdot}1$. This gives 1·812 and so $t = 1{\cdot}812$ and $-t = -1{\cdot}812$.

(c) If the area shaded in the upper tail is 0·01 then the area shaded in the lower tail will be 0·01. Therefore the total area shaded will be 0·02 and looking down the column headed $A = 0{\cdot}02$ we get 2·764. Therefore $t = 2{\cdot}764$.

(d) If the unshaded area between $-t$ and $t = 0$ is 0·45 then the area shaded in the lower tail will be 0·05. The total area shaded will be 0·1 and $-t = -1{\cdot}812$ from (b).

Note.

In (a) the total area shaded is 0·05, that is 5%, and the lower and upper values of t are $-2{\cdot}228$ and $+2{\cdot}228$. This means that if samples of 11 are taken and the t scores calculated and then this t score lies outside the range $-2{\cdot}228$ to $+2{\cdot}228$, we say that this value of t is significant at the 95% level of confidence. Therefore we would only expect a t score outside this range 5 times out of 100. A similar remark applies to other t scores and other levels of confidence.

Example 2: The t-curve for 15 degrees of freedom is shown in the diagram

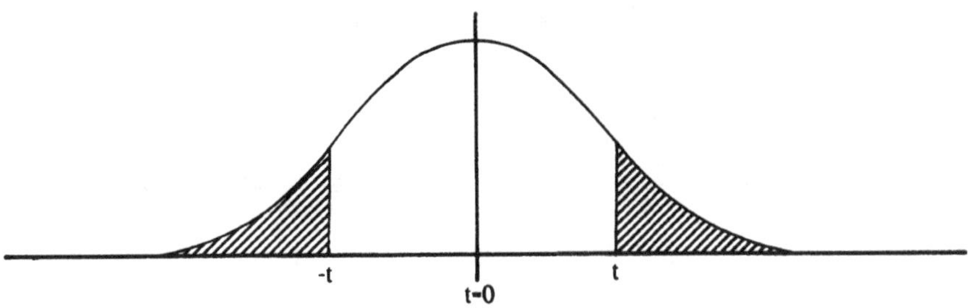

Fig. 9.5(c)

Find the area shaded for the following values of t.

(a) $t = 4{\cdot}073$

(b) $t = -2{\cdot}602$

(c) $t = 2{\cdot}36$

Answer

(a) Since there are 15 degrees of freedom (samples of 16) we are concerned only with the entries in the horizontal line level with $\nu = 15$. For $t = 4{\cdot}073$ we look along the horizontal line for $\nu = 15$ until we find it. Having found it we now look at the column headed $A = 0{\cdot}001$ the area shaded is 0·001.

(b) Since t is negative we know that it lies in the left hand half of the curve. Ignoring the negative sign we look in the table level with $\nu = 15$ until we find 2·602. Having found this entry we look at the column heading and find $A = 0{\cdot}02$, so that for $t = -2{\cdot}602$ the area shaded is 0·02.

(c) Again looking along the line level with $\nu = 15$ we see that 2·36 is between 2·131 and 2·602. We therefore have to use interpolation. 2·36 is roughly half way between 2·131 and 2·602 but is slightly closer to 2·131 than 2·602. Interpolating between $A = 0{\cdot}05$ and $A = 0{\cdot}02$ we arrive at 0·037. Thus 0·037 is the area shaded for $t = 2{\cdot}36$.

Example 3: A machine cuts wood into 29 centimetre lengths. A sample of 16 lengths was found to have a mean of 28 cms and a standard deviation of 3 cms. Is the machine working properly?

Answer

We proceed to calculate the t score for this sample.

$$s^2 = 9$$

$$\hat{s}^2 = \frac{n}{n-1}s^2 = \tfrac{16}{15} \times 9 = \tfrac{144}{15}$$

$$\hat{s} = \frac{12}{\sqrt{15}}$$

Now
$$\frac{\hat{s}}{\sqrt{n}} = \frac{\hat{s}}{\sqrt{16}} = \frac{\hat{s}}{4} = \frac{1}{4} \times \frac{12}{\sqrt{15}} = \frac{3}{\sqrt{15}} = 0{\cdot}78$$

$$t = \frac{\bar{x} - \mu}{\frac{\hat{s}}{\sqrt{n}}} = \frac{28 - 29}{0{\cdot}78} = \frac{-1}{0{\cdot}78} = -1{\cdot}28$$

We now consider −1·28. The minus sign tells us that this reading falls on the left hand side of the t curve.

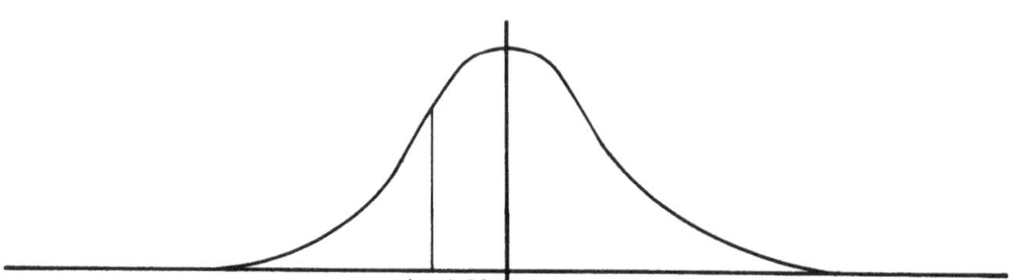

Fig. 9.5(d)

but for the purpose of the t table we have to ignore the minus sign and consider 1·28.

Looking in the table for the horizontal line level with $\nu = 15$ we see that the lowest reading is 1·753 and this is in the column headed $A = 0{\cdot}1$.

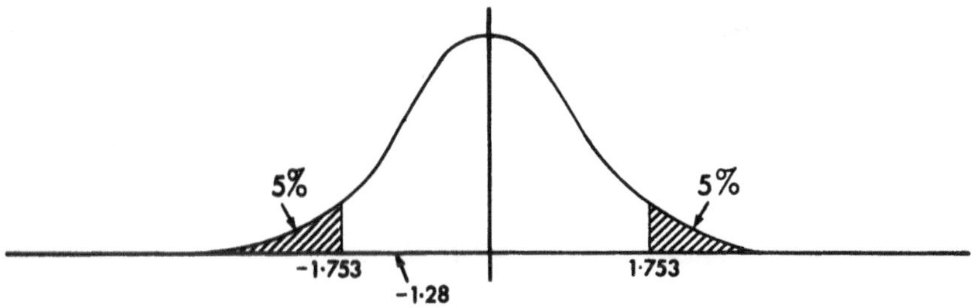

Fig. 9.5(e)

This means that as our reading is only –1·28 it is within the unshaded area which represents 90% of the total area under the curve. This in turn means that the reading of –1·28 is not significant at the 90% level of confidence.

For this situation any t score will be significant at the 90% level only if $|t| \geqslant 1{\cdot}753$. For any t score to be significant at the 95% level then $|t| \geqslant 2{\cdot}131$. For any t score to be significant at the 98% level then $|t| \geqslant 2{\cdot}602$, and so on.

If in practice a machine was being run and tested at the 95% level and a test sample produced a t score of 2·1 which is only slightly less than the 95% confidence level of 2·131 then this would be regarded as a warning sign that something might have gone wrong and another sample would be taken immediately to check. If the t score of this second sample was much smaller then the machine would not be stopped, it being realised that one of the rarer samples had been found. If however the t score was still high then the machine would be stopped and checked.

9.6 Confidence limits for means

The work of this section is analogous to the work of Sections 8.5, 8.6, and 8.7, on the confidence limits for an unknown mean μ using the fact that $\bar{x}$ for large samples is normally distributed. The problem for smaller samples when a t distribution has to be used is approached by example.

Example 1: A sample of 26 was found to have a mean of 38 and a standard deviation of 3. Find the 95% confidence limits for the mean of the population.

Answer

The first point to note is that as the sample size is 26 there will be 25 degrees of freedom and so we are concerned with a t distribution with 25 degrees of freedom. From the t table we get the limits for 95% of the area under the curve to be ±2·06.

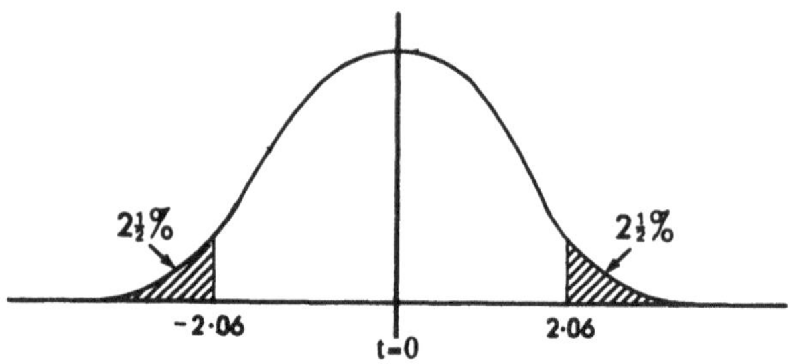

Fig. 9.6(a)

We now argue that 95% of the samples will produce a value of t lying in this interval, so that the probability of any single sample producing a value of t within this interval is 0·95, that is $P(-2{\cdot}06 \leqslant t \leqslant 2{\cdot}06) = 0{\cdot}95$. From this we get

$$P\left(-2{\cdot}06 \leqslant \frac{\bar{x} - \mu}{\frac{\hat{s}}{\sqrt{n}}} \leqslant 2{\cdot}06\right) = 0{\cdot}95$$

Taking the expression in the bracket

$$-2{\cdot}06 \leqslant \frac{\bar{x} - \mu}{\frac{\hat{s}}{\sqrt{n}}} \leqslant 2{\cdot}06$$

this becomes

$$-2{\cdot}06 \times \frac{\hat{s}}{\sqrt{n}} \leqslant \bar{x} - \mu \leqslant 2{\cdot}06 \times \frac{\hat{s}}{\sqrt{n}}$$

$$\therefore \quad -\bar{x} - 2{\cdot}06 \times \frac{\hat{s}}{\sqrt{n}} \leqslant -\mu \leqslant -\bar{x} + 2{\cdot}06 \times \frac{\hat{s}}{\sqrt{n}}$$

multiplying through by −1 and changing the direction of the inequality signs gives

$$\bar{x} + 2{\cdot}06 \times \frac{\hat{s}}{\sqrt{n}} \geqslant \mu \geqslant \bar{x} - 2{\cdot}06 \times \frac{\hat{s}}{\sqrt{n}}$$

and we now have, by rearranging,

$$P(\bar{x} - 2{\cdot}06 \times \frac{\hat{s}}{\sqrt{n}} \geqslant \mu \geqslant \bar{x} + 2{\cdot}06 \times \frac{\hat{s}}{\sqrt{n}}) = 0{\cdot}95$$

We now calculate the required figures for the example.

$$s^2 = 9$$

$$\therefore \hat{s}^2 = \tfrac{26}{25} \times 9$$

giving

$$\hat{s} = \tfrac{3}{5}\sqrt{26}$$

$$\frac{\hat{s}}{\sqrt{n}} = \frac{3}{5}\frac{\sqrt{26}}{\sqrt{26}} = \frac{3}{5} = 0{\cdot}6$$

Substituting in the above

$$P(38 - 2{\cdot}06 \times 0{\cdot}6 \leqslant \mu \leqslant 38 + 2{\cdot}06 \times 0{\cdot}6) = 0{\cdot}95$$

giving

$$P(38 - 1{\cdot}236 \leqslant \mu \leqslant 38 + 1{\cdot}236) = 0{\cdot}95$$

that is

$$P(36 \leqslant 764\,\mu \leqslant 39{\cdot}236) = 0{\cdot}95$$

Thus the confidence interval for the mean at a 95% level of confidence is 36·764 to 39·236.

Thus we see that small samples are treated in just the same way as large samples but that the normal curve for the large samples is replaced by a t distribution with the required number of degrees of freedom.

Example 2: Show that the confidence limits for a mean can be written

$$\bar{x} \pm t_c \times \frac{\hat{s}}{\sqrt{n}}$$

where t_c is the value of t for a given confidence level obtained from the t table for $n - 1$ degrees of freedom.

Answer

We leave this for the reader. (Hint: start with $P(-t_c \leqslant t \leqslant t_c) = c$)

9.7 Restrictions

Unfortunately the t test is not of universal application. Strictly speaking it can only be applied to samples taken from normal populations but in practice if a population is nearly normal the t test can be used without too much difficulty. The reason for this restriction is to be found in the mathematical theory which develops the t distribution.

Although limited to normal or nearly normal populations the t test is used a great deal because so many populations are in fact normally distributed.

It should be noted that it is often suggested that a better name than *small sampling theory* would be *exact sampling theory* because the results obtained apply to large as well as small samples.

9.8 Historical

The problem concerned with determining what effect substituting s for σ had in sampling situations was first studied by the statistician W.S. Gossett who was employed by Guinness' Brewery in Dublin. At that time this brewery did not permit research done by its staff to be published under their own names so Gossett chose the pen name 'Student', and the t distribution is frequently called 'Student-t distribution'.

Exercise 9

1. For the normal curve the 95% confidence limits are given by $z = \pm 1{\cdot}96$. Find the corresponding t values for the t distribution if the number of degrees of freedom is (a) 5 (b) 10 (c) 15 (d) 30

Answer

(a) $\pm 2{\cdot}57$ (b) $\pm 2{\cdot}23$ (c) $\pm 2{\cdot}13$ (d) $\pm 2{\cdot}04$

2. Repeat the previous question for 99% confidence intervals.

Answer

(a) $\pm 4{\cdot}03$ (b) $\pm 3{\cdot}17$ (c) $\pm 2{\cdot}95$ (d) $\pm 2{\cdot}75$

3. A sample of 5 six-inch nails gave a mean of $6{\cdot}01''$ and $s = 0{\cdot}04''$. Find the 95% and 99% confidence limits for the population mean length.

Answer

95% limits $5{\cdot}96''$ to $6{\cdot}06''$.

4. If large sampling methods were used for the previous example what would the difference be? Can you justify using these methods in the case?

5. A sample of 5 produced a mean of 35 and $s^2 = 8$. Find the 95% confidence interval for the population mean.

Answer

23·9 to 46·1

6. Repeat the previous question for samples of (a) 10 (b) 15 (c) 20 assuming each sample produces a mean of 35 and $s = 8$. What do you notice as the sample size increases?

7. A population has a standard deviation of 4. A sample of 6 had a mean of 28. Find the 90% confidence limits for the population mean. Justify in writing your method.

Answer

24·71 to 31·29

8. A population has a standard deviation of 16. A sample of 8 gave values 113, 121, 117, 102, 111, 131, 135, 119. Find the 95% confidence limits for the population mean.

Answer

105·24 to 132·02

9. Repeat the previous question assuming that the population standard deviation is not known.

10. A sample of 5 produced 95% confidence limits for the population mean of 11·45 and 17·78. Find the mean and standard deviation of the sample.

Answer

$\bar{x} = 14{\cdot}615, \ \hat{s} = 3{\cdot}187$

11. Repeat the previous question assuming that the given figures are (a) 90% and (b) 99% confidence limits.

12. A machine produces 5″ screws. To check that the machine is working under control a sample of 10 screws is taken. This sample gave a mean of 5·3″ and $s = 0{\cdot}3''$. Do these results indicate the machine is still under control and what action should be taken?

Answer

These figures are significant at the 95% level but not at the 99% level. The machine is *possibly* out of control, but another sample should be taken immediately to confirm or deny the first sample results.

13. Five fishing lines with a reputed breaking strength of 30lbs broke under the following pressures: 32, 33, 35, 36, 38lbs. Find the 95% confidence limits for the actual mean of the breaking strengths. Is the manufacturer giving his customers good value?

Answer

34·8 ± 3. Yes.

14. A watch was tested over a 5 day period and its gain or loss to the nearest second was recorded as –3, 12, 0, 1, 3 secs. Find the 2 limits – at the 99% level – between which you would expect this watch to work in the future.

Answer

–4·7 to 5·1 secs.

15. A manufacturer claims a lifetime of 750 hours for his light bulbs. Twelve of his bulbs are tested and produce a mean of 738 hours and $s = 124$ hours. Does this evidence support the manufacturer's claim?

Answer

It does not dispute the manufacturer's claim.

16. In the previous question what sample mean would dispute this manufacturer's claim? (Assume the standard deviation of the sample remains the same).

17. A manufacturer has a machine set to produce 1″ bolts. Previous sampling has shown that the mean length of the bolts produced is 1″ with $\sigma = 0{\cdot}05''$. Samples of size n are taken and 95% confidence bands are set up. Find those confidence bands if n is equal to (a) 5 (b) 7 (c) 11.

Answer

Assuming the population is not exactly normal (why?) (a) 1″ ± 0·062″ (c) 1″ ± 0·052″.

10 Chi Squared

10.1 Introduction

In Chapters 3, 4 and 5 we considered, for the binomial, Poisson and normal distributions respectively, the problem of fitting theoretical curves to empirircal data. In each case we were content to let the similarity of the two sets of figures be sufficient conviction for their match. However in all cases in statistics the fact that sets of figures *seem* to match is not enough and this qualitative assessment has to be replaced by a quantitative assessment. It is the exposition of this quantitative assessment which occupies this chapter.

10.2 Example

Suppose we are given a die and asked the question, 'Is this a fair die?' how would we decide the answer? Our reply would no doubt be along the following lines, – 'We know that if the die is fair then we would expect in a long run that the numbers 1 to 6 would occur an equal number of times, so if this die is not fair then in a long run we will not expect the numbers 1 to 6 to occur with equal frequencies'. But we also know that it is highly unlikely that in a long run, say 600 throws, we would get exactly 100 of each number appearing. We might well get something like

1	2	3	4	5	6
101	97	99	107	102	94

and looking at these figures we would say that although we have not got exactly 100 of each the frequencies are close enough to 100 so as not to matter.

However, what if, changing only two figures, the result had been

1	2	3	4	5	6
101	97	99	109	102	92

Well again we would be inclined to say that these are the sort of figures we would expect from a fair die under these circumstances.

But if we again change only two figures to

1	2	3	4	5	6
101	97	99	112	102	89

we might be a little less ready to agree that the dice was fair. Why? Because the 112 fours and 89 sixes have departed a little too far from the expected 100. It is this idea of departure from the expected that is the basis of the work of this chapter.

We now have the task of devising a mathematical test that will enable us to decide specifically when observed values have departed so far from expected values that we can say that the die is unfair. This test must produce a number which will be low when the observed and expected values are in close agreement and high when they are in disagreement. The obvious thing to do first is to find the differences between the observed and expected values and add them up.

Consider the second set of figures and subtract 100 from each

	1	2	3	4	5	6
	101	97	99	109	102	92
−100	1	−3	−1	9	2	−8

but when we add these differences they come to zero and a little reflec tion will show that this will always be the case.

We recall now that we met a similar difficulty when considering measures of dispersion and that we overcame the difficulty by squaring We use the same technique again here. Squaring the third line in the above table we get

1	9	1	81	4	64

and now the total comes to 160. It will be readily seen that this process will always produce a positive number with the required properties. It now requires only a slight modification. These figures represent the actual deviations from expected frequencies and it is better to have a measure of the average deviations from the expected values. This is obtained by dividing by the expected frequencies. The following table shows the complete calculation.

X_i	Observed frequencies O_i	Expected frequencies E_i	$(O_i - E_i)$	$(O_i - E_i)^2$	$\frac{(O_i - E_i)^2}{E_i}$
1	101	100	1	1	0·01
2	97	100	−3	9	0·09
3	99	100	−1	1	0·01
4	109	100	9	81	0·81
5	102	100	2	4	0·04
6	92	100	−8	64	0·64
			0		1·60

The final figure obtained is 1·6 and we now have to decide when this is too large for us to say that the die is fair. Before we can do this however there are some points which must be looked at.

10.3 Definition of Chi-squared (χ^2)

A measure of the deviation between observed and expected frequencies is found by using the following statistic:-

$$\chi^2 = \frac{(O_1 - E_1)^2}{E_1} + \frac{(O_2 - E_2)^2}{E_2} + \dots + \frac{(O_n - E_n)^2}{E_n}$$

$$= \sum_{i=1}^{n} \frac{(O_i - E_i)^2}{E_i}$$

This statistic, χ^2, is called chi-squared (pronounced ky-squared).

As already noted chi-squared will always be positive if there is any disagreement between observed and expected figures, and if there is no disagreement $\chi^2 = 0$. The larger the disagreement the larger χ^2 will be.

10.4 Equation of Chi-squared

Referring again to the questions of fair die. If a box contained 500 die and each one was tossed a certain number of times and χ^2 for that die calculated, and then if these 500 values of χ^2 were tabulated and then graphed as a histogram, the result would look something like the following

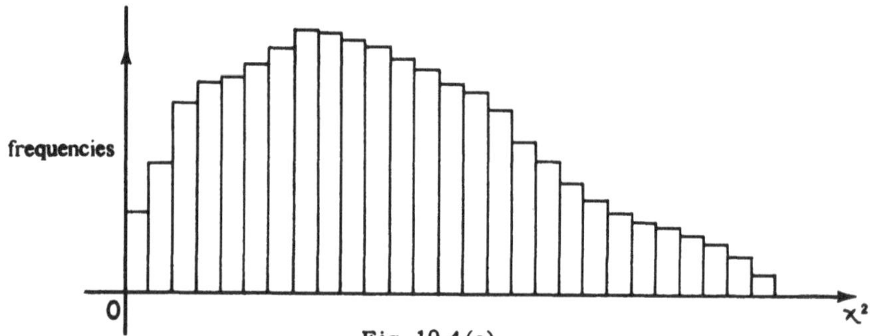

Fig. 10.4 (a)

It has been found that a probability curve or probability function which closely approximates this, and similar histograms, is the following

$$f(\chi^2) = K(\chi^2)^{(\nu-2)/2}\, e^{-(\chi^2/2)} \qquad \chi^2 \geqslant 0$$

where ν is the number of degrees of freedom, and K is a constant depending on ν and chosen in such a way as to make the area under the curve equal to unity. Just as in the case of the normal and t distributions, it is not necessary to fully understand the formula for the χ^2 distribution as tables have been produced giving required areas under the curve and between fixed limits.

The following graph shows curves for $\nu = 1$, 2, 3, 6 and 13.

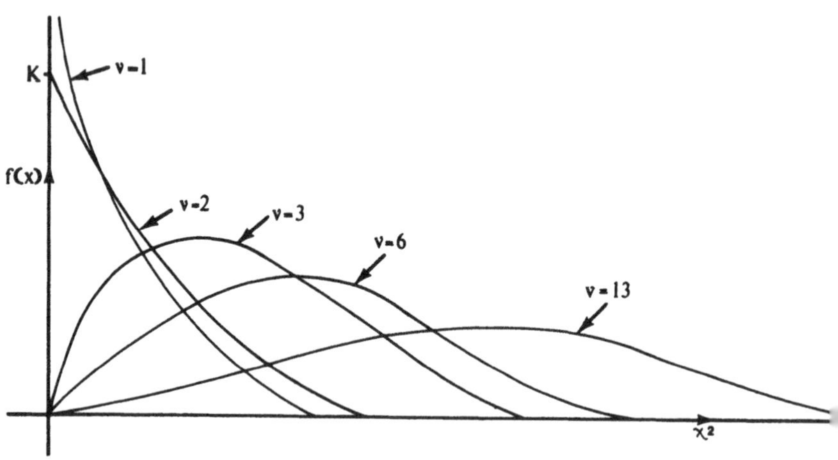

Fig. 10.4 (b)

It can be seen that theoretically χ^2 can take any value between zero and plus infinity. In practice of course, the calculation will produce a finite number. $f(\chi^2)$ generally takes smaller values than χ^2 and, except for $\nu = 1$, is finite. The mean and variance of the χ^2 distribution are ν and 2ν respectively.

For small values of χ^2 the curve is skewed to the right but for increasing ν becomes more symmetrically. When $\nu \geqslant 30$ χ^2 can be approximated with a normal distribution, see Example 1, section 10.9.

It will be noticed that for

(a) $\nu = 1$: the curve is asymptotic to the vertical and horizontal axes.

(b) $\nu = 2$: the highest point of the curve occurs at $\chi^2 = 0$ and is $f(0) = K$. The right hand tail is asymptotic to the horizontal axis.

(c) $\nu \geqslant 3$: for $\chi^2 = 0$ $f(\chi^2) = f(0) = 0$. The curves start at the origin, rise to a maximum, and then become asymptotic to the horizontal axis. For small ν the curve is skewed to the right; but as ν gets larger the curve becomes more symmetric.

Example 1: Prove that for $\nu = 2$, $f(0) = K$

Answer

For $\nu = 2$ $\quad f(\chi^2) = K(\chi^2)^0 e^{-(\chi^2/2)} = K e^{-(\chi^2/2)}$

and $\quad f(0) = K e^0 = K$

Example 2: Prove that for $\nu = 3$ the maximum value of $f(\chi^2)$ occurs at $\chi^2 = 1$, and is $\frac{6K}{10}$.

Answer

For $\nu = 3$ $\quad f(\chi^2) = K(\chi^2)^{\frac{1}{2}} e^{-(\chi^2/2)}$

Differentiating with respect to χ^2 gives

$$f'(\chi^2) = K\{\tfrac{1}{2}(\chi^2)^{-\frac{1}{2}} e^{-(\chi^2/2)} - \tfrac{1}{2}(\chi^2)^{\frac{1}{2}} e^{-(\chi^2/2)}\}$$

For a maximum $f'(\chi^2)$ must equal zero, so equating this to zero and cancelling $\frac{1}{2}K e^{-(\chi^2/2)}$ we get

$$(\chi^2)^{-\frac{1}{2}} = (\chi^2)^{\frac{1}{2}}$$

that is $\quad \chi^2 = 1$

Now $\quad f(1) = K e^{-\frac{1}{2}} = K \times 0{\cdot}6 = \frac{6K}{10}$

10.5 Area under the Chi-squared curve and use of Tables

The area under the χ^2 curve represents probabilities in just the same way that the area under the normal curve and t curve represent probabilities.

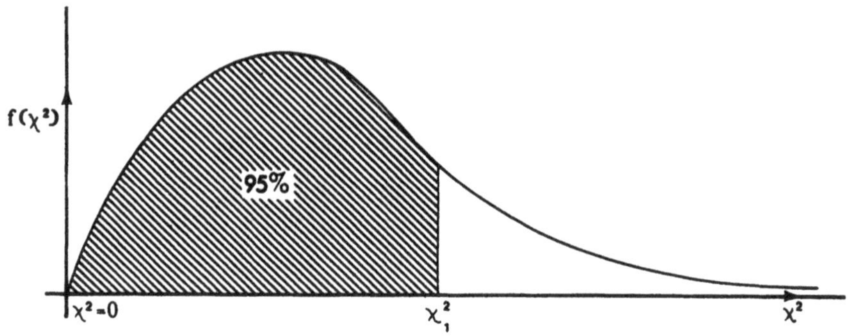

Fig. 10.5(a)

That is for a given value χ_1^2, a certain percentage of the area will lie under the curve and between $\chi^2 = 0$ and χ_1^2. (With the necessary allowance for the number of degrees of freedom)

If, for example, χ_1^2 is such that 95% of the area under the curve lies between $\chi^2 = 0$ and χ_1^2, then we can be 95% certain that any value of χ^2 obtained from a sample will lie between 0 and χ_1^2. If χ^2 should be higher in value than χ_1^2 we say that it differs significantly at the 95% level of confidence. A similar remark applies for other levels of confidence.

As stated in the previous section the chi-squared distribution has been extensively tabulated and the figures are shown in Appendix 5.

Notice that unlike the normal and *t* curves chi-squared is not symmetric so the tables will not be of the form that allows for symmetry. The area and it's relation to different values of χ^2 will have to be considered as in the following examples.

Example 1: The χ^2 curve for 12 degrees of freedom is shown in the diagram.

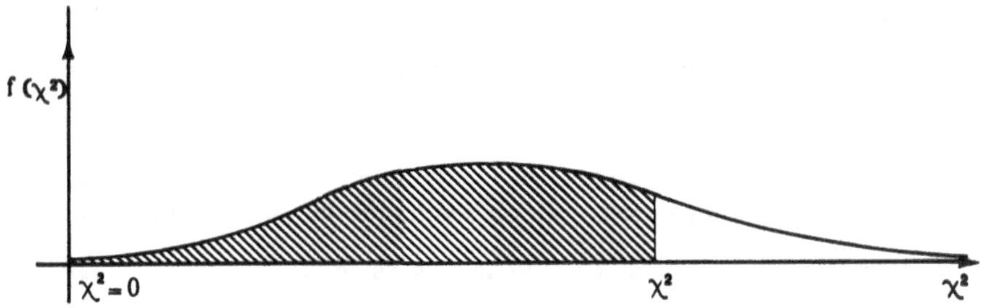

Fig. 10.5 (b)

Find the values of χ^2 for which

(a) The total area shaded is 0·5

(b) The total area unshaded is 0·80

(c) The total area shaded is 0·99

Answer

(a) Since there are 12 degrees of freedom we are concerned only with the entries in the table on the horizontal line level with $\nu = 12$. Since the total area shaded is 0·5 we look down the column headed $A = 0{\cdot}50$ until we come to the line $\nu = 12$. This gives the reading 11·340 so $\chi^2 = 11{\cdot}34$.

(b) Since 0·80 of the area is unshaded 0·20 of the area is shaded. We therefore repeat the process of part (a) but this time look in the column headed $A = 0{\cdot}20$. This procedure results in $\chi^2 = 7{\cdot}807$.

(c) Mimicking the above but using the $A = 0{\cdot}99$ column we get $\chi^2 = 26{\cdot}217$.

Note: If we took a sample and calculated χ^2 and this value of χ^2 was greater than 26·217 then we would say that the difference between the observed and expected frequencies was significant at the 99% level of confidence.

Example 2: Using the χ^2 curve of Example 1 find the area shaded for the following values of

(a) $\chi^2 = 21$. (b) $\chi^2 = 19$.

Answer

(a) Looking along the horizontal line opposite $\nu = 12$ we see that 21 is in the column headed $A = 0{\cdot}95$. The area shaded is therefore 0·95.

(b) Looking along the horizontal line opposite $\nu = 12$ we see that 19 comes in between 21 and 18·549. Using linear interpolation between 0·95 and 0·90 we get 0·91. The area shaded is therefore 0·91.

10.6 Degrees of freedom I

The number of degrees of freedom in connection with a situation involving a χ^2 test is found by considering *only the expected frequencies.*

If the expected frequencies can be calculated without reference to any population parameter which has had to be estimated from a sample, then $\nu = n - 1$, where n is the same n as in $\sum_{i=1}^{n} \frac{(O_i - E_i)^2}{E_i}$. Referring to the example of Section 10.2 where we calculated the expected values of the numbers 1 to 6 for 600 throws of the dice. We used a priori probability calculations to get the frequency of 100 for each of the numbers 1 to 6; we did not have to throw the dice 600 times (that is, take a sample) in order to calculate these probabilities. Thus since $n = 6$, $\nu = 6 - 1 = 5$. Note that 1 is subtracted from 6 because if we know five of the probabilities then the sixth probability must be such that the total of the probabilities must be unity. Again we have the idea that five numbers may be assigned freely but the sixth is allowed no such free choice. Generalising this we say that for n probability frequencies $n - 1$ may be freely assigned and so there are $n - 1$ degrees of freedom.

We are now in a position to complete the test for the example of Section 10.2. We recall that $\chi^2 = 1{\cdot}6$ and that $\nu = 5$. Looking in the table level with $\nu = 5$ we see that 1·6 is just below 1·61, and 1·61 is in the column headed $A = 0{\cdot}10$.

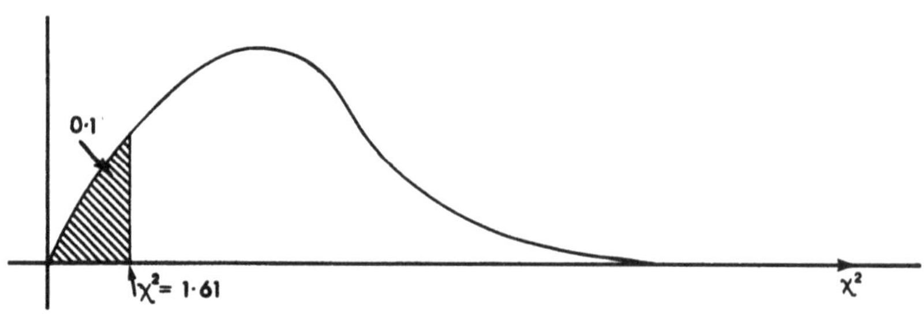

Fig. 10.6 (a)

Thus 1·6 is within the 10% shaded area in the diagram and is not significant. We therefore conclude that the dice is fair.

10.7 Degrees of freedom II

If the expected frequencies cannot be calculated without reference to population parameters, which in turn have had to be estimated from a sample, then $\nu = n - 1 - k$, where k is the number of population parameters estimated from the sample.

Example 1: Calculate χ^2 for Example 1 of Section 5.6 and comment.

Answer

The calculations are shown in the following table:-

Height Class Boundaries	Observed No. of Students	Expected No. of Students	$(O_i - E_i)^2$	$\frac{(O_i - E_i)^2}{E_i}$
59·5 -	3	5	4	0·8
62·5 –	10	10	0	0·0
65·5 –	23	20	9	0·45
68·5 –	12	10	4	0·4
71·5 – 74·5	2	5	9	1·8
				3·45

In the calculations involved in the completing of the table in Example 1 of Section 5.6 the mean and the standard deviation were calculated for the sample of 50 students. These results were then used to obtain a normal curve with the same mean and standard deviation. In other words they were being used as estimates of μ and σ for the population. As the figures in the above table have been taken from the table in Section 5.6 the calculation of χ^2 involves using estimated population parameters. Therefore to find the number of degrees of freedom for χ^2 we need to use $\nu = n - 1 - k$, which gives $\nu = 5 - 1 - 2 = 2$. At the 95% level of significance $\chi^2 = 5{\cdot}991$ for 2 degrees of freedom and as $3{\cdot}45 < 5{\cdot}991$ then the above value of χ^2 is not significant at the 95% level. We conclude therefore that the normal curve is a good fit for the data.

Example 2: A set of 5 coins was tossed 64 times and the number of heads each throw counted. The results were as tabulated in the table below where the expected results are also shown. Is there any doubt about the fairness of these coins.

No. of heads	0	1	2	3	4	5
Actual frequencies	4	10	14	28	6	2
Expected frequencies	2	10	20	20	10	2

Answer

If the number of items in a theoretical frequency class, E_i, is small then the fraction $\frac{(O_i - E_i)}{E_i}$ will be unduly large and therefore give χ^2 an inflated value. To avoid this it is essential that each theoretical frequency class contains at least 5. Any class or classes which do not can be combined with adjacent classes until this condition is satisfied. Thus the above table now becomes:-

Number of heads	0 or 1	2	3	4 or 5
Actual frequencies	14	14	28	8
Expected frequencies	12	20	20	12

Working out χ^2 in the usual way give $\chi^2 = 7{\cdot}32$.

Now the number of degrees of freedom will be $\nu = n - 1 - k = 4 - 1 - 1 = 2$, since the original 6 classes have been reduced to 4 and the parameter $p = \frac{1}{2}$ was used in the computation of the expected frequencies.

From the χ^2 table we see that the 95% level is $\chi^2 = 5{\cdot}991$ and as $7{\cdot}32 > 5{\cdot}991$ we conclude that there is doubt about the fairness of some at least of the coins.

10.8 Correction for continuity

Let us consider the experiment of tossing a coin 20 times. The expected frequencies will be 10 heads and 10 tails. If in one experiment exactly 10 heads and 10 tails appeared then the value of χ^2 would be zero. If in the next experiment 9 heads and 11 tails appeared then χ^2 would be 0·2. It will now be seen that χ^2 cannot take any value between 0 and 0·2 because the change from 10 heads and 10 tails to 9 heads and 11 tails is the 'smallest' that could be made. The following table shows the value that χ^2 could take for this experiment:-

Heads	10	9	8	7	6	5	4	3	2	1	0
Tails	10	11	12	13	14	15	16	17	18	19	20
χ^2	0	0·2	0·8	1·8	3·2	5	7·2	9·8	12·8	16·2	20

and the values of χ^2 shown in the above table *are the only values possible* for this experiment.

This means that χ^2 as calculated from the formula of Section 10.3 is not a continuous variable, that is it cannot take *all* values between it's limits.

Now the curve given in Section 10.4 as approximating to χ^2 as defined by the formula of Section 10.3 is in fact a continuous curve, so we are in the situation of applying a continuous curve to a situation giving discrete data. It has been seen in earlier chapters that when continuous theory is applied to discrete data there has to be a correction for continuity. χ^2 is modified by redefining it as

$$\text{corrected-}\chi^2 = \sum_{i=1}^{n} \frac{(|O_i - E_i| - \frac{1}{2})^2}{E_i}$$

Example 1: A penny was tossed 20 times and 6 heads and 14 tails were recorded. Calculate corrected-χ^2 and comment.

Answer

	Observed	Expected	$\lvert O_i - E_i \rvert$	$\lvert O_i - E_i \rvert - \frac{1}{2}$	$\frac{(\lvert O_i - E_i \rvert - \frac{1}{2})^2}{E_i}$
Heads	6	10	4	3·5	1·225
Tails	14	10	4	3·5	1·225
					2·45

Thus corrected-χ^2 = 2·45 which compares with 3·2 if an uncorrected calculation is made. This shows that corrected-χ^2 is lower in value than uncorrected-χ^2.

Looking at the χ^2 table for $\nu = 1$ we see that at the 90% level a value of 3·2 is significant but if we use the corrected value of 2·45 it no longer appears significant at this level.

The correction shown above is called *Yate's correction for continuity* and it is only used when $\nu = 1$ and the sample size is small. For large samples corrected-χ^2 gives nearly the same result as χ^2 but there can be difficulties at critical values. In cases of doubt the best course is to compare both results. Note that when $\nu > 1$ corrected-χ^2 is not used.

10.9 Remarks

The χ^2 test of significance is one of the most widely used in statistical work. In all it's applications it used the principle of 'how much do the observed frequencies differ from the expected frequencies'.

Since for each value of ν the χ^2 curve, like the *t* curve, has a difference shape to tabulate the areas as fully as the normal curve has been done would involve a table like the normal curve table for each value of ν. This would be very cumbersome. Another reason why this tabulation has not been done is that in practice only values at the various commonly used levels of significance are needed and if intermediary values are required they can be found fairly accurately by interpolation.

It is rare in practice for χ^2 to be very low and if for any particular situation χ^2 was less than the critical value for $A = 0{\cdot}05$ or $A = 0{\cdot}01$ then the close agreement between observed and expected data should be viewed with some suspicion. Further investigation of the circumstances surrounding the situation may reveal the reason for the very close agreement.

The χ^2 test was first put forward by Karl Pearson about the turn of the present century.

When the number of degrees of freedom is over 30 it is possible to use normal tables to arrive at a decision in respect of a given value of chi-squared. This is because the quantity

$$\sqrt{2\chi^2} - \sqrt{(2\nu - 1)}$$

is distributed normally with mean 0 and variance 1.

Example 1: Suppose, for instance, that $\nu = 41$ and $\chi \ = 64{\cdot}2$. We calculate

$$\sqrt{(2 \times 64{\cdot}2)} - \sqrt{(82 - 1)}$$

and get 2·33.

We look for 2·33 in the normal tables and see that 0·4901 of the area lies between 2·33 and 0. This tells us that $\chi^2 = 64{\cdot}2$ is significant at the 95% level but not at the 99% level.

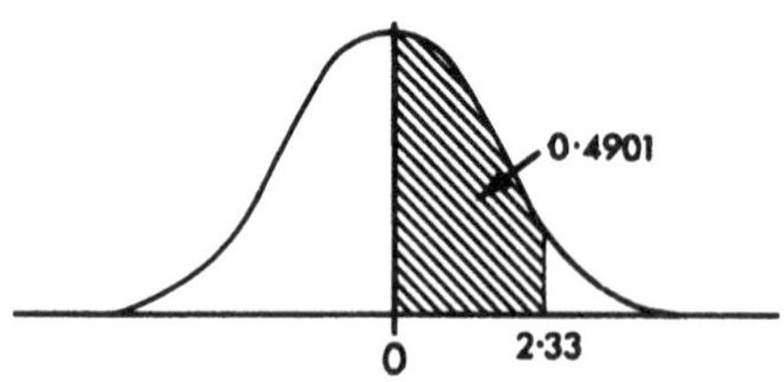

Fig. 10.9(a)

Alternatively we might recognise that 2·33 lies between 1·96 and 2·58 which we know to be the 95% and 99% levels for the normal distribution $N(0, 1)$, and arrive at the same conclusion.

Exercise 10

1. Draw a χ^2 curve (similar to the one at the head of Appendix 5) for 10 degrees of freedom. Find the values of χ^2 for which (a) the total area shaded is 0·9 (b) the total area shaded is 0·75 (c) the total area shaded is 0·05.

Answer
(a) 16·0 (b) 12·5 (c) 3·94

2. Repeat number 1 for 17 degrees of freedom.

Answer
(a) 24·8 (b) 20·5 (c) 8·67

3. Repeat number 1 for 30 degrees of freedom.

Answer
(a) 40·3 (b) 34·8 (c) 18·5

4. Draw a χ^2 curve (similar to the one at the head of Appendix 5) for 9 degrees of freedom. Find the area shaded for the following values of χ^2:- (a) 21·7 (b) 16·9 (c) 8·34 (d) 4·17

Answer
(a) 0·99 (b) 0·95 (c) 0·50 (d) 0·1

5. Repeat number 4 for 29 degrees of freedom with χ^2 values of (a) 30·1 (b) 18·3 (c) 10·1

Answer
(a) 0·95 (b) 0·5 (c) 0·05

6. The following table shows the figures obtained in throwing a die. Is the die fair?

1	2	3	4	5	6
32	46	34	50	30	48

Answer
The figures do not indicate the die is biased.

7. Experiment with the figures in the previous question and obtain a set of figures which cast doubt on the fairness of the die at (a) the 95% level and (b) the 99% level of confidence.

8. A pair of dice were thrown 180 times and the upper face numbers added. A total of 7 was recorded 36 times and a total of 3 was recorded 13 times. Use a χ^2 test to decide if the dice are fair.

Answer
There is no reason to suppose that the dice are unfair.

9. For the previous question find figures that cast doubt on the fairness of the dice at the 90% level but not at the 99% level.

10. Use a χ^2 test on number 20, Exercise 5, to determine if the theoretical curve is a good fit. Compare your value of χ^2 with the values of χ^2 in the table. Does this indicate anything?

11. The following table shows actual and expected frequencies. Test for 'goodness of fit' by using a χ^2 test at the 95% level.

Actual frequencies	12	16	18	25	52	78	59	35	28	22	14	11
Expected frequencies	11·2	14	21	34	49·5	60·1	59	46·6	31·1	19·3	14·2	10

Answer

Not a good fit.

12. Generate a set of random numbers by rolling a 10 sided die (or otherwise). Find the expected values and use a χ^2 test to determine if the numbers you generated are truly 'random'.

13. Generate random numbers by asking someone to write down the digits 0 to 9 'at random'. Perform a χ^2 test on the results to test for randomness.

14. A set of 5 coins were tossed 100 times and the following figures obtained. Use a χ^2 test to determine if the number of heads indicates the coins are fair.

Number of heads	0	1	2	3	4	5
Frequencies	2	9	21	35	22	11

Answer

Some at least of the coins are biased.

15. Perform a χ^2 'goodness of fit' test on the data from number 25, Exercise 3.

16. A survey of 250 families with four children produced the following figures:

Number of boys	0	1	2	3	4
Number of families	13	64	96	65	12

Are male and female births equally probable.

Answer

The figures do not dispute that male and female births are equally probable.

17. Calculate χ^2 for Example 1, Section 4.8, and hence comment on the goodness of fit of the theoretical data.

Answer

$\chi^2 = 1{\cdot}53$ (not $2{\cdot}025$)

18. Calculate χ^2 for number 16, Exercise 4, and hence comment on the goodness of fit of the theoretical data.

Answer

$\chi^2 = 0{\cdot}49$

19. Fit a Poisson distribution to the following data.

Number of impurities	0	1	2	3	4
Number of units	31	61	47	11	1

Test for goodness of fit using a χ^2 test.

Answer

Fit poor

20. The number of callers at an information desk during 100 days were distributed as follows:

Number of callers	0	1	2	3	4	5	6
Number of days	43	35	15	6	2	1	1

Fit a Poisson distribution to the data and then test for goodness of fit using a χ^2 test.

Answer

$\chi^2 = 1{\cdot}58$. Fit good at 95% and 99% levels

11 Some Connections in Statistical Theory

11.1 Introduction

This chapter is the most mathematical in the book. It is put in to show the power and beauty of mathematical statistics and it also points the way to the further development of this facet of statistics. It will also show how apparently different ideas in statistics can be traced to a common root.

11.2 The Gamma Distribution

One of the most important probability distributions of more advanced statistical theory is the so called gamma probability distribution, defined by

$$f(x) = \begin{cases} Ax^{k-1}e^{-x} & \text{for} \quad x > 0 \\ 0 & \text{for} \quad x \leqslant 0 \end{cases}$$

where $k > 0$, and A is chosen so that the area under the curve is unity. To find A we have to evaluate the integral in the equation

$$\int_0^\infty Ax^{k-1}e^{-x}\,dx = 1$$

This gives

$$A\int_0^\infty x^{k-1}e^{-x}\,dx = 1.$$

Now the integral in this equation in fact defines what is known as the gamma function, namely

$$\Gamma(k) = \int_0^\infty x^{k-1}e^{-x}\,dx$$

which is studied in more advanced analysis courses. It is because the evaluation of A involves the gamma function that the gamma probability distribution is so called.

It is not necessary to understand the deeper mathematical significance of the gamma function as the integral has been worked out for various values of k and the values can be read out of gamma function tables.

We now have

$$A\,\Gamma(k) = 1$$

giving

$$A = \frac{1}{\Gamma(k)}$$

This now gives the gamma distribution as

$$f(x) = \begin{cases} \dfrac{x^{k-1}\,e^{-x}}{\Gamma(k)} & \text{for} \quad x > 0 \\ 0 & \text{for} \quad x \leqslant 0 \end{cases}$$

The graphs of the gamma distributions for $k = 1$, 2 and 3 are shown in the following diagram:

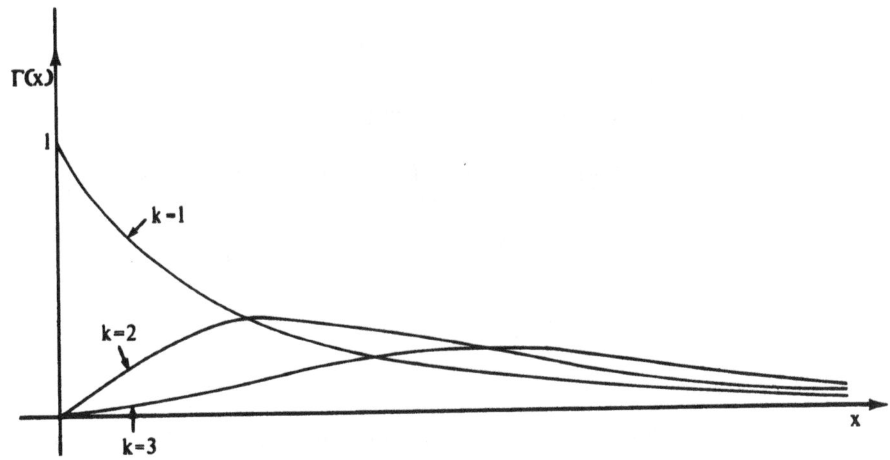

Fig.11.2 (a)

From the above diagram it can be seen that $f(x) \geqslant 0$ for all x and k. The graph of the gamma function for $k > 0$ is shown in Fig.11.2 (b).

11.3 Mean and Variance of the Gamma Distribution

The mean of the gamma distribution is found as follows.

$$\mu = E(x) = \frac{1}{\Gamma(k)} \int_0^\infty x.x^{k-1}\,e^{-x}\,dx$$

$$= \frac{1}{\Gamma(k)} \int_0^\infty x^k e^{-x}\,dx$$

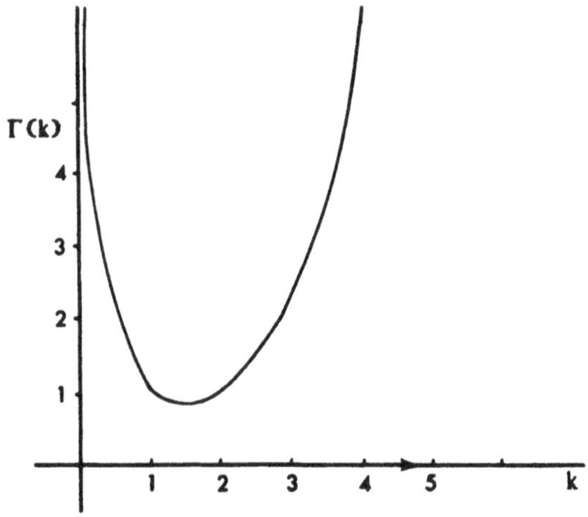

Fig.11.2(b)

and integrating this by parts we get

$$E(\underset{\sim}{x}) = \frac{1}{\Gamma(k)}\left\{\lim_{M\to\infty}[-x^k e^{-x}]_0^M - \int_0^\infty -e^{-x} k.x^{k-1}\, dx\right\}$$
$$= \frac{1}{\Gamma(k)}\left\{0 + k\int_0^\infty x^{k-1} e^{-x}\, dx\right\}$$
$$= \frac{k\,\Gamma(k)}{\Gamma(k)} = k$$

giving $\mu = k.$

It is left as an exercise for the reader to show that the variance of the gamma distribution is k.

11.4 The Moment Generating Function of the Gamma Distribution

The moment generating function of the gamma distribution is found as follows.

$$M_{\underset{\sim}{x}}(t) = \frac{1}{\Gamma(k)}\int_0^\infty e^{tx}\, x^{k-1}\, e^{-x}\, dx$$
$$= \frac{1}{\Gamma(k)}\int_0^\infty x^{k-1}\, e^{-x(1-t)}\, dx$$

changing the variable of integration by setting $y = x(1-t)$ we get

$$M_{\underset{\sim}{x}}(t) = \frac{1}{\Gamma(k)}\int_0^\infty \frac{y^{k-1}}{(1-t)^k}\, e^{-y}\, dy$$

$$= \frac{1}{\Gamma(k)(1-t)^k}\int_0^\infty y^{k-1}\, e^{-y}\, dy$$

and since the last integral is $\Gamma(k)$ we get

$$M_{\underset{\sim}{x}}(t) = \frac{1}{(1-t)^k} = (1-t)^{-k}.$$

11.5 Change of Variable

We have seen that when a random variable $\underset{\sim}{x}$ is given then other related random variables such as $\underset{\sim}{x} + 3$, $\tilde{x} + b$, $a\underset{\sim}{x}$, $a\underset{\sim}{x} + b$, and so on can be formed. Also given the probability distribution of $\underset{\sim}{x}$ then the probability distribution of the related random variables can be found. If, for instance, $\underset{\sim}{x}$ is distributed normally with mean 0 and variance 1, then $\underset{\sim}{x} + b$ will be normally distributed with mean b and variance 1, that is given x has probability distribution

$$\frac{1}{\sqrt{2\pi}}\, e^{\frac{-x^2}{2}}$$

then $\underset{\sim}{x} + b$ will have probability distribution

$$\frac{1}{\sqrt{2\pi}}\, e^{-\frac{(x-b)^2}{2}}$$

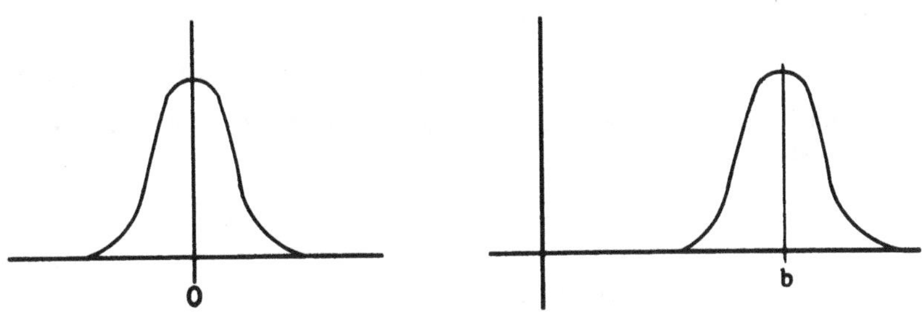

Fig.11.5 (a)

In simple cases finding the probability distribution of the related random variable is quite easy, but in less simple cases the problem can be quite difficult. The general problem of the probability distribution of related random variables is dealt with under the heading of change of variable and a full discussion is beyond the scope of this book. However this concept of related random variables has deep significance, and will be needed in the following sections.

11.6 Distribution of x^2 if x is Normally Distributed

It can be shown by the technique of change of variable that if x is normally distributed with mean 0 and variance 1, then x^2 is a gamma distribution. Thus we show a close connection between the normal distribution and the gamma distribution.

11.7 Distribution of Σx_i^2 if x_i is Normally Distributed

If $x_1, x_2, \ldots, x_n$ are independent random variables normally distributed with mean 0 and variance 1. then the random variable formed by adding their squares is a χ^2 distribution with n degrees of freedom.

that is $$x_1^2 + x_2^2 + \ldots + x_n^2 = \sum_i x_i^2$$

is distributed as a χ^2 distribution with n degrees of freedom. Again the result depends on the change of variable technique. We have now linked the normal distribution to the gamma and the χ^2 distributions.

11.8 Distribution of Σx_i if x_i has a Chi-squared Distribution

If we are given x_1 has a chi-squared distribution with ν_1 degrees of freedom

x_2 has a chi-squared distribution with ν_2 degrees of freedom

.

.

.

x_n has a chi-squared distribution with ν_n degrees of freedom

then it can be proved that the random variable formed by adding them together, that is

$$x_1 + x_2 + \ldots + x_n = \Sigma x_i$$

has a χ^2 distribution with

$$\nu_1 + \nu_2 + \ldots + \nu_n = \Sigma \nu_i$$

degrees of freedom.

11.9 The Chi-squared Distribution

If we take the gamma distribution with parameter k then we can form a whole set of gamma distributions by putting $k = \frac{n}{2}$ and letting $n = 1, 2, 3, \ldots$ in turn. If $n = 1$ then $k = \frac{1}{2}$ and the associated gamma distribution has mean and variance equal to $\frac{1}{2}$. If $n = 2, 3$, and so on, then similar remarks hold. To each of the gamma distributions so formed there will correspond a random variable.

If we now change the variable from $\underset{\sim}{x}$ to $\frac{x}{2}$, and, at the same time, allow the above variation in k, then the set of distributions so formed takes the form

$$f(n) = \begin{cases} \dfrac{1}{2^{n/2}\Gamma(\frac{n}{2})} x^{\frac{n}{2}-1} e^{-\frac{x}{2}} & \text{for} \quad x > 0 \\ 0 & \text{for} \quad x \leqslant 0 \end{cases}$$

and the random variable which has this distribution is called the chi-squared variable with n degrees of freedom.

It will now be seen that in Section 10.4 the constant in the definition of the probability distribution of chi-squared is

$$\left(\frac{1}{2^{n/2}\Gamma(\frac{n}{2})}\right)$$

and this constant, determined to make the area under the curve unity, is found by evaluating an integral involving the gamma function.

Thus we see that the χ^2 distribution is tracable to the gamma distribution.

11.10 The $\underset{\sim}{t}$ Distribution

Not only is it possible to take a random variable $\underset{\sim}{x}$ and derive from it random variables such as $a\underset{\sim}{x} + b$, $\underset{\sim}{x}^2$, and so on it is possible to take two different random variables $\underset{\sim}{x}$ and y and combine them to form random variables such as $\underset{\sim}{x} \times \underset{\sim}{y}$, $\underset{\sim}{x} + \underset{\sim}{y}$, and $\underset{\sim}{x}/\underset{\sim}{y}$. Having formed these random variables and knowing the probability distribution of $\underset{\sim}{x}$ and $\underset{\sim}{y}$ individually it is possible to find the probability distribution of these new random variables.

It is this technique which leads to the following result. If $\underset{\sim}{x}$ and $\underset{\sim}{y}$ are independent and $\underset{\sim}{x}$ has the standard normal distribution while $\underset{\sim}{y}$ has a chi-squared distribution with ν degrees of freedom, then we can form the random variable

$$\frac{\underset{\sim}{x}}{\sqrt{\frac{\underset{\sim}{y}}{\nu}}}$$

If we denote this random variable by $\underset{\sim}{t}$ then it can be shown that the probability distribution of $\underset{\sim}{t}$ is

$$f(t) = A\left(1 + \frac{t^2}{\nu}\right)^{-\frac{\nu+1}{2}} \quad \text{for} \quad -\infty < t < \infty$$

and this is the $\underset{\sim}{t}$ distribution we have already met, known as Student's t distribution with ν degrees of freedom.

It can be shown further that if A is chosen to make the area under the curve unity, then

$$A = \frac{\Gamma\left(\frac{\nu+1}{2}\right)}{\sqrt{\nu}\,\Gamma\left(\frac{1}{2}\right)\Gamma\left(\frac{\nu}{2}\right)}$$

and again the gamma function appears.

We have shown that the $\underset{\sim}{t}$ distribution is in fact a quotient formed from a normal random variable and a chi-squared random variable, and that the constant needed to make the area under the curve equal to unity involves three gamma functions.

We now recall that for $\nu \geqslant 30$ the t distribution can be approximated by the standard normal distribution, and so once again we see that ideas met earlier as separate items are connected in statistical theory.

Exercise 11

1. Find the maximum value of the gamma distribution for (a) $k = 1$ (b) $k = 2$ (c) $k = 3$
2. Show that for the gamma distributions with $k = 1$ and $k = 2$ the probability curves intersect at the maximum of one of the curves.
3. Repeat the previous example for $k = 1$ and $k = 3$.
4. Show that the variance of a gamma distribution is k.
5. Find the mean and variance of a gamma distribution by differentiating the moment generating function.
6. Find the mode of the gamma distribution where $k = 3$.
7. Generalise the previous question.
8. How does the mode of a gamma distribution compare with the variance.

9. Find the m.g.f. of the chi-squared distribution with ν degrees of freedom. By differentiating this find the mean and variance.

10. Use moment generating functions to show that if $\underset{\sim}{x}$ and $\underset{\sim}{y}$ are independent random variables normally distributed with means μ_x and μ_y, and variances σ_x^2 and σ_y^2, then $\underset{\sim}{x} - \underset{\sim}{y}$ is normally distributed with mean $\mu_x - \mu_y$ and variance $\sigma_x^2 + \sigma_y^2$.

Appendix 1

(a) The negative exponential function e^{-a}.

a	0·00	0·01	0·02	0·03	0·04	0·05	0·06	0·07	0·08	0·09
0·0	1·0000	0·9900	0·9802	0·9704	0·9608	0·9512	0·9418	0·9324	0·9231	0·9139
0·1	0·9048	0·8958	0·8869	0·8781	0·8694	0·8607	0·8521	0·8437	0·8353	0·8270
0·2	0·8187	0·8106	0·8025	0·7945	0·7866	0·7788	0·7711	0·7634	0·7558	0·7483
0·3	0·7408	0·7334	0·7261	0·7189	0·7118	0·7047	0·6977	0·6907	0·6839	0·6771
0·4	0·6703	0·6637	0·6570	0·6505	0·6440	0·6376	0·6313	0·6250	0·6188	0·6126
0·5	0·6065	0·6005	0·5945	0·5886	0·5827	0·5769	0·5712	0·5655	0·5599	0·5543
0·6	0·5488	0·5434	0·5379	0·5326	0·5273	0·5220	0·5169	0·5117	0·5066	0·5016
0·7	0·4966	0·4916	0·4868	0·4819	0·4771	0·4724	0·4677	0·4630	0·4584	0·4538
0·8	0·4493	0·4449	0·4404	0·4360	0·4317	0·4274	0·4232	0·4190	0·4148	0·4107
0·9	0·4066	0·4025	0·3985	0·3946	0·3906	0·3867	0·3829	0·3791	0·3753	0·3716

a	0·00	0·05
1·0	0·3679	0·3499
1·1	0·3329	0·3166
1·2	0·3012	0·2865
1·3	0·2725	0·2592
1·4	0·2466	0·2346
1·5	0·2231	0·2122
1·6	0·2019	0·1920
1·7	0·1827	0·1738
1·8	1·1653	0·1572
1·9	0·1496	0·1423
2·0	0·1353	0·1287
2·1	0·1225	0·1165
2·2	0·1108	0·1054
2·3	0·1003	0·0954
2·4	0·0907	0·0863
2·5	0·0821	0·0781
2·6	0·0743	0·0707
2·7	0·0672	0·0639
2·8	0·0608	0·0578
2·9	0·0550	0·0523
3·0	0·0498	0·0474
3·1	0·0450	0·0429
3·2	0·0408	0·0388
3·3	0·0369	0·0351
3·4	0·0334	0·0317

a	0·00	0·05
3·5	0·0302	0·0287
3·6	0·0273	0·0260
3·7	0·0247	0·0235
3·8	0·0224	0·0213
3·9	0·0202	0·0193
4·0	0·0183	0·0174
4·1	0·0166	0·0158
4·2	0·0150	0·0143
4·3	0·0136	0·0129
4·4	0·0123	0·0117
4·5	0·0111	0·0106
4·6	0·0101	0·0096
4·7	0·0091	0·0087
4·8	0·0082	0·0078
4·9	0·0074	0·0071
5·0	0·0067	0·0064
5·1	0·0061	0·0058
5·2	0·0055	0·0052
5·3	0·0050	0·0047
5·4	0·0045	0·0043
5·5	0·0041	0·0039
5·6	0·0037	0·0035
5·7	0·0033	0·0032
5·8	0·0030	0·0029
5·9	0·0027	0·0026
6·0	0·0025	0·0024

a	7	8	9	10
e^{-a}	0·00091	0·00034	0·00012	0·00005

To obtain values of e^{-a} for values of a between 1 and 6 not given, use interpolation

To obtain values of e^{-a} for values larger than 6 use the usual index laws.

for example $e^{-6\cdot5} = (e^{-6})(e^{-0\cdot5})$

$= (0\cdot0025)(0\cdot6065) = 0\cdot00152$

(b) The exponential function e^{a}

a	e^{a}
0·01	1·0101
0·02	1·0202
0·03	1·0305
0·04	1·0408
0·05	1·0513
0·06	1·0618
0·07	1·0725
0·08	1·0833
0·09	1·0942
0·10	1·1052
0·20	1·2214
0·30	1·3499
0·40	1·4918
0·50	1·6487
0·60	1·8221
0·70	2·0138
0·80	2·2255
0·90	2·4596
1·00	2·7183
2·00	7·3891
3·00	20·0886
4·00	54·598
5·00	148·41
6·00	403·43
7·00	1096·6
8·00	2981·0
9·00	8103·1
10·00	22026·0

Appendix 2

Reproduced from Chartwell Graph 5591A, with permission from H.W.Peel & Co. Ltd., Greenford, Middlesex.

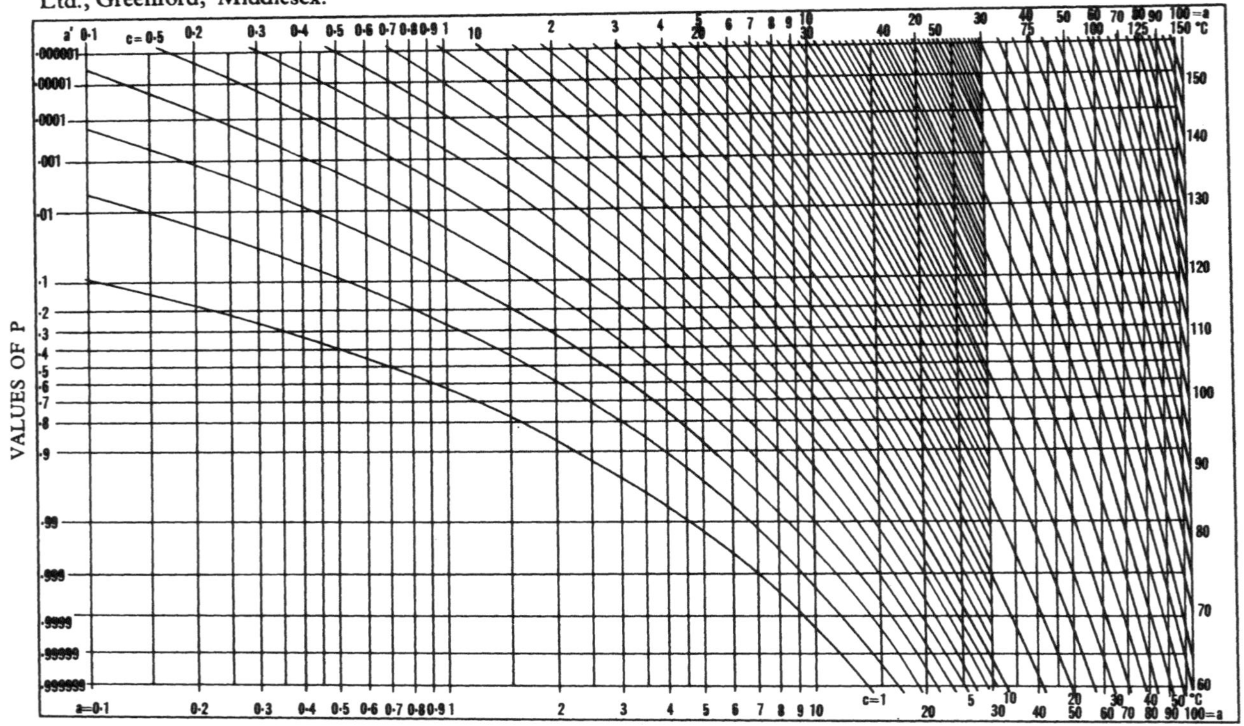

Fig. 1.-Probability curves showing Poisson's exponential summation

$$P = 1 - \left[1 + \frac{a}{1!} + \frac{a^2}{2!} + \cdots + \frac{a^{c-1}}{(c-1)!}\right] c^{-a}$$

for the probability P that an event occur at least c times in a large group of trials for which the average number of occurences is a. A scale proportional to the normal probability integral is used for P, a logarithmic scale for a

Appendix 3

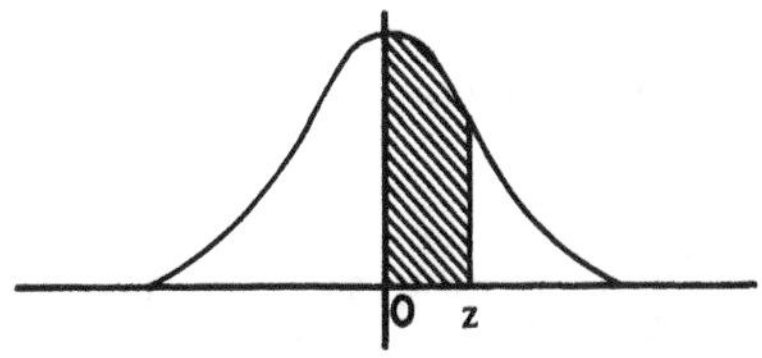

Areas under the normal curve between 0 and z where

$$z = \frac{x - \mu}{\sigma}$$

z	0·00	0·01	0·02	0·03	0·04	0·05	0·06	0·07	0·08	0·09
0·0	0000	0040	0080	0120	0160	0199	0239	0279	0319	0359
0·1	0398	0438	0478	0517	0557	0596	0636	0675	0714	0753
0·2	0793	0832	0871	0910	0948	0987	1026	1064	1103	1141
0·3	1179	1217	1255	1293	1331	1368	1406	1443	1480	1517
0·4	1554	1591	1628	1664	1700	1736	1772	1808	1844	1879
0·5	1915	1950	1985	2019	2054	2088	2123	2157	2190	2224
0·6	2257	2291	2324	2357	2389	2422	2454	2486	2517	2549
0·7	2580	2611	2642	2673	2704	2734	2764	2794	2823	2852
0·8	2881	2910	2939	2967	2995	3023	3051	3078	3106	3133
0·9	3159	3186	3212	3238	3264	3290	3315	3340	3365	3389
1·0	3413	3438	3461	3485	3508	3531	3554	3577	3599	3621
1·1	3643	3665	3686	3708	3729	3749	3770	3790	3810	3830
1·2	3849	3869	3888	3907	3925	3944	3962	3980	3997	4015
1·3	4032	4049	4066	4082	4099	4115	4131	4147	4162	4177
1·4	4192	4207	4222	4236	4251	4265	4279	4292	4306	4319
1·5	4332	4345	4357	4370	4383	4394	4406	4418	4429	4441
1·6	4452	4463	4474	4484	4495	4505	4515	4525	4535	4545
1·7	4554	4564	4573	4582	4591	4599	4608	4616	4625	4633
1·8	4641	4649	4656	4664	4671	4678	4686	4693	4699	4706
1·9	4713	4719	4726	4732	4738	4744	4750	4756	4761	4767
2·0	4772	4778	4783	4788	4793	4798	4803	4808	4812	4817
2·1	4821	4826	4830	4834	4838	4842	4846	4850	4854	4857
2·2	4861	4864	4868	4871	4875	4878	4881	4884	4887	4890
2·3	4893	4896	4898	4901	4904	4906	4909	4911	4913	4916
2·4	4918	4920	4922	4925	4927	4929	4931	4932	4934	4936
2·5	4938	4940	4941	4943	4945	4946	4948	4949	4951	4952
2·6	4953	4955	4956	4957	4959	4960	4961	4962	4963	4964
2·7	4965	4966	4967	4968	4969	4970	4971	4972	4973	4974
2·8	4974	4975	4976	4977	4977	4978	4979	4979	4980	4981
2·9	4981	4982	4982	4983	4984	4984	4985	4985	4986	4986
3·0	49865	49869	49874	49878	49882	49886	49889	49893	49897	49900
3·1	49903	49906	49910	49913	49916	49918	49921	49924	49926	49929

Appendix 4

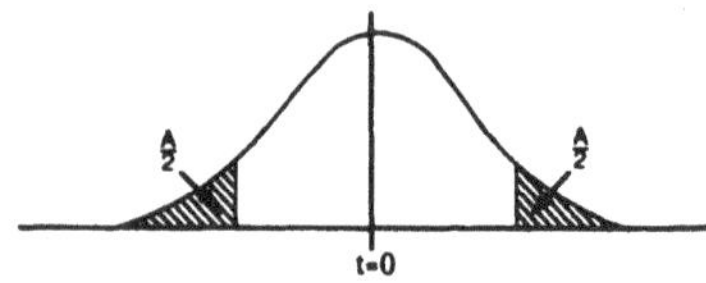

Student's *t* Distribution

ν \ A	0·9	0·8	0·7	0·6	0·5	0·4	0·3	0·2	0·1	0·05	0·02	0·01	0·001
1	0·158	0·325	0·510	0·727	1·000	1·376	1·963	3·078	6·314	12·706	31·821	63·657	636·619
2	0·142	0·289	0·445	0·617	0·816	1·061	1·386	1·886	2·920	4·303	6·965	9·925	31·598
3	0·137	0·277	0·424	0·584	0·765	0·978	1·250	1·638	2·353	3·182	4·541	5·841	12·924
4	0·134	0·271	0·414	0·569	0·741	0·941	1·190	1·533	2·132	2·776	3·747	4·604	8·610
5	0·132	0·267	0·408	0·559	0·727	0·920	1·156	1·476	2·015	2·571	3·365	4·032	6·869
6	0·131	0·265	0·404	0·553	0·718	0·906	1·134	1·440	1·943	2·447	3·143	3·707	5·959
7	0·130	0·263	0·402	0·549	0·711	0·896	1·119	1·415	1·895	2·365	2·998	3·499	5·408
8	0·130	0·262	0·399	0·546	0·706	0·889	1·108	1·397	1·860	2·306	2·896	3·355	5·041
9	0·129	0·261	0·398	0·543	0·703	0·883	1·100	1·383	1·833	2·262	2·821	3·250	4·781
10	0·129	0·260	0·397	0·542	0·700	0·879	1·093	1·372	1·812	2·228	2·764	3·169	4·587
11	0·129	0·260	0·396	0·540	0·697	0·876	1·088	1·363	1·796	2·201	2·718	3·106	4·437
12	0·128	0·259	0·395	0·539	0·695	0·873	1·083	1·356	1·782	2·179	2·681	3·055	4·318
13	0·128	0·259	0·394	0·538	0·694	0·870	1·079	1·350	1·771	2·160	2·650	3·012	4·221
14	0·128	0·258	0·393	0·537	0·692	0·868	1·076	1·345	1·761	2·145	2·624	2·977	4·140
15	0·128	0·258	0·393	0·536	0·691	0·866	1·074	1·341	1·753	2·131	2·602	2·947	4·073
16	0·128	0·258	0·392	0·535	0·690	0·865	1·071	1·337	1·746	2·120	2·583	2·921	4·015
17	0·128	0·257	0·392	0·534	0·689	0·863	1·069	1·333	1·740	2·110	2·567	2·898	3·965
18	0·127	0·257	0·392	0·534	0·688	0·862	1·067	1·330	1·734	2·101	2·552	2·878	3·922
19	0·127	0·257	0·391	0·533	0·688	0·861	1·066	1·328	1·729	2·093	2·539	2·861	3·883
20	0·127	0·257	0·391	0·533	0·687	0·860	1·064	1·325	1·725	2·086	2·528	2·845	3·850
21	0·127	0·257	0·391	0·532	0·686	0·859	1·063	1·323	1·721	2·080	2·518	2·831	3·819
22	0·127	0·256	0·390	0·532	0·686	0·858	1·061	1·321	1·717	2·074	2·508	2·819	3·792
23	0·127	0·256	0·390	0·532	0·685	0·858	1·060	1·319	1·714	2·069	2·500	2·807	3·767
24	0·127	0·256	0·390	0·531	0·685	0·857	1·059	1·318	1·711	2·064	2·492	2·797	3·745
25	0·127	0·256	0·390	0·531	0·684	0·856	1·058	1·316	1·708	2·060	2·485	2·787	3·725
26	0·127	0·256	0·390	0·531	0·684	0·856	1·058	1·315	1·706	2·056	2·479	2·779	3·707
27	0·127	0·256	0·389	0·531	0·684	0·855	1·057	1·314	1·703	2·052	2·473	2·771	3·690
28	0·127	0·256	0·389	0·530	0·683	0·855	1·056	1·313	1·701	2·048	2·467	2·763	3·674
29	0·127	0·256	0·389	0·530	0·683	0·854	1·055	1·311	1·699	2·045	2·462	2·756	3·659
30	0·127	0·256	0·389	0·530	0·683	0·854	1·055	1·310	1·697	2·042	2·457	2·750	3·646
40	0·126	0·255	0·388	0·529	0·681	0·851	1·050	1·303	1·684	2·021	2·423	2·704	3·551
60	0·126	0·254	0·387	0·527	0·679	0·848	1·046	1·296	1·671	2·000	2·390	2·660	3·460
120	0·126	0·254	0·386	0·526	0·677	0·845	1·041	1·289	1·658	1·980	2·358	2·617	3·373
–	0·126	0·253	0·385	0·524	0·674	0·842	1·036	1·282	1·645	1·960	2·326	2·576	3·291

This Table is taken from Table III of Fisher and Yates: *Statistical Tables for Biological, Agricultural and Medical Research*, published by Oliver and Boyd, Edinburgh, and by permission of the authors and publishers.

The Chi-squared Distribution

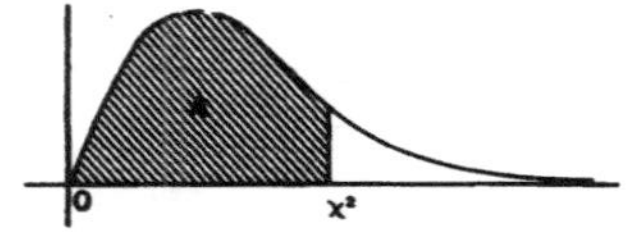

ν \ A	0·01	0·02	0·05	0·10	0·20	0·30	0·50	0·70	0·80	0·90	0·95	0·98	0·99
1	0·0002	0·0006	0·0039	0·0158	0·0642	0·148	0·455	1·074	1·642	2·706	3·841	5·412	6·635
2	0·0201	0·0404	0·103	0·211	0·446	0·713	1·386	2·408	3·219	4·605	5·991	7·824	9·210
3	0·115	0·185	0·352	0·584	1·005	1·424	2·366	3·665	4·642	6·251	7·815	9·837	11·345
4	0·297	0·429	0·711	1·064	1·649	2·195	3·357	4·878	5·989	7·779	9·488	11·668	13·277
5	0·554	0·752	1·145	1·610	2·343	3·000	4·351	6·064	7·289	9·236	11·070	13·388	15·086
6	0·872	1·134	1·635	2·204	3·070	3·828	5·348	7·231	8·558	10·645	12·592	15·033	16·812
7	1·239	1·564	2·167	2·833	3·822	4·671	6·346	8·383	9·803	12·017	14·067	16·622	18·475
8	1·646	2·032	2·733	3·490	4·594	5·527	7·344	9·524	11·030	13·362	15·507	18·168	20·090
9	2·088	2·532	3·325	4·168	5·380	6·393	8·343	10·656	12·242	14·684	16·919	19·679	21·666
10	2·358	3·059	3·940	4·865	6·179	7·267	9·342	11·781	13·442	15·987	18·307	21·161	23·209
11	3·053	3·609	4·575	5·578	6·989	8·148	10·341	12·899	14·631	17·275	19·675	22·618	24·725
12	3·571	4·178	5·226	6·304	7·807	9·034	11·340	14·011	15·821	18·549	21·026	24·054	26·217
13	4·107	4·765	5·892	7·042	8·634	9·926	12·340	15·119	16·985	19·812	22·362	25·472	27·688
14	4·660	5·368	6·571	7·790	9·467	10·821	13·339	16·222	18·151	21·064	23·685	26·873	29·141
15	5·229	5·985	7·261	8·547	10·307	11·721	14·339	17·322	19·311	22·307	24·996	28·259	30·578
16	5·812	6·614	7·962	9·312	11·152	12·624	15·338	18·418	20·465	23·542	26·296	29·633	32·000
17	6·408	7·255	8·672	10·085	12·002	13·531	16·338	19·511	21·615	24·769	27·587	30·995	33·409
18	7·015	7·906	9·390	10·865	12·857	14·440	17·338	20·601	22·760	25·989	28·869	32·346	34·805
19	7·633	8·567	10·117	11·651	13·716	15·352	18·338	21·689	23·900	27·204	30·144	33·687	36·191
20	8·260	9·237	10·851	12·443	14·578	16·266	19·337	22·775	25·038	28·412	31·410	35·020	37·566
21	8·897	9·915	11·591	13·240	15·445	17·182	20·337	23·858	26·171	29·615	32·671	36·343	38·932
22	9·542	10·600	12·338	14·041	16·314	18·101	21·337	24·939	27·301	30·813	33·924	37·659	40·289
23	10·196	11·293	13·091	14·848	17·187	19·021	22·337	26·018	28·429	32·007	35·172	38·968	41·638
24	10·856	11·992	13·348	15·659	18·062	19·943	23·337	27·096	29·553	33·196	36·415	40·270	42·980
25	11·524	12·697	14·611	16·473	18·940	20·867	24·337	28·172	30·675	34·382	37·652	41·566	44·314
26	12·198	13·409	15·379	17·292	19·820	21·792	25·336	29·246	31·795	35·563	38·885	42·856	45·642
27	12·879	14·125	16·151	18·114	20·703	22·719	26·336	30·319	32·912	36·741	40·113	44·140	46·963
28	13·565	14·847	16·928	18·939	21·588	23·647	27·336	31·391	34·027	37·916	41·337	45·419	48·278
29	14·256	15·574	17·708	19·768	22·475	24·577	28·336	32·461	35·139	39·087	42·557	46·693	49·588
30	14·953	16·306	18·493	20·599	23·364	25·508	29·336	33·530	36·250	40·256	43·773	47·962	50·892

Note: For values of ν greater than 30 the quantity $\sqrt{2\chi^2} - \sqrt{(2\nu - 1)}$ may be taken as being normally distributed with mean 0 and variance 1. See Example 1, Section 10.9.

This Table is taken from Table IV of Fisher and Yates: *Statistical Tables for Biological, Agricultural and Medical Research*, published by Oliver and Boyd, Edinburgh, and by permission of the authors and publishers.

www.ingramcontent.com/pod-product-compliance
Lightning Source LLC
LaVergne TN
LVHW020639300926
849161LV00004B/751
9781041076766